Climate Justice

The link between justice and climate change is becoming increasingly prominent in public debates on climate policy. This clear and concise philosophical introduction to climate justice addresses the hot topic of climate change as a moral challenge.

Using engaging everyday examples, the authors address the core arguments by providing a comprehensive overview of this heated debate, enabling students and practitioners to think critically about the subject and to promote discussion on questions such as:

- Why do anything in the face of climate change?
- How should we distribute the burden of climate action between industrialized and developing countries?
- Which means of reducing emissions are permissible?
- Should we put hope in technological solutions?
- Should we redesign democratic institutions for more effective climate policy?

With chapter summaries, illustrative examples, and suggestions for further reading, this book is an ideal introduction for students in political philosophy, applied ethics, and environmental ethics, as well as for practitioners working on one of the most urgent issues of our time.

Dominic Roser is a Research Fellow in the Oxford Martin Programme on Human Rights for Future Generations at the University of Oxford, UK.

Christian Seidel is a Lecturer in Philosophy at the Friedrich-Alexander University of Erlangen-Nürnberg, Germany.

Climate Justice

An Introduction

Dominic Roser and Christian Seidel

Translated by Ciaran Cronin

Routledge
Taylor & Francis Group

LONDON AND NEW YORK

First published in 2017
by Routledge
2 Park Square, Milton Park, Abingdon, Oxon OX14 4RN

and by Routledge
711 Third Avenue, New York, NY 10017

Routledge is an imprint of the Taylor & Francis Group, an informa business

Translation © 2017 Routledge

© Original Edition
Ethik des Klimawandels. Eine Einführung, 2013
By WBG (Wissenschaftliche Buchgesellschaft), Darmstadt, Germany

The translation of this work was funded by Geisteswissenschaften International –
Translation Funding for Humanities and Social Sciences from Germany, a joint
initiative of the Fritz Thyssen Foundation, the German Federal Foreign Office,
the collecting society of VG WORT and the Börsenverein des Deutschen
Buchhandels (German Publishers & Booksellers Association).

British Library Cataloguing in Publication Data
A catalogue record for this book is available from the British Library

Library of Congress Cataloging in Publication Data
A catalog record for this title has been requested

ISBN13: 978-1-138-84528-2 (hbk)
ISBN13: 978-1-138-84527-5 (pbk)
ISBN13: 978-1-315-61796-1 (ebk)

Typeset in Times New Roman and Gill Sans
by Sunrise Setting Ltd, Brixham, UK

MIX
Paper from
responsible sources
FSC
www.fsc.org   FSC® C013056

Printed and bound in Great Britain by
TJ International Ltd, Padstow, Cornwall

Contents

List of illustrations

Figures

Tables

Preface

Climate policy is a complex ethical challenge that calls for cooperation among numerous agents. On a somewhat smaller scale, this book about the ethical challenge of climate change is also a cooperative undertaking: While the overall line of argument was developed jointly by both authors, Christian Seidel is primarily responsible for Chapters 1–4 and 10–16, and Dominic Roser, for Chapters 5–9 and 17–21.

This book also represents a collaborative effort because we received valuable feedback and support from a variety of sources. We would like to thank the following in particular: Andreas Allemann, Christian Baatz, Gregor Betz, Barbara Bleisch, Michael Bock, Sabine Burkhardt, Nils Carqueville, Ruth Denkhaus, Jonathan Erhardt, Alexander Hauri, Clare Heyward, Markus Huppenbauer, Ulrike Kaps, Roger Koch, Andreas Kugler, Ariane Lissel, Axel Michaelowa, Benito Müller, Doreen Müller, Chukwumerije Okereke, Veronika Philipps, Eugen Pissarskoi, Dominique Reber, Matthew Rendall, Daniel Roser, Elisabeth Roser, Lienhard Roser, Miriam Roser, Ulrike Saul, Thomas Schinko, Hubert Schnüriger, Fabian Schuppert, Ivo Wallimann, Konstantin Weber, Joshua Wells, and an anonymous reviewer. The whole project was made possible by the generous support of the Mercator Foundation Switzerland, the University Research Priority Program for Ethics at the University of Zurich, and the Oxford Martin School at the University of Oxford. Ciaran Cronin translated the book into English, and we would like to thank him for the skill and effort he put into this.

The book is also a collaborative effort in that it is based on the ideas and arguments developed by the research community in recent years. We cite only the most important references to the literature in the text itself. Those who want to explore the individual questions and themes further will find the most important contributions in a thematic list of suggested readings under http://climate-justice-references.christianseidel.eu.

Our main aim in this book is to offer an evenhanded presentation of the pros and cons of different positions. In addition, we also try to make an overall assessment of the persuasiveness of the arguments and thus to take positions of our own. Our hope is that it will be sufficiently clear where the presentation ends and our own position begins. We will, of course, be gratified if we manage to persuade our readers of our own position—but, in the first instance, we hope that the arguments presented will enable our readers to form and examine their own opinions. Our main ambition, however, is that we the authors, our readers, and humanity as a whole will not be content simply to argue, but will go on to actively promote just climate protection. In this spirit, we dedicate this book to two young people who will benefit from these efforts, Russell Fronda and Maximilian Saul, as representatives of all future generations.

Acknowledgements

This book was supported by the Mercator Foundation Switzerland

1 Climate change as an ethical challenge

There is no avoiding the issue of climate change: When summer temperatures rise, hurricanes bear down on the US coast, Europe's rivers burst their banks, or the receding polar ice caps open up new shipping lanes, people often ask whether these are already indications of climate change. The energy transition—restructuring the energy supply system to increase the proportion of renewable energies aimed at bringing climate change to a halt—is a permanent item on the political agenda and, once a year, we read about major international climate negotiations. In our everyday lives, we encounter the topic of climate change at the gas station in the form of biofuel, at the supermarket when we read instructions about the carbon footprint of certain products, and when the travel agent asks us if we want to fly climate-neutral. And maybe you have also asked yourself, when hiking in the Alps, what has actually happened to the glaciers.

But climate change also confronts us with a whole series of open questions, many of them scientific in nature: Is climate change already occurring? How extreme will it be? To what extent is it caused by human activity? These are empirical issues that science can answer. But there is another range of questions that has more to do with politics and our everyday actions: What measures *should* the government undertake against climate change? What would a *just* international climate treaty look like? Do we have a *duty* to limit our prosperity in order to protect future generations against climate damage? Is it still *acceptable* to drive to the supermarket or fly to Spain for a short holiday? These questions are not about what is in fact occurring, and what politics and each of us is in fact doing, regarding climate change; rather, they are about what *should* happen and what we *ought* to do when faced with climate change. Questions about what one ought to do are normative, not empirical, questions. When it comes (as in the present case) to clarifying what is just, what is our duty, what is allowed, and what is forbidden, then we are dealing more precisely with *moral* questions. What is at stake in this second range of questions, therefore, is the correct moral response to the problem of climate change: How should political institutions and individual lifestyles be adapted? That is the topic of this book.

Three key questions of climate ethics

Why do we even ask moral questions regarding climate change? Is it not simply a natural phenomenon like the rotation of the moon around the Earth? If we do not ask moral questions in the case of other natural phenomena, why should we do so with regard to climate change? It is true that very few people have ever wondered what they or their political representatives should do about the rotation of the moon around the Earth. This is because human beings play no role here: They neither caused the motion of the moon nor can they influence it. So no moral questions arise concerning the moon either.

However, the case of climate change is different. Climate change is a "natural" phenomenon only insofar as it occurs "in nature." Unlike the movement of the moon, climate change is largely man-made and as such can be stopped, slowed down, or accelerated by human action. How exactly do human beings influence the climate? This can be explained very briefly as follows (see Maslin 2004 and Archer and Rahmstorf 2010 for more detailed introductions). Our planet is surrounded by the atmosphere, which acts as an insulating layer: It allows the sun's radiation in, but not to the same extent back out. This is the so-called *greenhouse effect*, which, on a natural scale, makes possible the climate and the temperature level we have experienced on the Earth until now. However, the greenhouse effect depends on the concentration of greenhouse gases in the atmosphere. When this concentration increases, less radiation is released back into space and, as a result, it becomes hotter in "greenhouse earth." The most important greenhouse gases are water vapor, carbon dioxide (CO_2), and methane (CH_4). There have been constant fluctuations in the atmospheric concentration of greenhouse gases during the course of the Earth's history. With the onset of industrialization, however, human beings began to burn fossil fuels (coal, oil, and natural gas) on an enormous scale and to cut down forests for settlements or agricultural use. Although rice cultivation, automobiles, airplanes, oil- or gas-fired heating, cement and steel production, and coal-fired power plants for industrial production have contributed to high levels of prosperity, they also mean that human beings have increased the atmospheric concentration of greenhouse gases in two ways simultaneously: On the one hand, burning fossil fuels sets free large amounts of greenhouse gases; on the other hand, forests serve as natural CO_2 sinks, so fewer forests means more free CO_2 in the atmosphere.

As a result, the concentration of CO_2 has increased by more than 35 percent from 280 parts per million (ppm) since the onset of industrialization. This exceeds by far the natural fluctuation over the past 650,000 years. There has been a continual increase in emissions in recent decades, because the human population is both growing and becoming increasingly affluent, and hence is producing more and more emissions. The most well-known result is an increase in temperature. And this trend is continuing: If no further efforts are made to reduce emissions, then a rise in temperature of between 2.5 and 7.8°C compared to the second half of the 19th century is expected in the year 2100 (IPCC 2014).

However, climate change and the rotation of the moon around the Earth differ not only in terms of the causal role played by human beings, but also in terms of how they *affect* human beings. The moon may influence sleepwalkers and, through the tides, also fishermen. Climate change, by contrast, has much more far-reaching effects on our lives. When temperatures rise, glaciers, which serve as water reservoirs for the summer, begin to melt and the melt water ends up in rivers that supply human beings with water. Without glaciers, there is less water in summer for agriculture, energy production, and daily use. At higher temperatures, the polar ice caps melt and the water spreads into the oceans; owing to the resulting rise in the sea level, land masses contract and the groundwater becomes salinated near the coast where a large proportion of mankind lives. Ocean currents and precipitation patterns change; the resulting increase in the frequency of extreme weather events such as hurricanes, floods, and droughts will make people homeless and destitute, and will aggravate famines resulting from declines in crop yields. Lower crop yields are synonymous with migration, less (and lower quality) water is synonymous with more conflicts. More frequent heat waves will lead to an increase in suffering and mortality among the old and weak. More people will be affected by tropical diseases because, in a warmer climate, the insects that serve as vectors for these diseases will gain a foothold in new regions.

Viewed in this way, it is obvious that climate change raises moral questions. Some of the effects to be expected, such as poverty, famine, death, and suffering, clearly give rise to a need for action—in particular, it seems that we should do our utmost to *prevent* climate change. We should, it seems, reduce greenhouse gas emissions, and conserve and expand the natural sinks for greenhouse gases (such as forests). In other words, we have a *moral duty to protect the climate*.

For some, however, this inference is overly hasty. It might be contended that the science may be wrong and that climate change will not occur at all, or that it may also have positive aspects that outweigh the negative. One might also take the view that climate change is a remote prospect that does not affect any living human being and that one cannot have any obligations toward people who do not exist. Therefore we must examine more closely whether we have a duty to do anything at all when confronted with climate change. This is the first fundamental moral question raised by climate change. We will discuss it in Part I.

Let us assume that the answer to this first question is in the affirmative: We do have to protect the climate. Climate protection is not an all-or-nothing affair, however, but a matter of degree: One can do more or less to protect the climate. Thus, even if it were established *that* we must do something when faced with climate change, it would still remain open *how much* should be done. How far must we go to protect the climate? How extensive should our efforts be? We will discuss this second fundamental moral question concerning climate change in Part II.

This then leads to a further issue: Even if we were to know how much climate protection we needed to perform, this would not tell us anything about how the amount of climate protection required should be distributed across different shoulders. *Who* must do what exactly? Which contributions must individual countries make and which costs must they bear? This is the third fundamental moral question concerning climate change and it will be treated in Part III.

The role of ethics between science and politics

Three fundamental questions, therefore, play a central role in the ethical controversy over climate change and hence are central to this book:

(1) Do we have a duty to do anything at all in the face of climate change?
(2) Assuming that we are obliged to do something, how much should we do?
(3) How should these duties be distributed?

As already stated, these are *moral* questions. It is not the role of science to answer them: Science can tell us only how the world *is*. But from statements about how the world is nothing follows about how the world *ought to* be. This means that science can make only statements such as the following (see IPCC 2014: 20): "Emissions scenarios leading to CO_2-equivalent concentrations in 2100 of about 450 ppm or lower are *likely* to maintain warming below 2°C over the 21st century relative to pre-industrial levels." (Here, "CO_2-equivalent" refers to a unit of measurement for comparing the different climatic effects of various greenhouse gases.) But science cannot answer the question of whether we *should* avoid warming of more than 2°C. Such questions—moral questions—belong instead to ethics. This is why we will also call the three abovementioned fundamental moral questions concerning climate change the "three key questions of climate ethics."

That these three ethical questions cannot be answered by science does not mean, of course, that scientific findings are irrelevant for answering them. On the contrary—ethics is a matter of *evaluating* individual conduct and climate policy measures from a moral point of view. For this, we need to know the properties and effects of these actions and measures, because our moral evaluation depends on this. And science provides us with *descriptions* of just these properties and effects. Thus ethical evaluation presupposes scientific description.

There is a close connection not only between science and ethics, but also between ethics and politics—for what is ethically right in the face of climate change should also ultimately be translated into practice. This is, on the one hand, a matter of individual action, but also, on the other, a matter of the political design of the social, legal, and economic framework within which this action takes place—in other words, of climate policy. For example, countries are reorienting their energy policies in the light of climate change and are concluding international climate treaties, such as the United Nations Framework Convention on Climate Change (UNFCCC) adopted in 1992, the 1997 Kyoto Protocol, or the 2015 Paris Agreement. Politicians and voters ask themselves which climate policy is the right one, all things considered, and hence which measures *should* be taken in the face of climate change. Aside from economic aspects, ethical considerations are clearly relevant here—in particular, the aspect of justice. Presumably, politicians and voters do not opt for a specific climate policy based solely on considerations of justice. However, few of them would advocate a climate policy that they consider to be extremely unjust. Thus ethics helps politicians and voters in their deliberations, and as such it is certainly relevant for practice. In addition, a proposed international climate agreement that was perceived to be unjust (for example one that imposed the main burdens on the poor developing countries that have hardly any responsibility for climate change) would be rejected *for this reason alone* and hence would not be implemented. Thus the ethical category of justice is also a criterion for successful climate policy—although by no means the only one—and this also makes ethics relevant for politics. This means that ethical reflection is, in a certain sense, the bridge between science and policy: Building on the scientific description of the facts, ethics evaluates different options from a moral point of view and makes recommendations for the morally correct climate policy.

But we should not expect too much from ethics either. It goes without saying that ethical reflection *alone* does not change the world; the world will become a better place only if we also *do* the right thing. Careful ethical reflection is, however, the first step in that direction, because if we are to do the right thing, we first need to know what the right thing is. That is precisely the aim of ethical reflection. It uses conceptual analysis and the critical examination of arguments to distinguish good from bad answers to the key questions of climate ethics. In this way, it equips every individual—and, in particular, political decision-makers—with a moral compass that can provide orientation for climate policy (but also, of course, for each individual in his or her actions).

However, it is not at all easy to follow this compass in political practice as well. The concrete implementation of the morally ideal climate policy gives rise to complications that raise a series of further ethical questions. For example, not all countries are willing to act cooperatively and some ignore their climate protection duties altogether. How should a "conscientious" country respond when other countries fail to do their part to protect the climate? Does it have to redouble its efforts or might it likewise reduce them? Which emission reduction strategy should the country adopt then: reducing population growth, reducing economic growth, or adopting cleaner technologies? And what does the much-vaunted policy instrument of emissions trading look like from an ethical point of view? Can it be legitimate for rich people to continue to produce emissions without qualms as long as they pay an "indulgence"? Or should we each not put our own house in order first? Also, given that we disagree about the best course of action to be taken, how should we design collective decision-making procedures? Are democratic procedures an obstacle or an asset when it comes to solving climate change? We will discuss these ethical complications of political practice in Part IV, after we have constructed a "moral compass" for the ideal climate policy by answering the three key questions of climate ethics in Parts I–III.

The ethical peculiarities of the problem of climate change

Unfortunately, constructing this moral compass is no easy matter either. Climate change exhibits a number of peculiarities that mean that it is difficult to answer the key ethical questions that it poses. Consider the following example:

> It is night. You are riding your bicycle and, to get home faster, you take a shortcut across the field of a neighboring farmer, thereby damaging his crops. Was it wrong to take the shortcut?

Now consider another situation:

> It is night and, to get home faster, you take your car instead of going by bike. In the process, you emit CO_2 and, together with emissions of many other people, this slowly changes the climate. Decades later, this leads to crop losses for farmers in remote developing countries. Was it wrong to take the car?

Many answer the first question spontaneously with "yes," but, after long reflection, answer the second with a "Well … "Although these two situations seem very similar at first sight, we are less sure of our moral judgments in the case of climate change than in everyday situations. Climate change seems to turn our sense of right and wrong on its head. But what is so morally peculiar and confusing about climate change?

When we examine the two situations more closely, several differences emerge. The first is that the effects of your action occur much later in the case of climate change than in that of your cross-country bike ride: You may even be long dead by the time the farmers in the developing countries suffer harvest losses. This is because the effects of many greenhouse gas emissions are time-delayed: The climate change observable today can be traced back in large part to past emissions and it will be decades before current emissions exert their full effects. Therefore the actions we take today do not necessarily affect those who are alive today, but above all affect future generations—including our children and grandchildren. This means that climate change is an *intergenerational problem* between the past, the present, and the future (see Fig. 1.1). In particular, it means that the costs and benefits of actions that harm the climate are not borne by the same person: Flying on vacation today benefits us, but harms our descendants. Conversely, protecting the climate (by not taking a flight) constitutes a sacrifice for us, while it benefits our descendants (by preventing climate damage). This time lag between cause and effect makes climate change morally complicated because our everyday ethics are tailored to short time spans. When we make moral judgments about murder, theft, or lies, then it is always a matter of actions the effects of which (a corpse, an empty safe, or a bitter disappointment) follow the cause more or less directly. With climate change, by contrast, there are decades and centuries in between.

Second, the causes and effects of climate change are separated not only temporally, but also spatially. The farmer in the first case is your neighbor; the farmers who are affected in the second case, by contrast, are unknown to you and are dispersed across the globe. Climate change is a *global phenomenon* in two respects. On the one hand, since greenhouse gases are dispersed in the atmosphere, it is immaterial from a

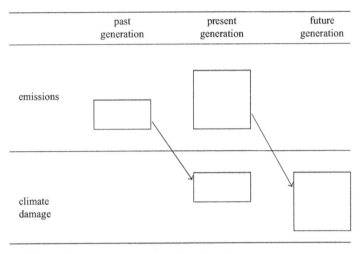

Figure 1.1 Climate change as an intergenerational problem

causal perspective where in the world the emissions are produced: A flight in Europe is just as much a contributory factor to global climate change as is meat consumption in Australia or rice cultivation in India. On the other hand, the effects are felt throughout the world, because virtually every global region is affected by them in one way or another. As with the time lag, the spatial gulf between causes and effects also means that the costs and benefits of actions that harm the climate do not fall on the same persons. When you take a flight, you enjoy the benefits, while the associated disadvantages are borne by others; if you forgo the flight, you suffer a disadvantage, while others enjoy the benefits of a protected climate. This spatial gulf also makes climate change morally complicated, because our everyday ethics are tailored to our immediate vicinity. The well-being of the people with whom we are directly acquainted moves us much more directly than the well-being of strangers living in other regions of the world. We are enjoined to "love thy neighbor," not to love those who are distant from us. And social redistribution generally occurs within and not between communities.

However, the cross-country bike ride and climate change differ not only in that the causes and effects are proximate, in the one case, and spread across the globe, in the other; the most important difference is that the causes and effects of climate change are distributed *unevenly* across the globe. When you ride your bicycle across your neighbor's field, the action of one well-off person harms another relatively well-off person. The farmers whose harvest is reduced as a result of the emissions of your car, by contrast, live in the developing countries and are comparatively poor. Thus poor farmers in the developing countries are affected by the emissions of a citizen from a rich industrialized country. This turns climate change into a problem of *global inequalities*. On the one hand, in the past, people in the industrialized countries contributed more per capita to climate change than people in the developing countries—and they continue to do so today. In 2011, the per capita CO_2 emissions in high-income countries were more than three times higher than in low- and middle-income countries (World Bank 2015: table 3.8). While one cannot claim in general that every single wealthy country has higher per capita emissions than every poor country, because some developing and emerging countries (such as Malaysia, Indonesia, and Brazil) have made significant contributions to climate change through deforestation, on the whole, the causes of climate change are located disproportionately in the industrialized countries with their high per capita emissions. On the other hand, however, the developing countries are much more severely affected by present and future climate-related damage: They are more reliant on agriculture, which is extremely vulnerable to climate change, and many developing countries are situated in climatically sensitive regions, such as drought- or flood-prone areas, where climate change gives rise to additional problems. Moreover, developing countries are poorer and, as a result, have fewer resources with which to adapt successfully to climate change. On the whole, therefore, climate damage affects the developing countries disproportionately, while the emissions that cause it are located disproportionately in the industrialized countries. In other words, there is a *twofold* inequality (see Fig. 1.2)—and this actually triggers a third inequality. While men are likely to pursue more energy-intensive lifestyles and thus cause more emissions than women (Räty and Carlsson-Kanyama

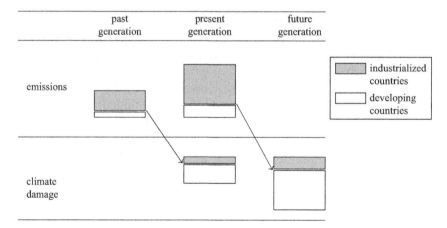

Figure 1.2 Climate change as a problem of twofold global inequality

2010), women (particularly in developing countries) are more heavily affected by climate damages such as natural disasters (Neumayer and Plümper 2007).

A third difference between taking a shortcut across a field and climate change concerns the *fragmentation of the causes*. Climate change is caused by many small everyday actions: We take a hot shower, drive by car, take a flight, eat a steak, or leave the lights on. Taken in isolation, these actions seem harmless, because we cannot directly perceive the harm caused, for example, by a hot shower in the morning; only the combined effects of many actions lead to perceptible climate damage. There is no immediate connection between a single action and a concrete harm in the case of climate change. However, our moral sense is designed for cases in which we can clearly see the harm, we can easily identify a person responsible for the harm, and we can specify the action that caused it. If you ride across the farmer's field—moreover, intentionally—then the harm is plain to see, the person responsible is easy to identify, and the offending action can be specified without any problem.

But what if 100,000 people were to ride across the field with you? Should we then say that you are not responsible because you have not caused any damage that would not have occurred anyway? You could say the same about anyone and thus, in the end, nobody would be considered to be responsible. Should we not rather say that you are responsible for a fraction (1/100,000th) of the damage? Such questions give us pause for reflection, because our everyday ethics are not designed for problems such as climate change, the causes of which are fragmented.

A fourth complication arises from the fact that our knowledge of the effects of our actions is fraught with considerable uncertainty. Not to mince words, from a scientific perspective, there is no longer *any* uncertainty about the fact *that* climate change is occurring and that human beings are the chief contributors to it through greenhouse gas emissions. Popular presentations in the media can easily create the impression that climate research is far from conclusive about this or that it is split into two equally large camps. However, scientific surveys of the consensus within climate science itself have concluded that (a) 97–98 percent of the most globally active publishing climate researchers expressly agree with the view that climate change is a man-made phenomenon and (b) the reputation of those who do not agree with this view is significantly worse among climate researchers (Anderegg et al. 2010). Viewed in this light, it can be seen to be a myth that there is disagreement and uncertainty about these scientific findings. Most of the concerns that have misled some people into denying climate change are relatively easy to dispel: Balanced and clear refutations can be found, for example, in the background information provided by the ProClim Forum for Climate and Global Change of the Swiss Academy of Sciences (ProClim 2010).

Even if there is no uncertainty about the man-made character of climate change, there is considerable uncertainty about exactly *how much* climate change we will cause. Estimates of how many degrees temperature will increase, by the end of the 21st century, absent additional measures to mitigate climate change, range from 2.5°C to 7.8°C (IPCC 2014). And even these estimates involve controversial assumptions—meaning that the increase could also end up being larger or smaller. The simple fact is that the climate system is extremely complex and therefore statements about how it will develop are always fraught with uncertainty. No one is more aware of this than the scientists themselves. In order to gain a better understanding of the current state of climate science, the Intergovernmental Panel on Climate Change (IPCC) was founded in 1988 by institutions of the United Nations. The IPCC is neither a political nor a research organization; rather, its task is to examine, summarize, and evaluate the state of research every five to seven years. In this context, the IPCC not only goes to great lengths to present estimates of important climatic changes, but also, in recent times, it attaches a "label" to many of these estimates that provides information about the level of uncertainty, the consensus among the experts, and the quality of the evidence in the case of specific data.

This kind of uncertainty over precisely how much climate change is being caused by our emissions is of major relevance for ethics. If we assume that climate change means that we, in fact, have a moral duty to prevent certain effects—for example an increase in temperature of more than 2°C above preindustrial levels—then we must reduce our emissions. But if there is uncertainty about what level of emissions in particular will have what effects, then we are also inevitably taking a certain *risk* with every climate policy. After all, that there is uncertainty means nothing other than that any level of emissions can also give rise to warming of *greater* than 2°C with some probability. And that raises the—ethical—question of what level of risk is actually permissible from a moral point of view. In this context, climate science can make statements such as "Limiting cumulative CO_2 emissions over 2000–50 to 1,000 Gt CO_2 yields a 25% probability of warming exceeding 2°C" (see Meinshausen et al. 2009: 1158). From an ethical perspective, we must then ask: Is this 25 percent risk morally defensible? With this, the question of our duties in the face of climate change immediately becomes more complicated. Now we not only have to make an ethical evaluation of the expected consequences, but we also have to reflect on how to deal with the risks associated with these consequences and on which risks are morally acceptable. Thus climate change is also a *problem of dealing with uncertainty*. And again, our familiar everyday ethics are not designed for this. While it is relatively uncontroversial that one must not do anything that will *certainly* cause the deaths of innocent people, it is much more difficult to decide how the line should be drawn between permissible and impermissible conduct if the conduct will lead to the deaths of innocent people with only *a probability*. If we drive to the supermarket in our car, there is a small probability that we will kill other people in a car accident; in the normal course of events, this is an acceptable risk and it is permissible to drive to the supermarket. However, if we drive along a twisting country highway at night at 75 mph in a fatigued state, then there is a substantially increased probability that we will cause an accident in which others will be killed. Is that still morally acceptable? And what would be the answer if we were not only fatigued, but also drunk and driving at 110 mph? If we want to know what probability of causing a certain harm—what risk—is still acceptable, then rules formulated for cases in which we are all but certain of what will happen are simply of no use to us. Yet climate change is precisely such a case in which the limits of acceptable risks are also at stake.

Thus, all told, there are four complicating factors when it comes to the ethical assessment of climate change: Climate change is a problem of how to deal with global inequalities and major uncertainties, the causes of which are fragmented and the repercussions of which affect future generations. This is a far cry from a familiar, everyday "normal" ethical problem (cf. Gardiner 2011: ch. 1)—and this is why it is completely understandable that we have to think long and hard when we try to make ethical sense of climate change. In fact, this seems to call for a kind of "ethics 2.0." But where should this "new" kind of ethical reflection on climate change begin? How should we proceed?

Where to begin?

Sometimes, ethical reflection comes to a halt before it has really got going. Occasionally, moral questions are brushed aside on the grounds that they cannot be answered objectively. The claim is that they are ultimately subjective matters, that everyone has their own opinion about them and that that is all there is to it. So is reflecting on answers to the key ethical questions of climate change even worthwhile?

We do, however, often deal with moral questions on the basis of an assumption that one side could be right and the other wrong. If the person next to you at dinner were to declare that it was perfectly right from a moral point of view to exploit the colonies, then you would hardly say "Well, that's your opinion. I see it differently. But what of it? Let's stop arguing." On the contrary, you would be more inclined to say that your neighbor is wrong, is mistaken, or is in error. You would argue with your neighbor and try to persuade him or her to the contrary with reasons. This is the difference between answers to moral questions and judgments of taste such as "I like the blue shirt." In that latter case, we do not object, begin to argue, or try to persuade, and we do not speak of a mistake or error.

The reference to the supposedly subjective character of ethical reflection is sometimes more of an excuse when things become complicated. Granted, ethical questions are all too often difficult. But this holds for other questions as well: For example, it is also difficult to determine whether 131,071 is a prime number. Nevertheless, it would not occur to anyone to conclude that there is no objective answer to this question. The decisive point is that there are often clear answers to ethical questions: Is it permissible to kill someone in cold blood? Is it wrong to set fire to a cat? Or, to return to our previous example, is it wrong to ride your bicycle across the farmer's field? These are also moral questions, but we have no difficulty in answering them.

But are not moral questions often answered in different ways and, moreover, with different justifications? Just think of controversial issues such as assisted suicide: How is an objective answer supposed to be possible where there are major disagreements and conflicts of opinions? It is true that, in many moral questions, several answers are defended and argued for. But that does not mean that all of the answers and justifications put forward are equally good. Just as in other areas, in ethics there are also good and less good arguments, and convincing and less convincing justifications. And this is what ethics is all about—namely, distinguishing well-justified answers to moral questions from badly justified answers by means of conceptual distinctions and, above all, with arguments. "Doing ethics" means asking what speaks for and against certain answers to moral questions, and establishing when a position is poorly grounded or when it leads to conclusions that contradict other central moral convictions. Therefore, ethical reflection on climate change involves justifying and testing specific answers to the key questions of climate ethics based on arguments. And that sounds like a decidedly "objective" matter.

But which arguments and justifications are we talking about here? To what do we appeal in moral discussions? On what do we base our arguments? One argumentative resource to which many people appeal is self-interest. Self-interest is indeed often invoked by calls to protect the climate. The damage caused by climate change is very severe, it is claimed, and the costs of avoiding it are relatively small; anyone who does the math will reduce emissions because it is in his or her interest. However, this appeal to self-interest has a catch: It fails to take into account the intergenerational and global character of climate change. When we reduce emissions today, it is not we who enjoy the benefits, but primarily future generations across the globe. The reference to self-interest is misleading, therefore, insofar as it is not a matter of off-setting costs and benefits in our *own* interest, but rather of striking a balance between the interests of *all* present and future human beings. It is not our own well-being, our own interests and concerns, therefore, but the well-being, interests, and concerns of all human beings that constitute the argumentative resource for answering the key ethical questions of climate change.

There is a further argumentative resource to which calls to protect the climate can appeal: Instead of making human welfare the sole argumentative point of reference, we could also include the welfare of animals. The animal world will also be severely affected by climate change. As sentient beings, animals also suffer under climatic stress factors such as extreme weather events. Since the habitats and refuges of many species will change more rapidly as a result of climate change than those species can adapt, massive extinctions are also to be expected. You may already have heard that polar bears are drowning because the pack ice at the North Pole is shrinking. Many marine animals will also become extinct as a result of changes in the oceans (for example acidification), and if high temperatures force lizards to remain in the shade longer during the day, they will not be able to search for food and will die more quickly, which will have repercussions for bird species via the food chain. All of this provides us with additional reasons for doing something about climate change.

We could even go a step further and also include plants, inanimate nature, or entire ecosystems. We will exclude such an "ecocentric" conception from our purview for the most part. There are two reasons for this. On the one hand, it is more difficult to justify than an "anthropocentric" argument geared to human welfare and concerns, or even than including animals. It is hard to deny that human and animal welfare count; is this also true of the loss of plant diversity or the disappearance of glaciers *taken in itself*—in other words, even if no human beings were affected by it? That is already more controversial. On the other hand, there is no need to fall back on an ecocentric argumentative strategy because (other than in two brief instances cited in Chapters 4 and 18), it does not make much difference in the final analysis. *If* we can show that a moral duty to protect the climate can be justified solely on the basis of the less contentious appeal to human (and animal) welfare and interests, then a lot has already been gained and we do not have to concern ourselves further with the moral status of plants or of inanimate nature in connection with our duties to protect the climate. We will now go on to examine *whether* this can be shown. Let us turn, therefore, to the first of the key ethical questions raised by climate change.

References

Anderegg, W. R. L., Prall, J. W., Harold, J., and Schneider, S. H. (2010) "Expert credibility in climate change," *Proceedings of the National Academy of Sciences*, 107(27): 12107–9.

Archer, D., and Rahmstorf, S. (2010) *The Climate Crisis: An Introductory Guide to Climate Change*, Cambridge: Cambridge University Press.

Gardiner, S. (2011) *A Perfect Moral Storm: The Ethical Tragedy of Climate Change*, New York: Oxford University Press.

Intergovernmental Panel on Climate Change (IPCC) (2014) *Summary for Policymakers: Climate Change 2014—Synthesis Report*, available online at http://www.ipcc.ch/pdf/assessment-report/ar5/syr/AR5_SYR_FINAL_SPM.pdf [accessed April 29, 2016].

Maslin, M. (2004) *Global Warming: A Very Short Introduction*, Oxford/New York: Oxford University Press.

Meinshausen, M., Meinshausen, N., Hare, W., Raper, S. C., Frieler, K., Knutti, R., Frame D. J., and Allen, M. R. (2009) "Greenhouse gas emission targets for limiting global warming to 2°C," *Nature*, 458(7242): 1158–62.

Neumayer, E., and Plümper, T. (2007) "The gendered nature of natural disasters: the impact of catastrophic events on the gender gap in life expectancy, 1981–2002," *Annals of the Association of American Geographers*, 97(3): 551–66.

ProClim (2010) "Arguments from global warming sceptics," *Climate Press*, 29, available online at http://proclimweb.scnat.ch/portal/ressources/1994.pdf [accessed April 29, 2016].

Räty, R., and Carlsson-Kanyama, A. (2010) "Energy consumption by gender in some European countries," *Energy Policy*, 38(1): 646–9.

World Bank (2015) *World Development Indicators 2015*, available online at http://data.worldbank.org/products/wdi [accessed April 29, 2016].

Suggested further reading for Introduction

Gardiner, S. M. (2010) "Ethics and climate change: an introduction," *Wiley Interdisciplinary Reviews: Climate Change*, 1(1): 54–66.

A short, critical introductory overview of the emerging field of climate ethics.

Gardiner, S. M. Caney, S., Jamieson, D., and Shue, H. (eds.) (2010) *Climate Ethics: Essential Readings*, Oxford/New York: Oxford University Press.

A collection of articles written by some the most influential figures in the field.

Intergovernmental Panel on Climate Change (2014) *Climate Change 2014: Synthesis Report—Contribution of Working Groups I, II and III to the Fifth Assessment Report of the Intergovernmental Panel on Climate Change,* available online at https://www.ipcc.ch/report/ar5/syr [accessed April 29, 2016].

This is the broadest and most authoritative overview of climate research. Of particular relevance is Working Group III's ch. 3, which treats ethical questions. The "Summary for policymakers" summarizes the essence of the three volumes in short form.

Palmer, C. (2011) "Does nature matter? The place of the nonhuman in the ethics of climate change," in D. G. Arnold (ed.) *The Ethics of Global Climate Change,* Cambridge/New York: Cambridge University Press, 272–91.

This chapter discusses a theme that does not receive extensive attention in our book: the role of species, ecosystems, nonconscious living organisms, and conscious, sentient animals in climate ethics.

A more comprehensive list of further readings for this part is available at http://climate-justice-references.christianseidel.eu

Part I

___

DO WE NEED TO DO ANYTHING AT ALL? MORAL JUSTIFICATION OF THE NEED TO ACT

2 Three reasons for skepticism about the duty to mitigate climate change

We had emphasized that there is a fundamental gap between scientific findings on climate change, on the one hand, and ethical conclusions (for example that we should mitigate climate change), on the other. However, the step needed to bridge this gap does not seem excessively large or difficult. Science tells us what consequences we will have to live with in the future if we continue as we have been doing: heat waves and droughts, inundations and rising sea levels, species extinction and the spread of tropical insects—and as a result poverty, famine, migration, disease, and death. These findings already seem to suggest an ethical conclusion: We should avoid climate change. In other words, we have a moral duty to mitigate climate change. Thus the first key question of climate ethics—"Do we have a duty to do anything at all in the face of climate change?"—seems to be easy to answer.

For some, however, this step from the scientific findings to answering the first key question is not so obvious. Again and again, one encounters voices that deny that there is an obligation to mitigate climate change. In this chapter, we will begin by distinguishing between three typical versions of this denial and then go on to examine one version in greater detail. At the end of the chapter, we take up a question that is especially relevant for journalists and lobbyists: Is it permissible to deny the duty to mitigate climate change and how should one—morally speaking—deal with people who nevertheless do so?

Three ways in which to deny the duty to mitigate climate change

Those who maintain that we have a moral duty to mitigate climate change generally mean that climate change is a moral problem to which we—the members of the current generation—have to respond by taking measures to mitigate climate change. Therefore, the thesis that we have a duty to mitigate climate change actually involves three theses: first, the assertion that climate change is, in principle, a *moral problem* to which someone must respond in some way; second, the assertion that it is *we*—the members of the current generation—who must respond; and third, the assertion that what we have to do is to *mitigate climate change*—that is, reduce emissions. This also holds quite generally in other contexts. Someone who maintains that Frieda has a duty to buy groceries for a sick neighbor is claiming that someone must respond in some way to the neighbor's illness (hence that the illness constitutes a moral problem), that it is Frieda who must do something here, and that what she has to do is to buy groceries for her neighbor.

Correspondingly, one can distinguish between three different "opponents" of the assertion that there is a moral duty to mitigate climate change. First, there are those who dispute that climate change is *even a moral problem* and hence that climate change requires anybody to do anything. Someone who thinks, for example, that climate change is a fiction or that it will not have negative consequences will also deny that there is a moral imperative to take action. If there is nothing to which to respond, then there is no need to respond at all.

Second, however, there are also those who concede that climate change is a moral problem, yet deny that it is *we* in particular who have to do something about it. Here, what is disputed is not that climate change demands something of somebody, but only that it demands something of *us*. For example, one could take the view that climate change does not concern us as members of the current generation, but only people in the distant future. And one might believe in addition that we cannot owe these people anything, because we cannot have any relationships of any kind with people in the distant future: When they exist, we will be long dead. So someone who is of the opinion that current generations cannot, in principle, have any moral obligations toward future generations will also take the view that we do not have a duty to mitigate climate change.

Finally, third, there are those who concede that climate change is a moral problem and, in addition, that it is we who have to do something about it, but deny that what we have to do is specifically to *mitigate climate change*. Thus they do not deny that we have to do something in the face of climate change, but only that this something is climate mitigation in particular. One might take the view, for example, that we merely owe it to future generations to ensure that they are able to adapt to climate change or to mitigate its effects through technical solutions. That would not be a duty to mitigate climate change, but a duty to facilitate adaptation to climate change.

So there are, in fact, three different ways in which to deny that there is a duty to mitigate climate change:

(1) denying the *basis* of the duty to mitigate climate change—"We don't have a moral duty to mitigate climate change, because climate change is not a moral problem at all";
(2) denying the *addressee* of the duty to mitigate climate change—"We don't have a moral duty to mitigate climate change, because climate change is a moral problem that affects only future generations and we don't have duties toward future generations as a matter of principle"; or
(3) denying the *content* of the duty to mitigate climate change—"We don't have a moral duty to mitigate climate change, because our obligation toward future generations regarding climate change is of a completely different kind (for example to leave them the resources they need to adapt to climate change)."

When arguing with someone who thinks that we do not have a duty to mitigate climate change, one should first ask which of these three positions is being defended if one is to be able to respond appropriately. Here, we will examine in greater detail to what arguments the first denial of the duty to mitigate climate change could appeal. In Chapters 3 and 4, we will go on to examine the reasons for—and against—the other two forms of denial.

Is climate change even a moral problem that calls for a response?

What arguments might one cite in support of the claim that the duty to mitigate climate change lacks any basis? Let us first consider a different case:

> Your neighbor knocks furiously on your door and maintains that your daughter is in the process of laying waste to his vegetable patch. He demands that you do something to stop her as a matter of urgency.

Evidently, your neighbor thinks that you have a duty to prevent your daughter from destroying his vegetable patch. How could you respond if you were to want to deny that this duty has any *basis*—namely, to deny that your daughter is, in fact, in the process of destroying the neighbor's vegetable patch?

There are at least four options open to you. First, it may be that your daughter is much too small to cause the damage feared, or that your neighbor is a bit confused and has forgotten that he no longer even has a vegetable patch. Thus the impending harm that the neighbor is calling on you to prevent does not exist and hence you do not have a duty to protect the vegetable bed either.

Let us assume, however, that your daughter is quite capable of causing the damage feared and also that the neighbor does have a vegetable patch in which someone is, in fact, currently rampaging. Then, second, it could be that this someone is not your daughter at all and you could tell your neighbor that he is confusing a wild boar with your daughter and that hence, because it is not, in fact, your child who is laying waste to his vegetable patch, you are not under any obligation either.

Let us assume, though, that it is indeed your daughter who is present in the vegetable patch. Then, third, you might respond that perhaps your daughter is not causing any damage or that, although she is trampling on some lettuce leaves, by playing in the vegetable bed she is also loosening the soil and collecting snails, thereby relieving the neighbor of part of the gardening work that still needs to be done. Your daughter, you might thus claim, is also doing something good and this outweighs the bad. As a result, she should be free to play and you, in turn, are not under an obligation to prevent her from doing so.

But let us now assume, finally, that your daughter is, in fact, causing damage and also that this damage is, in fact, greater than the benefits of her cavorting. Then, fourth, you might respond to your neighbor that it is, in any case, too late to do anything about it: You no longer have a duty to prevent your daughter from laying waste to the garden because the damage has already been done. Of course, this does not mean that you could not have other duties—for example to pay compensation or to bake a cake to show that you are sorry—but you no longer have a duty to prevent damage to the vegetable patch. Again, you are off the hook as regards this duty.

Let us apply this reasoning to the more serious topic of climate change. Someone who wants to deny that there is a general duty to mitigate climate change might argue along very similar lines. First, he or she might maintain that climate change is not occurring or will not occur at all—just as you claimed that no damage was being caused in the vegetable patch because the neighbor did not even have a vegetable patch or your daughter was still too small.

Second, he or she might maintain that, although climate change will occur, it is a natural process and human beings are not to blame—just as you claimed that a wild boar and not your daughter was to blame for the damage to the vegetable patch.

Third, he or she might maintain that, although climate change will occur and is being caused by human beings, it will not have any—or it will not have exclusively—negative effects; rather, it will also have positive effects and these will more or less cancel out the negative effects—just as you previously claimed that the good deeds of your cavorting daughter would not cause any damage or would outweigh the damage to the vegetable patch.

Finally, fourth, he or she might maintain that it is, in any case, too late to prevent or reverse climate change—just as you previously claimed that the damage was already done and that the vegetable patch was beyond repair.

If only one or several of these considerations were to apply in the case of climate change, then we could not have a duty to mitigate climate change as a matter of principle—just as previously the duty to protect the vegetable bed would be null and void if one of your claims were true.

But how cogent are these arguments? The first denies that climate change constitutes a moral problem by denying that climate change is even occurring—and we already pointed out in the last chapter that this denial of climate change is untenable. There may be uncertainties about the precise extent of global warming, but it is certain *that* global warming is occurring—that it has, in fact, already begun. Moreover, the assertion one sometimes hears that concerns about climate change are politically motivated, and that the work of climatologists is motivated by their personal interest in attracting attention and research funding, is likewise untenable: It is simply not plausible that 97–98 percent of climate researchers—moreover, of researchers working independently of each other—have manipulated their findings to serve their diverse individual interests and have nevertheless arrived at the same conclusion.

Similarly one can dispel the second reason for denying that the duty to mitigate climate change has any basis. Someone who asserts that we do not have a duty to mitigate climate change because the climate change that is occurring is not caused by us human beings, but is instead a natural process, is asserting something that is simply at odds with the current state of scientific knowledge. There is no longer any uncertainty that the climate change that has occurred or is going to occur is in large part man-made ("anthropogenic"). All natural climate-warming factors taken together are not sufficient to explain the observed increase in the global temperature; only when the influence of human activities is taken into account can one explain the observations. Thus the second argument does not provide a cogent reason for denying that climate change is a moral problem either.

So what about the third reason, the assertion that climate change does not have any morally bad consequences or that, even though it entails something bad, it also entails something good that cancels out the bad?

Here, it is helpful to distinguish between two cases. First, someone who maintains that climate change does not have *any* morally problematic consequences is either ignorant of the scientific facts or is making an incorrect moral judgment about their moral significance. Predictions of the impacts of climate change leave no room for doubt that at least *some* of these impacts are morally problematic: People will be driven from their homelands, drought and water shortages will foment wars and aggravate famines, tropical diseases will become endemic in formerly temperate climate zones, and extreme weather events will lead to home-lessness and destitution. Anyone who thinks that these effects will not materialize is ignorant of the facts. And those who are aware of the facts, but think that they are not so bad, have a false (and questionable) moral conception. We generally regard expulsion, war, starvation, disease, death, homelessness, or destitution as morally bad. One cannot deny, therefore, that there is at least something morally bad about climate change.

Second, someone who admits this, but nevertheless maintains that there is also something good about climate change that cancels out the bad, is right in one respect and wrong in another. It is true that climate change will also have some positive effects: For example, it will become possible to grow wine in Norway, previously inhospitable steppes in Russia will be opened up to cultivation, and sales of ice cream will probably increase. However, it is not true that these advantages counter-balance, or even outweigh, the disadvantages. Someone who seriously maintains that clearing new farmland and an increase in ice-cream con-sumption counterbalance famine, death, and disease clearly has a dis-torted moral view of things. The negative side has far greater moral weight than the positive side. And even if this were not so, sometimes one has to avoid doing something bad even if, as a result, one could do something good that outweighs the bad: If a doctor could save five human lives by sedating someone who happens to be passing by, then removing her heart, lungs, liver, and both kidneys, and transplanting them into five sick people, then the good (five lives saved) would seem to outweigh the bad (one life sacrificed)—yet, morally speaking, the doctor should *not* do this. Even when the good outweighs the bad, there-fore, one may nevertheless have to avoid the bad. In the case of climate change, this means that even if the "net balance" of climate change might turn out to be positive, this does not necessarily cancel out the duty to mitigate climate change (and hence to avoid evil). Thus the third argument for the claim against a duty to mitigate climate change also lacks any basis and is not convincing.

This brings us to the fourth argument: Can one avoid the duty to miti-gate climate change by pointing out that it is already too late and that climate change can no longer be checked? It is indeed true that greenhouse gases will lead to global warming only with a time delay. Therefore, even if humanity as a whole were to stop emitting greenhouse gases overnight, a certain increase in average global temperatures is still to be expected. But this objection fails to recognize that the duty to mitigate climate change is not about avoiding *any* climate change, but rather about avoiding a *dangerous* or *morally problematic* change in the climate. What level of climate change is dangerous and what is not is itself an ethical question, closely bound up with the second key question of climate ethics that we will examine in more detail in Part II. Here, the important point is that it is indeed still possible to avoid dangerous climate change, which could correspond, for example, to a rise in temperature of greater than 2°C. Admittedly, the window of opportunity is gradually closing—but at least there is still such a window, if we follow the estimates of the relevant climatologists (Meinshausen et al. 2009; Knutti and Rogelj 2015). It is simply not true, therefore, that it is already too late to avoid dangerous climate change. And even if this should turn out to be the case, it would still be possible to *limit* dangerous climate change, because more emissions means a greater increase in temperature (and hence more damage), while fewer emissions also means a lower increase in temperature (and hence less damage). This applies even if the extent of the damage exceeds what is morally permissible. Although, in this case, one would not avoid all morally problematic damage by reducing greenhouse gas emissions, one would limit the damage as much as possible. In the final analysis, therefore, the fourth argument does not refute the duty to mitigate climate change either.

So it is difficult to deny that climate change is a moral problem and that something has to be done about it. Nevertheless, there is no shortage of people who do just that. For people working in the media or politics who often find themselves confronted with such cases, another set of moral questions arise: Is it permissible to deny that climate change is a moral problem? And should one pay attention to people who do precisely that?

Is it permissible to deny climate change? Ethics for climate lobbyists and journalists: a brief

We have seen that there are no good reasons to deny the need for moral action with regard to climate change. Yet even if an opinion is unreasonable, this in itself does not mean that expressing this opinion in public (for instance as a lobbyist) or reporting on it (for instance as a journalist) should be forbidden. Nevertheless, one might wonder whether there is something morally wrong with spreading views that deny climate change: Is it not somehow objectionable to cast doubt on something that is supported by overwhelming scientific evidence? Is it not even *dangerous* to deny that climate change is a moral problem, when this will lead to delays in implementing corresponding measures to mitigate climate change?

These questions about the moral character of the denial of climate change affect two occupational groups above all: first, those who are involved either directly or indirectly in shaping the political response to climate change, whether as representatives of nongovernmental organizations (NGOs), as public servants, as politicians, or as members of interest groups; and second, those who report on climate change and climate policy in the media. The appeal to free speech, or alternatively to *freedom of opinion*, plays a key role in both contexts: We should be free to defend and discuss even unreasonable opinions. Someone who thinks that all swans are black, for example, believes something that is untrue and unreasonable. Needless to say, however, it is not morally forbidden to assert that all swans are black in public. Freedom of speech guarantees us the right to express our opinions (about swans, historical facts, political decisions, people's behavior, or fundamental values) in public, even when they are false. And those who deny that climate change is a moral issue (especially in the version that denies that there is even such a thing as climate change) often invoke freedom of speech and opinion. Are they justified in doing so? And how should one respond to public denials of climate change?

First, it is important to recognize that there are limits to freedom of speech. Hate speech directed against a particular group, denying the Holocaust (in Germany and some other countries), and incitements to murder are forms of public expression that are not only subject to criminal prosecution, but also morally wrong. Evidently, therefore, freedom of speech has certain limits. It is a difficult ethical question where exactly these limits should be drawn and according to what criteria the public expression of an opinion should be forbidden. However, here, there is no need to develop a comprehensive catalog of criteria for the limits of freedom of speech (see McGowan 2013 for an overview), because it seems evident that denying climate change is not on a par with incitement to murder or denying the Holocaust. That restrictions should not be placed on freedom of speech in the case of denials of climate change is hardly in need of argument. Therefore those who publicly deny the existence of climate change can rightly appeal to freedom of speech in the first instance.

But it is also important to recognize that this does not resolve all the questions. Even if it is not a matter of placing restrictions on free speech with regard to climate change and legally prohibiting denials of the existence of climate change, it nevertheless remains an open question whether such denials reflect a right or a wrong exercise of free speech to which one is, in principle, entitled. Here, the situation is exactly the same as with other civil liberties: It is up to us (and, to that extent, part of our freedom) whether we are indifferent toward the community or support it actively, whether we cultivate our children's musical talents or not, and whether we serve others in our professional lives or only our own bank balances. However, there are better and worse options within the scope of the freedom to which we are entitled. The use we make of our freedom is not morally neutral. This is also true in the context of climate change: We are free to publicly defend any position we like with regard to climate change—but it may be better to defend one position rather than another. Even though some of those who deny climate change paint a different picture, what is at stake here is not whether one has a right to deny climate change (insofar as it falls under freedom of speech, which is one's right); rather, the issue is whether one is making the correct use of one's right to free speech when one publicly denies climate change.

When it comes to *this* question, we have to weigh up two conflicting considerations. On the one hand, being skeptical and critical by publicly challenging an established consensus and advocating the opposing view has fundamental value for the process of acquiring knowledge and establishing the truth. In this respect, skepticism about climate change is a good thing. On the other hand, there is an imminent danger of intellectual arson, because denying climate change has negative consequences. It leaves politicians and the public with the vague impression that "things are not so certain with climate change" and, as a result, contributes to ensuring that measures to mitigate climate change are never, or only belatedly, implemented. In this respect, there is something bad about skepticism concerning climate change.

How should we strike a balance between these two considerations? In our opinion, two cases must be distinguished—namely, *sincere* and *insincere* denials of climate change. When it comes to the first of the considerations (skepticism has value for ascertaining the truth), the *motive* for adopting a skeptical position plays an important role. There is nothing wrong in principle with questioning and challenging the prevailing consensus because you find the arguments, data, and evidence presented unconvincing and want to discover the truth. By contrast, someone who casts doubt on a position for personal gratification, to provoke, or for pecuniary reasons cannot appeal to the value of skepticism for discovering the truth, since he or she is not even interested in the truth. Thus only someone who is really interested in discovering the truth can invoke the first consideration in his or her defense. This is bound up with the fact that freedom of speech protects something quite specific: the right to be able to publicly defend one's *convictions*. But being convinced of something means taking it to be *true*. For this very reason, many of the denials of climate change actually encountered cannot appeal to freedom of speech or the value of skepticism. It is not uncommon for representatives of certain interest groups to deliberately pepper their public denials of climate change with selective evidence against climate change, in full awareness that the evidence in question is selective and that the whole truth looks very different (on which, see Oreskes and Conway 2010). Neither is it uncommon for certain publicity-hungry scientists to adopt a position that is at odds with the prevailing consensus and to play devil's advocate for personal gratification or to provoke. But someone who knowingly mouths untruths, half-truths, or distorts the truth, who deliberately manipulates evidence, or who places something in question that, in reality, he or she believes him or herself, evidently does *not* consider that public proclamation to be true. In this case, the denier him or herself is not convinced of what he or she defends toward the outside world—so that, here, one can speak of *insincere* denial of climate change.

The first consideration (the value of skepticism for discovering the truth) is irrelevant for this latter kind of denial. It is to be feared, however, that some of the negative consequences of denying climate change that underlie the second consideration (intellectual arson) will materialize. When high-ranking lobbyists or mercenary scientists deny climate change, this discourages certain people—in the worst case, decision-makers—from taking climate change seriously and doing something about it, and this can lead to delays in implementing appropriate countermeasures. Weighing up the two considerations, therefore, it is wrong to make an insincere use of one's freedom of speech. (Of course, this applies to *all* lobbyists, not only to those who represent the interests of the oil, electricity, and industrial concerns. Lobbyists from a "green" NGO cannot appeal to free speech either if they suppress or deny facts that they know to be prejudicial to their cause.) Certainly, there are also sincere deniers—people who are convinced that there is insufficient evidence for climate change and really believe that climate change is a fiction. These people cannot be accused of being dishonest or insincere.

Insincere public denial is an abuse of freedom of speech; sincere public denial is not. There is a further ethical issue that is the mirror image of the issue of sincerity: How should those who report on climate change in the media deal with people who deny climate change? In this context, one sometimes hears it said that a journalist's duty is to provide coverage of both those who support and those who oppose an issue. That is true. But it is a misconception that journalists can simply be content to present "both sides of the story" or to grant all voices equal time or space in their reports. In the context of climate change, this creates the impression that the horde of climate scientists can be divided into two equally large camps: those who deny climate change and those who do not. As we have already repeatedly stressed, however, that this is simply not the case. Moreover, it contradicts the ideal to which journalism is committed—namely, the truth. In the case of climate change, therefore, journalistic commitment to the truth means more than only providing exposure for two conflicting views and their arguments; it also means informing the public about the relative *weights* and *levels of justification* of these views. In a report on climate change, one certainly *may* point out that there are also dissenting voices and one may even cite the arguments of these climate change deniers— but one *must* also point out that this is a minority position and that the arguments of the deniers have been refuted. Regrettably, sometimes this is does *not* happen, leaving readers or viewers with the impression that the camp of climate scientists is divided into two equally large factions, which is simply not true.

Conclusion

This chapter examined more closely the step that leads from the scientific findings to an initial answer to the key question of whether we need to do anything at all in the face of climate change. For many, this is an obvious step: In view of the consequences of climate change, we *have an obligation* to do something about it and to mitigate climate change. Some people do not draw this conclusion, however, but instead deny that climate mitigation is morally required. This denial can assume the form of denying the *basis* of the duty to mitigate climate change (that climate change is a moral problem), denying the *addressee* of the duty to mitigate climate change (the current generation), or denying the *content* of the duty to mitigate climate change (that mitigation is what is required rather than adaptation). In this chapter, we have taken a somewhat closer look at the first version of the denial and explored the different reasons one might cite in support of the claim that climate change is not a moral problem. From this, it emerged that none of these reasons is ultimately convincing (see Arguments box 1). In the next two chapters, we will examine how things stand with the second and third versions of the denial.

Arguments box 1: denial of the basis of the duty to mitigate climate change

The first way in which to deny a general duty to mitigate climate change casts doubt on whether there is any basis for such a duty and hence whether a moral problem of climate change exists to which someone has to respond in some way. There are four reasons why one might take this view, as follows.

(1) *Objection*: "Climate change does not exist."
    Reply: That contradicts the scientific findings.
(2) *Objection*: "Climate change is not a man-made problem; we are not to blame."
    Reply: That also contradicts the scientific findings.
(3) *Objection*: "Climate change is not all bad."
    Reply: The good aspects do not outweigh the bad. Moreover, sometimes one has to avoid doing something that is very bad even if, as a result, one could achieve an even greater good.
(4) *Objection*: "Climate change can no longer be avoided; it's already too late."
    Reply: That is false: It is not too late to avoid the dangerous consequences of climate change. And even if it were too late, we would still have to try to limit the damage as far as possible.

References

Knutti, R., and Rogelj, J. (2015) "The legacy of our CO_2 emissions: a clash of scientific facts, politics and ethics," *Climatic Change*, 133(3): 361–73.

McGowan, M. K. (2013) "Speech, freedom of," in H. LaFollette (ed.) *The International Encyclopedia of Ethics*, Chichester: Wiley-Blackwell, 4981–91.

Meinshausen, M., Meinshausen, N., Hare, W., Raper, S. C., Frieler, K., Knutti, R., Frame D. J., and Allen, M. R. (2009) "Greenhouse gas emission targets for limiting global warming to 2°C," *Nature*, 458(7242): 1158–62.

Oreskes, N., and Conway, E. M. (2010) *Merchants of Doubt: How a Handful of Scientists Obscured the Truth on Issues from Tobacco Smoke to Global Warming*, New York: Bloomsbury Press.

3 Fundamental doubts about our responsibility for the future

The second way in which to deny the duty to mitigate climate change does not dispute that climate change is a moral problem and that something has to be done about it; rather, it disputes that it is we—the present generation of human beings—who have to do something. This doubt is rooted in a much more fundamental doubt about whether one can have any moral obligations toward future human beings at all. You may have heard someone say in a discussion about world poverty: "That's terrible about the poor and starving children in Africa—but, to be honest, what does it have to do with me? What are these distant people to me?" Just as here the speaker denies that duties exist across *spatial* distances, so too one can deny that duties exist across *temporal* distances—that is, that there are duties between different generations: "That's terrible for the people living 100 years from now—but, to be honest, what does it have to do with me? What are these people in the distant future to me?"

At first sight, there seems to be something to this argument. After all, climate mitigation is an intergenerational problem (see Chapter 1), because future generations are the main beneficiaries. Every ton of CO_2 we save *today* will mainly protect the climate *in the future*. In this respect, climate mitigation can be viewed as something that we do for future generations. Why, one might ask, should we have moral obligations toward these people in the future? We do not know them and will never have anything to do with them. If we take measures to ensure their well-being, they will never be able to do anything for us in return. And if it is, in fact, true that we do not owe future generations anything at all, then there does not seem to be any need *for us* to take moral action with regard to climate change either: *We* do not have to do anything.

But is it true that we cannot have *any* obligations toward future generations? Even a cursory glance at our everyday morality casts doubt on this claim: For example the pension system in some developed welfare states is based on the idea of solidarity between generations. Evidently, we do not think that every generation has to earn and set aside its own provision for retirement; on the contrary, we consider it morally justifiable that the younger working part of the population should make payments to the older retired part. In so doing, the younger generation in turn acquires a claim to be financed in its old age by the then younger part of the population. This is what is meant by the "intergenerational contract": The present generation fulfills a duty that follows from the right of an earlier generation and, in doing so, it in turn acquires a right that the future generation has an obligation to guarantee. But if present-day generations can have rights vis-à-vis future generations, why can they not also, in principle, have duties toward them? Doubts about the possibility of duties toward future generations do not seem to be so easy to reconcile with our everyday morality. Thus proponents of this version of the denial that there is a duty to mitigate climate change have to present *arguments* to persuade us that, contrary to our initial impressions, we cannot have duties toward future generations.

We will now examine in turn the three main arguments that play a role in the discussion of this issue in climate ethics.

"Only if we have direct dealings with each other": relational conceptions of justice

The first argument takes up the notion of the intergenerational contract and generalizes the idea of intergenerational solidarity. What, one might ask, is the real basis of our justice-based obligations toward other persons? It is tempting to say, for example, that the intergenerational contract in the pension system gives rise to duties only because the generations that have duties toward each other via this contract overlap for a certain period during which they stand in a close *relationship*: Parents care for their children; teachers educate their pupils; in every large company, several generations of employees contribute to the company's success or lack of success; retirees volunteer in associations and local groups that also benefit young people; and people in need of care are looked after by their relatives and by professional caregivers. In short, the social network is permeated by relationships between members of different generations from which both sides benefit—the "young" as well as the "old." One could now argue that this specific circumstance is a precondition of the existence of duties between young and old: By contributing to the well-being of the community, one part of society (young or old) acquires a claim that ought to be met by the other part (old or young), which benefits from this contribution. And this, one might argue, is always the case when we owe someone something: There must be a prior *relationship* between the one who has to fulfill a duty and the one to whom the performance of the duty is owed.

This is the idea underlying the "relational conception of justice": Justice-based obligations come into play where—and only where—persons or communities stand in relationship with each other. The specific kind of relationships in question is spelled out differently in different versions of this conception. It might be relationships in which people cooperate for their mutual benefit, relationships within public institutions, or relationships within a community held together by shared descent and culture. The key point according to this conception is that some such relationship is *necessary* if justice-based obligations are to be possible.

Imagine a case of two islands that are completely isolated from each other: The inhabitants of the one island are virtually swimming in affluence because of their mineral resources, whereas the inhabitants of the other island scratch out the bare minimum from the barren land to ensure their survival. There is neither exchange, nor cooperation, nor any kind of relationship between the two islands. If we follow the relational conception, then the inhabitants of the wealthy island do not have any justice-based obligations toward the inhabitants of the poor island (for example a duty to achieve a balance between their relative levels of affluence)—they do not owe them a thing. Of course, that does not preclude the inhabitants of the wealthy island from engaging in voluntary assistance out of compassion—but it would be just that: a *voluntary* act and not a duty.

Taking such a relational conception of justice as our point of departure, we can now construct a first argument for the second version of the denial—that is, the claim that we do not have any duties toward future generations. Evidently, people living today do not stand in *any relationship whatsoever* with the people who will exist in the distant future: We do not produce any goods with people who are not yet born; we do not assist them when crossing the street and they do not look after us when we are sick; they do not volunteer in our clubs and we do not help them to organize block parties. People from the distant future are more like strangers: We neither know them nor have anything to do with them. But if the present and future generations do not stand in a relationship, and if a relationship is a necessary precondition of justice-based duties, then the present-day generation does not have any such duties toward future generations. This is really just a way of spelling out the question already raised at the beginning: "What on earth do *I* have to do with people in distant countries and in the distant future?" Here, too, the assumption is that duties can exist only where there are relationships.

Is there a plausible response to this argument? There is. In the first place, even relational conceptions of justice cannot deny that we also have certain minimal duties toward strangers. They have to concede, for example, that the inhabitants of the wealthy island are not permitted to drop a bomb on the inhabitants of the poor island. At least the duty not to *harm* others and the duty to respect their *human rights* seem to be independent of relationships, even if all duties that go beyond these are based on relationships. And one might ask whether some of the things that we owe future generations cannot also be derived from such minimal duties. Do we not harm future generations when our greenhouse gas emissions contribute, for example, to the increased frequency and destructiveness of tropical hurricanes in the future?

Second, it does not require much imagination to justify—albeit indirectly—certain duties toward the future even within relational conceptions. Although we do not cooperate with our descendants in the distant future, we do cooperate with the members of generations that overlap with our own. We cooperate with our parents and grandparents, but also with our children and our children's children. Therefore, within the relational conception, one can justify duties toward the immediately preceding and following generations with whom we coexist for a certain period—and if every generation fulfills such duties and cares for the following generation (with whom they are directly acquainted), the result is a series of interlinked generations that take care of each other. This chain ultimately ensures that *all* generations, including those in the distant future, are cared for. It would then indeed be true that we do not have any *direct* duty toward people in the distant future, but such a duty would arise indirectly, as it were, because we have a duty toward the next generation, which in turn has a duty toward the following generation, and so on. Now, one could object that such a chain of obligations does not exist in the case of climate change, because the detrimental climatic effects of current emissions do not affect our direct descendants, but only later generations. The effects of our actions "skip," as it were, the next link in the chain of obligations. This objection rests on the empirical assumption that our current emissions will not have any problematic repercussions for the generation coming directly after us. As some climate studies show, however, this is not entirely true: Even the emissions resulting from the activity of a 30-year-old woman *today* will lead to discernible global warming in as little as 50 years (see Friedlingstein and Solomon 2005; Hare and Meinshausen 2006). Therefore, that woman's son, born today, who will then be 50 years old, will be affected by the emissions resulting from his mother's activity. So our current emissions *will*, in fact, have problematic consequences for the generation coming immediately after us.

Third, one can turn the tables and ask why we should assume that issues of justice arise only when human beings stand in relationship with one another or interact in certain ways. Is the simple fact that one is a *human being* not sufficient to bring one within the scope of justice, independently of the specific relationship in which one stands to others? Is it not unjust that the child of a wealthy Wall Street banker can spend as much on alcohol in a single night of binge drinking as the child of a Chinese migrant laborer earns in five years as a harvest worker—independently of whether the two children know each other? To pose this question is to challenge the central premise of the relational conception of justice and to pull the rug out from under the first argument against the possibility of future-oriented duties.

Taking all three replies together, then, there is not much left of the first argument. It is *not* a sufficient reason to assume that duties toward future generations are impossible.

"And if you did not exist?" The nonidentity problem

A second argument for the view that we cannot have duties toward future generations goes a step further. It starts from the observation that our actions also have unintended consequences:

> You buy a newspaper at the kiosk and slip it into your pocket. By chance, a passerby sees the front page and decides to buy the newspaper and, while he is at it, a lottery ticket. He wins the jackpot: a lifelong monthly pension that assures himself and his family a comfortable life.

In a certain sense, in this example, a side effect of your buying the newspaper has been to transform the life of the passerby and to influence the course of the world in a way that you did not intend.

Translated into the context of climate mitigation, this leads to the following thought. One of the unexpected side effects of climate policies is that, through these policies, we also influence *which* human beings will exist in future. Imagine a person called Laura in the year 2200. Climate change has become a reality and the global average temperature has risen by 5°C. Laura is suffering as a result and complains that nothing was done about this 200 years ago. But if we, as her ancestors, had taken measures to reduce emissions in time, we would not only have mitigated climate change, but would also have changed many other things as well: Companies would have made different investments and implemented energy efficiency measures; certain sectors (for example the oil industry) would have experienced less growth, while others (for example the renewable energies sector) would have grown even more rapidly; tax revenues would have been funneled into different areas of research, leading to different technological developments; people would have chosen different professions, earned different salaries, and purchased different goods; certain social developments (for example a discussion about climate mitigation measures) would never have taken place; and certain human beings would never have met each other either privately or professionally. If one adds up all of these effects over the years, it is extremely unlikely that the very two people who were destined to become Laura's parents would have met each other and conceived a child on the same night with precisely the same ovum and sperm cell that determine Laura's DNA. Then Laura would never have been born either. Thus Laura would not have been better off in the scenario in which we took prompt measures to mitigate climate change, because she would never exist! Completely different people from Laura would have existed—and while *these other human beings* would have been better off as a result of the climate mitigation measures than Laura would be without them, Laura *herself* would not.

Through climate policy, therefore, we influence not only how good things will be for people in the distant future, but also who exactly these future human beings will be. At first sight, this train of thought may seem to be an empty abstraction. But it leads to a serious problem that has come to be known in the literature as the "nonidentity problem" (Parfit 1984: ch. 16). Our duty to mitigate climate change seems to be based on the fact that we would *harm* some people living in the future if we were to fail to implement climate mitigation measures today. However, harming these people seems to mean that *they* would be worse off without climate mitigation than *they* would be with it. Thus duties to mitigate climate change seem to be based on the idea that the people affected in the future will be worse off if we do nothing and will be better off if we do something to mitigate climate change. But, in so arguing, we assume that the people affected in the two scenarios are *identical*: *They* are better off with, rather than without, climate mitigation. As we have just seen, this precondition is not fulfilled, because the people who would do well in the scenario in which we take measures to mitigate climate change are *completely different people* from those who would do badly if we do nothing. Therefore the people whom we are talking about in the scenario "with climate mitigation" versus the scenario "without climate mitigation" are not identical. This is why it is called the "nonidentity problem": In the distant future, there will be nobody who can complain that he or she would have been better off if we had protected the climate, because had we done so he or she would not exist. It would seem, therefore, that our current greenhouse gas emissions do not, in fact, harm anybody—and hence there cannot be a duty toward future generations to mitigate climate change either.

The strange conclusion of the argument from nonidentity has prompted a wide-ranging debate (see Roberts 2009; Boonin 2014). Among the various responses, here we will single out that which seems to us to be the most promising. The nonidentity problem rests, first, on the assumption that the duty to mitigate climate change is based on the fact that people would be *harmed* if we were to do nothing to mitigate climate change. Second, this argument assumes a conception of harm in which we consider one and the same person in two different scenarios and ask whether *this* person would be better or worse off in the one scenario than *the same* person would be in the other. Thus the idea of harm always seems to involve a comparison between two states of one and the same person.

But is the assumption that climate mitigation duties can be based only on the idea of harm plausible? And, even assuming that it is, should harm be conceived as the relative worsening of the position of one and the same person? As long as someone has crossed a certain threshold of well-being, it is often less crucial from a moral point of view whether he or she is better or worse off above this threshold; the more important question is whether people are even able to cross this threshold and to lead sufficiently good lives. Moreover, the decisive issue is not *who in particular* is denied this opportunity by our actions, but only that our actions deny *someone* this opportunity. A good illustration of this is how we think about rights. We often assume that every human being has certain rights, for example human rights (the rights to life, to choose where to live, or to own property), or claims derived from considerations of distributive justice (such as a claim to a certain share of natural resources). If one argues in terms of rights, then whether one is permitted to do something or not depends on whether it does or does not violate the corresponding rights—and whether rights are violated does not depend crucially on *whose* rights they are, but only that they are somebody's rights.

Imagine that a mad scientist sends a rocket into the atmosphere today that is programmed to spread a highly toxic substance across the entire planet exactly 200 years from now, which will kill large numbers of people. The scientist informs the whole world of what he has done, so that everyone knows what they and their descendants must expect. With this decision, the scientist also certainly influences which human beings will exist 200 years from now. Some people may think: "If everything is going to come to an end soon anyway, then there is no point in having children." There will be research projects aimed at preventing this catastrophe and certain people will get to know each other who would never have met if the rocket had not been launched. Thus the world in 200 years will be a different place from the world that would have existed if the rocket had not been launched. But this is irrelevant for the question of whether it is *morally permissible* for the scientist to launch the rocket. The reason why he should not is simply that, in doing so, he violates the *right to life* of some human beings who will be alive in 200 years' time. It does not matter who exactly these people will be. The only thing that is important is *that* the action violates the right to life; *whose* right to life it violates is immaterial to the justification of the duty not to launch the rocket.

One could argue analogously in the case of climate mitigation that our emissions are like the mad scientist's rocket in that they also violate the rights of future human beings. If our actions lead, for example, to more frequent and more violent hurricanes that kill or injure future human beings, make them destitute and homeless, and force them to migrate, then our actions violate the rights to life, to bodily integrity, to property, and to the free choice of where to live. The crucial point is not whether it is Laura's or Mauro's rights that are violated, but simply that rights are violated *as such* while we had alternatives available that would have avoided any right violation. That seems already enough to conclude that we have to mitigate climate change. If this is correct, then duties toward future generations can also be justified in ways that are not—or at least are less—vulnerable to the nonidentity problem. Hence the second argument also fails to support the conclusion that future-oriented duties are not possible as a matter of principle.

"Do we know too little?" Ignorance of the future

We still have to consider a third argument for the view that future-oriented duties are impossible in principle. The version that you may have encountered in your daily life goes as follows:

> This is all well and good—but we have no idea what the future holds! Maybe it will be as the climate scientists claim. But it may also be completely different. Why should we make efforts to mitigate climate change when it is not clear what will come of them?

The basic idea here is that we do not have absolute certainty about what the future holds and hence we cannot have future-oriented duties.

This argument is relatively easy to refute. The fact that we know nothing with absolute certainty about the future does not of itself imply that we do not have any duties regarding future states of the world. This is shown by the following example:

> Your neighbor is becoming extremely annoyed that your daughter still has not left his garden. He reaches for a gun and takes aim at your daughter. Is he allowed to pull the trigger?

The answer is obvious: No, certainly not! Your neighbor has a moral obligation not to do so. It makes no difference if he points out that it is not certain that the gun will fire (perhaps the trigger will jam), or that the shot—if one goes off—will hit your daughter (perhaps a bird will fly into the line of fire at that very moment and be hit instead), or that your daughter, if she is hit, will even be wounded (perhaps she is wearing a locket that will deflect the bullet). It is true that nobody knows with absolute certainty that your neighbor will injure your daughter if he pulls the trigger—but that in no way alters the fact that he simply should not do so.

The point of the argument from ignorance of the future cannot be that *absolute certainty* about the future is a necessary precondition to a duty to do something. If that were what was meant, we would not have *any* duties, because we never have absolute certainty about the future. Presumably what was meant is the somewhat weaker claim that, for there to be a duty, one must have *sufficient* and *sufficiently certain* information about the future. What is crucial for our moral duties is not absolute certainty, but the extent of our (un)certainty. In the case of the neighbor with the gun, the factors that could prevent your daughter from being injured are simply very improbable. Therefore it is very likely that your daughter will be injured, or even killed, if your neighbor pulls the trigger. However, in the case of climate change—on a suitably modified interpretation of the argument—it is not equally certain that the problematic consequences that are feared will actually materialize: We do not know how many people will be forced to migrate by the rise in sea levels, how many people will become homeless as a result of more frequent hurricanes, or how high the losses suffered by farmers will be. Although we know *something* about future climate change, we do not know *everything*, and the question is whether we know *enough* to place us under an obligation.

However, even in this version, the argument based on ignorance of the future does not provide a compelling reason to reject a duty toward future generations to mitigate climate change in principle. Of course, there is no doubt that the extent of our knowledge about the future influences what we ought to do. If it were extremely unlikely that climate mitigation could prevent climate change in the slightest, then things would indeed look different from a moral point of view. But, first, the best available findings of climate science tell us that it is not extremely unlikely that climate mitigation can prevent climate change; on the contrary, it is quite probable that the lack of measures to mitigate climate change will have problematic consequences. It may not be as likely as your daughter being injured by your neighbor shooting at her, but it is nevertheless very probable.

Therefore doubting it amounts to doubting the scientific findings (and we already dealt with and refuted this form of denial in the previous chapter).

Second, it is not so clear that we have fewer duties under conditions of uncertainty, as the objection assumes, rather than even more demanding duties. Imagine that you have promised a colleague that you will mail her a book you borrowed from her and, in particular, that she will receive it in two days at the latest because she needs it urgently for a talk. The postal worker now informs you that it normally takes two days to deliver such a package, but that it is not unusual for it to take a day more (or less). Alternatively, you can send the book with a private courier service, which is more expensive, and then your colleague is certain to receive it within two days. So you have two options: either to send a normal package, but take a risk that the book will not arrive on time, that you will not keep your promise, and that your colleague will not be able to prepare her talk properly; or to send the package by courier and pay more, but without running the risk that it will arrive late. What should you do?

It seems that you are obliged to take the more expensive option and send the package by courier. This means, however, that, in this situation, you have to do *more* when it is uncertain that you will achieve the goal to which you are obligated (here, keeping your promise). In some contexts, therefore, ignorance of the future means that one ought to do more and not less or nothing at all. We will discuss the ethical significance of uncertainty in greater detail in Chapter 8. At this point, it suffices to note that behind the objection based on ignorance of the future ultimately lurks skepticism concerning the scientific findings or a questionable assumption about how our duties change under conditions of uncertainty. Either way, the argument based on ignorance of the future does not demonstrate that we cannot have any duties toward future generations in principle.

Conclusion

In this chapter, we have examined arguments for and against the second way of denying the duty to mitigate climate change. The second form of denial takes the addressee of the putative duty to mitigate climate change—the current generation—as its point of departure and questions whether this generation can have duties toward future human beings. Three arguments are generally adduced in support of this doubt: that based on the relational conception of justice, that based on the nonidentity problem, and that based on ignorance. We have shown that none of these arguments provides a compelling reason for taking radical doubt concerning duties toward future generations seriously (see Arguments box 2).

Arguments box 2: denial of the addressee of the duty to mitigate climate change

The second version of the denial of a general duty to mitigate climate change casts doubt on the claim that it is *we*—the members of the present generation—who must do something. People living today cannot have any kind of moral duties toward human beings living in the future. Three arguments can be cited in support of this view, as follows.

(1) *Relational conceptions of justice*: "Questions of justice arise only when people stand in relationships to one another. But this is not the case with regard to future generations."
   Reply: First, even a proponent of this view should acknowledge certain minimal duties that are not relational; second, an indirect duty toward future human beings can also be deduced within relational conceptions via a chain of obligations; and third, it is simply not true that questions of justice arise only in the context of relationships.

(2) *The nonidentity problem*: "If we were to take measures to mitigate climate change, then the people whom we would supposedly harm by failing to mitigate climate change would not even exist."
   Reply: The duty to mitigate climate change does not rest on the fact that we harm future human beings, but on the fact that we violate rights—and, for this, it does not matter which human beings in particular will exist in future. The decisive point is that some people's rights will be violated.

(3) *Ignorance of the future*: "We have no idea what the future holds. How can we have an obligation to mitigate climate change if it is not clear what will come of it?"
   Reply: First, absolute certainty is not a precondition for having a duty to do something; second, our knowledge of the future impacts of climate change is by no means so unreliable; and third, it is not true that the efforts we have a duty to make always become less when our knowledge of the future is incomplete—on the contrary, sometimes they even become greater.

References

Boonin, D. (2014) *The Non-Identity Problem and the Ethics of Future People*, Oxford: Oxford University Press.

Friedlingstein, P., and Solomon, S. (2005) "Contributions of past and present human generations to committed warming caused by carbon dioxide," *PNAS (Proceedings of the National Academy of Sciences of the United States of America)*, 102 (31): 10832–6.

Hare, B., and Meinshausen, M. (2006) "How much warming are we committed to and how much can be avoided?" *Climatic Change*, 75(1–2): 111–49.

Parfit, D. (1984) *Reasons and Persons*, Oxford: Clarendon Press.

Roberts, M. (2009) "The nonidentity problem," in E. N. Zalta (ed.) *The Stanford Encyclopedia of Philosophy*, Fall 2009 edition, available online at http://plato.stanford.edu/archives/fall2009/entries/nonidentity-problem/ [accessed April 29, 2016].

4 Mitigation, adaptation, or climate engineering

Do many roads lead to the desired goal?

There is a third way in which one might deny the moral duty to mitigate climate change. This does not focus on the basis or on the addressee of the supposed duty, but instead on its content. According to this we do not have a duty to avoid (that is, to mitigate) climate change; instead, we have a duty to enable future generations to adapt to climate change or to use new technologies to intervene in the climate system to offset the greenhouse effect. Rather than reducing emissions (that is, *mitigation*), the proponents of this position argue, we should aim at *adaptation* or at additional large-scale interventions in the climate system (so-called *climate engineering*).

In this chapter, we want to examine whether there are good moral arguments for the claim that we have a duty to facilitate adaptation or interventions in the climate system rather than to take measures to mitigate climate change. For this purpose, we will first examine the two alternative proposals in greater detail and then show that these alternatives have moral drawbacks in comparison with mitigation.

The alternative proposals to climate mitigation

Assuming that we want to avoid the problematic impacts of our current emissions on future generations, then we do, in fact, have a number of options. Consider the chain of effects leading from our current emissions to their problematic effects in the future (see Fig. 4.1). Our emissions are accumulating in the atmosphere. The atmospheric concentration of greenhouse gases will increase accordingly, leading—via the greenhouse effect—to an increase in the average global temperature over time. This increase in temperature will ultimately lead to droughts, more frequent extreme weather events, the melting of the glaciers, and so forth—all of which will, in turn, directly affect people in the future.

As we have seen, the effects on people in the future are morally problematic, which means that we should avoid them. The assumption until

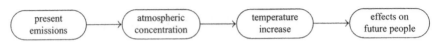

Figure 4.1 Schematic representation of the chain of effects leading from current green-house gas emissions to their impacts on future human beings

now has been that we must start at the beginning of the chain of effects and reduce emissions. That was the "mitigation" option. But one can also start with one of the three *intermediate stages* in the causal chain. This is what is involved in the options "adaptation" and "interventions in the climate system" (see Fig. 4.2). The adaptation strategy starts with the last connecting link in the chain. It allows climate change to take its course until the third link of the chain, the increase in temperature, but then intervenes to reduce the impact on future human beings or to prevent it entirely: Barriers and dams will help against rising sea levels and new drought-resistant types of crop will provide sufficient yields even during longer periods of drought; water shortages can be met with rain water reservoirs and desalination plants; early warning systems and the controlled release of water from glacial lakes will prevent flooding, and the expansion of areas under forestation will prevent soil erosion; and finally, improvements in health care and vaccinations will mitigate the health effects of higher temperatures. Insofar as these "adaptation measures" reduce the threat posed by global warming to future human beings, they involve humanity adapting to the changes in climatic conditions brought about by our current emissions.

At this point, we must make a differentiation. Over the past century, our emissions have already led to warming of approximately 0.75°C. Moreover, since the effects of emissions are time-delayed, a further increase in temperature is to be expected even if we bring emissions to a halt overnight. This means that a certain amount of climate change is inevitable and that corresponding adaptation measures are needed in any case. When we discuss adaptation as an alternative to mitigation in what follows, what is up for debate are not these measures that are necessary to adapt to the climate change that has already occurred or is inevitable; rather, the question is whether additional adaptation measures should be implemented instead of measures to mitigate climate change—and hence whether adaptation can serve as a *substitute* for climate mitigation.

The measures that can be called further interventions in the climate system (climate engineering) focus on the first and second intermediate stages. Hence they can be divided into two main categories (see Royal Society 2009). The first of these involves technologies, such as fertilizing the oceans or the large-scale diffusion of silicates, which bind already

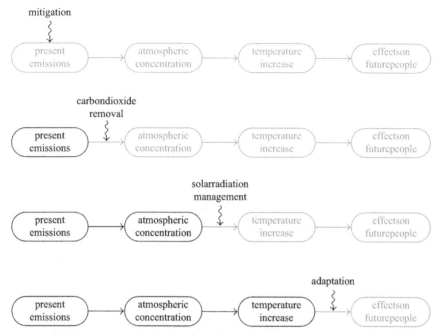

Figure 4.2 Mitigation, climate engineering, and adaptation as different ways of breaking the chain of effects

emitted greenhouse gases and consequently reduce the atmospheric concentration of greenhouse gases. These so-called CO_2 *removals* block the first intermediate stage in the chain of effects. The second category involves the use of technologies such as large sunshades for deployment in space, brightening the surface of the Earth, artificial cloud production, or spraying cooling aerosols into the atmosphere. The aim of this so-called *solar radiation management* is to block the second intermediate stage in the chain of effects by changing the Earth's radiation balance: Although the atmospheric concentration of greenhouse gases would remain unchanged, either less solar radiation would reach the Earth or the Earth would be able to release more radiation back into space, so that the temperature would not rise. Since both classes of technologies share many ethical properties (and measures from both classes could be implemented simultaneously), we will not distinguish further between CO_2 removals and solar radiation management, and will instead speak simply in terms of climate engineering (which does not imply that all of the various specific climate engineering technologies are ethically on a par).

How should we evaluate these proposed alternatives? Is it better, morally speaking, to start at the beginning of the causal chain? Or do we also fulfill our duty if we start at the last intermediate stage of the chain (adaptation) or at the first two intermediate stages (climate engineering)? In what follows, we will argue that climate mitigation is the better option from a moral point of view and that it should not be replaced by adaptation or climate engineering. To this end, we will first examine and refute a number of arguments that, at first sight, seem to *support* adaptation or climate engineering. We will then go on to present three arguments that speak *against* adaptation or climate engineering. (A detailed reconstruction of the arguments can be found in Betz and Cacean 2011, especially ch. 3.)

What speaks for the alternatives?

Let us first examine the considerations that speak *in favor of* adaptation or climate engineering. The first reason why one might take this view is that both adaptation measures and the technical modification of the climate system through CO_2 removals and solar radiation management could prove to be cheaper than mitigation. This argument involves two elements: an empirical assertion ("The alternatives are cheaper than mitigation") and a moral assertion ("The fact that one option is cheaper than another is morally relevant"). Both elements are open to doubt. The financial cost of a course of action in itself says nothing about its moral value: Slavery may have been cheaper than a system in which everyone could choose their work freely and earn an appropriate wage for it—but that, of course, does not justify slavery from a moral point of view. The costs entailed by an option become morally relevant only when they are morally unacceptable for those who have to foot the bill. However, that is certainly not true of the costs that we would have to pay for climate mitigation. A range of studies in climate economics (Stern 2009; Edenhofer et al. 2010; IPCC 2014) conclude that these costs do not exceed a very low single-digit percentage of annual economic output. Of course, the precise level of the costs depends on *how much* climate mitigation we have to perform—an issue that we will address in Part II. However, it is already clear that the level of the costs of climate mitigation is far below what would be morally unacceptable. This holds at any rate as long as no country has to bear these costs alone and they are instead allocated fairly among the present-day generation—an issue that we will address in Part III. In addition (and this brings us to the empirical part of the argument), it should be noted that the alternatives "adaptation" and "climate engineering" also entail certain risks: Dams could burst or turn out not to be high enough; the fertilization of the oceans could have unforeseen effects via changes in the food chain; the development of drought-resistant cereal varieties could prove to be a long time coming. If we want to minimize or even exclude these risks, then the adaptation measures and climate engineering will be quite complex, and hence expensive. And in that case it is far from clear that these alternatives are really cheaper than mitigation.

A second consideration that speaks in favor of adaptation and climate engineering over climate mitigation can be presented as follows:

> Climate mitigation is effective only if many, or even all, countries do their part. But that presupposes a political consensus and, as the failure of climate negotiations in the past shows, this is not easy to achieve. By contrast, it is easier to achieve a political consensus on adaptation measures and climate engineering. This is why we should favor these alternatives.

This argument also has two components: on the one hand, the empirical assertion that it is easier to reach a political consensus on the alternatives than on climate mitigation; on the other, the normative assertion that one should prefer a more consensual option over less consensual options. As regards the latter, one should bear in mind that the normative assertion is not necessarily a *moral* consideration. The claim is not that whether we have a duty to do something or not depends directly on whether the relevant course of action is capable of commanding consensus. That would be a rather absurd position (because then one could avoid any duty that a person or group disagrees with, perhaps out of convenience). What is meant is rather that it would be reasonable or prudent to invest one's time and resources in the alternatives if the option of mitigating climate change had little prospect of political success. But this would not alter the fact that our moral duty is actually to mitigate climate change.

In Chapter 17, we will discuss the problems that arise when ideal moral requirements are confronted with nonideal political realities. Here, it suffices to note that it is not obvious that feasibility considerations (like considerations of cost-effectiveness in the first argument) can really justify moral duties. In addition, concerning the first, empirical, part of this argument, one should not forget that it is not so clear that it is easier to reach a consensus on the alternatives "adaptation" and "climate engineering" than on climate mitigation. After all, measures like a space sunshade first have to be financed, and when it comes to financing, every country has an incentive to let the others make their contributions and then fail to contribute itself. If the sunshade were to be financed, even countries that failed to contribute would benefit from its cooling effect. In this respect, the interactions between the countries involved are quite similar to those in the case of climate mitigation.

This holds in an analogous way for the alternative "adaptation." Adaptation measures also have to be financed and the contentious issue is *who* should finance them. The arduous and inconclusive negotiations on this issue in the recent climate conferences testify to the fact that it is no easier to achieve an inclusive consensus on this issue than on climate mitigation.

A third reason for favoring the alternative proposals over climate mitigation might be that, in future, we could find ourselves in a situation in which the window of opportunity for climate change has closed and implementing adaptation measures or climate engineering is the lesser of two evils (the other being to allow climate change to take its course). This is certainly relevant: We *could*, in fact, find ourselves in this situation—and then it would be good if corresponding technologies had been researched and were ready to be deployed. But it does not follow that we have a duty to facilitate adaptation or climate engineering *instead of* a duty to mitigate climate change. If there is such a duty, then it is more a supplement to the duty to mitigate climate change than a replacement for it.

Consider the following comparison:

> You have promised your mother to bring a *homemade cake* to her birthday party tomorrow. Since one should keep one's promises, you have a duty to bake a cake yourself. But you know that lately your oven has been unreliable. Therefore it is quite possible that, tomorrow morning, you will find that you are simply not in a position to bake the cake yourself, in which case you would be able to bring only a cake from the bakery (which then, of course, would *not* be homemade).

In this situation, a store-bought cake would be the lesser evil, compared to not bringing a cake at all. But, in order to be able to bring a cake from the bakery tomorrow, you must take appropriate measures today (that is, place an order, have sufficient cash on hand, etc.). Of course, here too it is not the case that you now have a duty to take preventive measures for the eventuality that your oven fails *instead of* the duty to bring a homemade cake; on the contrary, you continue to have the duty to bake a cake yourself. The duty to take precautions is at most an additional duty and does not replace the original duty. And this also seems to hold for the duties to mitigate climate change and to facilitate adaptation and climate engineering.

A fourth argument for favoring the alternative proposals is that adaptation measures or climate engineering are the only way that still remains open—the last resort—for preventing the morally problematic impacts on future human beings. Here, the argument is not that the window of opportunity for adequate climate mitigation *could* soon be closed, but that it *is* already closed. Thus the assumption is that it is no longer possible to avoid dangerous climate change by reducing emissions (by means of climate mitigation). We saw in Chapter 2, however, that this view does not reflect the current state of scientific knowledge: We still have time to mitigate climate change (even if time is running out). Therefore the fourth argument also fails to convince.

What speaks against the alternative proposals and for climate mitigation?

Thus far, we have found no compelling reasons to favor "adaptation" and "facilitating climate engineering" over climate mitigation. However, there are a number of reasons that speak specifically against these alternatives. First, the foregoing discussion assumed that the only morally relevant factor is to prevent the problematic repercussions for future human beings (the last link in the causal chain—see Fig. 4.1). But, from a nonanthropocentric perspective (see Chapter 1), morally relevant factors already come into play at other parts of the causal chain: For example, if we concentrate our efforts on the adaptation option, then the effects of the increase in temperature on human beings can indeed be mitigated. What cannot be prevented in this way, however, are the effects on ecosystems: The oceans will become more acidic; aquatic plant and animal species will die out; the polar ice caps will disappear and, with them, the polar bears; it will be possible to admire many alpine glaciers only on old photos; and desertification will change the appearance of the landscape in southern Europe. If you believe that not only human beings count from a moral point of view, but that the suffering of animals, the reduction of species diversity, and the transformation of the landscape are also morally relevant, then climate mitigation seems to be the better option compared to adaptation (at any rate if it is a question of implementing adaptation measures as a substitute for climate mitigation), because climate mitigation would provide much more protection for ecosystems. This problem does not arise in the same way for the other alternative proposal—namely, conscious intervention in the climate system (climate engineering)—but it cannot be excluded either. Fertilizing the oceans would also have an impact on species diversity and artificially brightening the Earth's surface (to increase the amount of radiation reflected back by the Earth) would likewise profoundly change the natural appearance of the landscape. From an ecocentric perspective, therefore, climate mitigation should be preferred to the alternative proposals.

The second argument for preferring climate mitigation focuses on the side effects of the alternative proposals and points out that they could lead to neglect of climate mitigation. Implementing adaptation measures or conducting research on climate engineering could, by itself, already lead individuals and states to reduce their efforts to prevent climate change. Facilitating adaptation and climate engineering could be regarded as a kind of insurance that leads us to drag our heels on what we should actually be doing (namely, mitigating climate change). Moreover, every dollar that is spent on research on climate engineering or on adaptation instead of climate mitigation is no longer available for mitigation. Therefore one would do better not to focus on the alternative proposals as substitutes for climate mitigation.

A third argument for the primacy of climate mitigation—actually, more a complex of several considerations—concerns the risks associated with implementing the alternative proposals. Above all, two risks are relevant here: on the one hand, the risk that the catastrophic consequences that we want to avoid could arise *in spite of* our implementing the alternative proposals; on the other, the risk of *new* unsuspected side effects resulting from the implementation of the alternative proposals. Let us call the former the "residual risk of ineffectiveness" and the latter, "the risk of new dangers."

Let us first consider the residual risk of ineffectiveness. It is important to recognize that neither adaptation nor climate engineering will be able to exclude *all* risks of catastrophic consequences. The adaptation strategy has limits in the case of hurricanes, for example. Houses, trains, and infrastructure can indeed be built to be less susceptible to damage in the case of a hurricane, but it will never be possible to exclude all potential climate damage in this way. Another example of the problem of residual risk is the so-called *termination problem* (Royal Society 2009: 24). Imagine that humanity focused its efforts on climate engineering, built gigantic sunshades in space, and then continued to produce emissions for another two centuries, and in this way increased the concentration of greenhouse gases without a rise in the global average temperature. One day, a meteor shower destroys all of the sunshades. These cannot be replaced overnight and, because of the by now extremely high concentration of greenhouse gases in the atmosphere, extreme warming occurs in a very short time. In this scenario, neither nature nor humanity has enough time to adapt to this drastic and abrupt change: It would be as if someone had shoved the Earth into a 200°C oven. The repercussions would be extremely grave. Thus there is a residual risk that the alternative proposals will fail and not fully protect us against those consequences against which they were supposed to protect us. Moreover, this risk is greater than if we had opted for climate mitigation. But if what is morally required is precisely to minimize this risk for future human beings, then ambitious climate mitigation is to be preferred to climate engineering or adaptation.

Let us now consider the second risk: the risk of new dangers. Adaptation measures and, in particular, climate engineering call for large-scale interventions in ecosystems and in the man-made infrastructure. The sheer scale of these interventions could have unintended side effects, even if the objective (avoiding global warming) were to be achieved: The fertilization of the oceans might lead to drastic changes in the maritime food chain; sunshades could become instruments of political power and blackmail around which wars break out, or they could lead to a reduction in crop yields because the reduced intensity of solar radiation prevented cereals from ripening fully; or the large-scale deployment of aircraft for spraying aerosols or silicates could increase the global energy demand. Given these new threats, it seems safer not to let the chain of effects to run its course in the first place (and hence to reduce emissions) than to allow it to unfold to a certain extent and then to try to bring it under control. In the latter case, it might not be possible to put the genie back into the bottle once it has escaped.

Dealing with risks and uncertainties complicates the ethical analysis of climate change, a topic to which we will return in Chapter 8. When it comes to the question of whether we owe future generations the possibility of adaptation or of climate engineering rather than climate mitigation, the following answer suggests itself at any rate: The fact that the proposed alternatives to climate mitigation involve a non-negligible residual risk of failure and a risk of new, unanticipated side effects speaks against them. Morally speaking, therefore, climate mitigation takes precedence.

Conclusion

In this chapter, we examined more closely the third way in which to deny that we have a duty to mitigate climate change. This version of the denial asserts that we—the present generation of human beings—do not owe future generations climate mitigation, but instead the opportunity to adapt to climate change or to intervene in the climate system. We began by explaining what these two alternatives involve, and went on to examine what speaks for and against them. It turned out that none of the arguments that are supposed to justify the primacy of the alternative proposals over climate mitigation is ultimately successful. Conversely, there are three strong arguments for taking measures to mitigate climate change instead of backing the possibility of adaptation or of climate engineering (see Arguments box 3). However, none of the considerations presented implies that adaptation and climate engineering should not be entertained as supplements to climate mitigation. The important point is that this cannot replace the duty to mitigate climate change. Therefore the primary moral duty of the present generation is to mitigate climate change.

This shows that none of three forms of denial of the duty to mitigate climate change is ultimately convincing. Thus the answer to the first key question of climate ethics— "Do we have a duty to do anything at all in the face of climate change?"—is "Yes, we have to do something: Specifically, we have to take measures to mitigate climate change. This is what we owe future generations." Of course, this does not tell us exactly how much we have to do in order to fulfill our duty (the second key question of climate ethics) and how we should spread the burden of what has to be done (the third key question of climate ethics)—the questions to which we will now turn.

Arguments box 3: denial of the content of the duty to mitigate climate change

The third way in which to deny the duty to mitigate climate change casts doubt on whether we have a duty *to mitigate climate change.* According to the proposal, we instead owe future generations the opportunity to adapt to climate change or to neutralize its effects through technical interventions in the climate system (climate engineering).

Four arguments are often cited for this view, but each of them can be rebutted, as follows.

(1) *Argument*: "The alternative proposals are cheaper than climate mitigation."
   Reply: Financial costs in themselves are not morally relevant; moreover, if one wants to minimize all risks, the alternative proposals become very expensive.

(2) *Argument*: "The alternative proposals are more likely to command consensus than climate mitigation."
   Reply: Whether one has a duty to do something is not contingent on whether it can command consensus; moreover, the funding of the alternative proposals could also be thwarted by a lack of political will or by failure to reach a consensus.

(3) *Argument*: "The alternative proposals could prove to be the lesser evil in the future."
   Reply: This speaks at most for backing other strategies in addition to climate mitigation, but not for abandoning climate mitigation altogether.

(4) *Argument*: "The alternative proposals are the last resort."
   Reply: The argument presupposes that it is already too late to prevent dangerous climate change by reducing emissions— but this contradicts the current state of scientific knowledge.

In contrast, there are three arguments that *support* the primacy of climate mitigation over the alternative proposals.

(1) Viewed from a nonanthropocentric ethical standpoint, adaptation measures and climate engineering are morally worse than climate mitigation, because they intervene more profoundly in ecosystems.
(2) Research on climate engineering and adaptation technologies (as a substitute for measures to mitigate climate change) could lead to neglect of climate mitigation.
(3) The alternative proposals involve a non-negligible residual risk of catastrophic consequences and are themselves a source of new risks.

References

Betz, G., and Cacean, S. (2011) *Ethical Aspects of Climate Engineering*, Karlsruhe: KIT Scientific Publishing.

Edenhofer, O., Knopf, B., Barker, T., Baumstark, L., Bellevrat, E., Chateau, B., Criqui, P., Isaac, M., Kitous, A., Kypreos, S., Leimbach, M., Lessmann, K., Magné, B., Scrieciu, Ş., Turton, H., and van Vuuren, D. P. (2010) "The economics of low stabilization: model comparison of mitigation strategies and costs," *The Energy Journal*, 31(1): 11–48.

Intergovernmental Panel on Climate Change (IPCC) (2014) "Summary for policymakers," in *Climate Change 2014: Synthesis Report—Contribution of Working Groups I, II and III to the Fifth Assessment Report of the Intergovernmental Panel on Climate Change*, available online at http://www.ipcc.ch/pdf/assessment-report/ar5/syr/AR5_SYR_FINAL_SPM.pdf [accessed April 29, 2016].

Royal Society (2009) *Geoengineering the Climate: Science, Governance and Uncertainty*, London: The Royal Society.

Stern, N. (2009) *The Global Deal: Climate Change and the Creation of a New Era of Progress and Prosperity*, New York: PublicAffairs.

Suggested further reading for Part I

Gardiner, S. M. (2010) "Is 'arming the future' with geoengineering really the lesser evil? Some doubts about the ethics of intentionally manipulating the climate system," in S. M. Gardiner et al. (eds.) *Climate Ethics: Essential Readings*, Oxford/New York: Oxford University Press, 284–312.

A forceful attack on the "lesser evil" argument that is often taken to decisively count in favor of (research on) climate engineering.

Gosseries, A. (2008) "On future generations' future rights," *The Journal of Political Philosophy*, 11(4): 446–74.

This paper carefully discusses four challenges to the idea of ascribing rights to future people and develops an interesting proposal (the chain of obligation) to address them.

Page, E. A. (2006) *Climate Change, Justice and Future Generations*, Cheltenham: Edward Elgar.

Chapters 5 and 6 of this book discuss aspects of relational conceptions of justice and the nonidentity problem in more detail.

A more comprehensive list of further readings for this part is available at http:// climate-justice-references.christianseidel.eu

Part II

HOW MUCH DO WE NEED TO DO? INTERGENERATIONAL JUSTICE

5 Equality for our descendants

The previous part has shown that it is hard to justify fundamental skepticism concerning the duty to mitigate climate change. Therefore we can now turn to the second key question of climate ethics: *How much* climate mitigation do we owe future generations? Is the threat to the climate so great that we must transform our current lifestyle from the bottom up? Or will we leave our descendants an acceptable inheritance even if we confine our climate mitigation efforts to measures that do not "hurt"?

A prominent answer to the question "How much climate mitigation?" can be found in the 1992 UNFCCC. Article 2 describes the goal as preventing "dangerous anthropogenic interference with the climate system." But what should be considered "dangerous" interference? If this vague term is intended to specify how much climate mitigation we *owe* future generations, it cannot be spelled out without reference to ethical claims concerning intergenerational justice. Therefore, in this part of the book, we will first ask quite generally—without explicit reference to climate mitigation—what our descendants are entitled to. What we owe them in the specific context of climate policy—in the sense of preventing "dangerous" interference in the climate system— will then depend on how we answer this general question.

We can compare successive generations with hikers who spend a night in a mountain hut (Gosseries 2008). Just as hikers face the question of how well they must tidy up the hut in the morning for the next visitors, so too each generation must ask in what state they must leave the Earth for the generations that follow. Different rules are common in mountain huts. Thus one rule might be: "Leave the hut as clean as you found it." In other huts, the rule might be: "Every user should make a small contribution to improving the hut." In yet others, it might simply be: "Leave the hut clean." Similar rules are conceivable in the domain of intergenerational justice. In this part of the book, we will consider three such rules: first, we must leave future generations *as much* as we have ourselves (Chapter 5); second, we must leave them *more* than we have (Chapter 6); or third, we must leave them *enough* (Chapter 7). But before examining these rules in turn we must consider the prior question: as much, more, or enough *of what*?

What is available for distribution?

The hiker example was a matter of the cleanliness of the hut, which can stand in for the quality of the Earth's environment. In the case of inter-generational justice, however, an even more general good must be taken into account. The good in question can be captured by the terms "well-being" or "quality of life." In this part, we consider specific goods—such as environmental quality or material prosperity—as relevant insofar as they are conducive or detrimental to well-being. The question to be addressed, therefore, is whether the *level of well-being* over time must be preserved, increased, or brought to a sufficient level. Viewed from this perspective, reductions in emissions transfer well-being from the present to the future as it were (and, conversely, ongoing emissions transfer well-being from the future to the present). While measures to reduce emissions cost us something today, the associated avoidance of climate change promotes future well-being.

However, well-being in general is difficult to grasp and, most importantly, it is difficult to measure. Therefore, in practice, we often do not speak *directly* in terms of levels of well-being; instead, it is often easier to use an *indirect* measure to determine the extent of our duties toward the future. A variety of measures can serve in this context as an approximation to the losses and increases in well-being as a result of climate mitigation. If we begin on the far right in Fig. 5.1 (which depicts the chain of effects that we saw in Fig. 4.1), then we can express the impact of current emissions on the future, for example as reductions in future *gross domestic product (GDP)*. Of course, this represents only a very imperfect approximation to well-being. Nevertheless, GDP is one of the most commonly used measures for capturing the present costs and the future benefits of climate mitigation. Thus the acclaimed British government report penned by former World Bank Chief Economist Nicholas Stern uses as a springboard the question of what costs would need to be incurred if we were to avoid climate-related losses corresponding to a reduction of 5–20 percent in global GDP (Stern 2007: 162). The underlying assumption

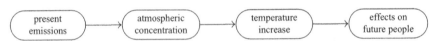

Figure 5.1 Schematic representation of the chain of effects leading from current greenhouse gas emissions to their impacts on future human beings

may be that such a reduction would be difficult to justify from the perspective of intergenerational justice.

Moving further to the left in the chain of effects, however, we might also adopt *increase in temperature* as the "currency" for approximating the losses in well-being of future generations. The call to keep the increase in temperature below 2°C is especially prominent in discussions of climate change. The *2°C target* is the benchmark used by many countries (including the European Union), and the Paris Agreement from 2016 even sets a temperature target well below this benchmark. Another way of expressing the scope of intergenerational duties can be found by going one step further back in the chain of effects. A familiar call is to stabilize atmospheric concentrations of CO_2 below 350 ppm (McKibben 2011: 15 and 19) or 450 ppm (often understood as a pendant to the 2°C target). Until the beginning of industrialization, this value lay around 275 ppm; to date, we have reached around 400 ppm. Taking the box on the far left as our guide, we could also quantify the required amount of climate mitigation in terms of a maximum admissible "emissions budget" for the current generation (or, conversely, in terms of the minimum required emissions reduction). A concrete example is the intuitively appealing call to limit the emissions budget to an average of 1 ton of CO_2 per person per year (see, for example, WBGU 2009: 2–3). That would be equivalent to a reduction in emissions to around a quarter of the status quo. A maximum admissible emissions budget can also be specified for longer periods of time. An example is the call to limit total emissions since the beginning of industrialization to less than 1 trillion tons of carbon. At the present point in time, we have already used up over half of this budget and could reach the trillionth ton before the middle of the 21st century (Allen et al. 2009). Instead of using an emissions budget, of course, one could also measure the duties of the present generation in terms of the costs that they would have to bear in order to reduce emissions.

Those who focus on the left end of the chain of effects are thinking about these obligations from the perspective of the present; by contrast, those who focus on right end are thinking in terms of the acceptable impacts on the future. The task of science is to generate conversions between the different stages of the cause-and-effect chain. To put it in concrete terms: How large can the emissions budget become while nevertheless avoiding an extreme increase in the atmospheric concentration of greenhouse gases—an increase that would lead in turn to a rise in temperature, which would result in climate damage corresponding to unacceptably high losses in well-being?

These conversions are fraught with enormous uncertainty. To simplify matters, we will disregard this aspect for the time being and take it up again later in Chapter 8 as a reason for additional emission reductions. In Chapter 9, another reason for reducing emissions will come into play that we will ignore for the time being—namely, that the impacts of climate change are not distributed evenly within future generations. Climate change will manifest itself in very different ways depending on levels of affluence, geographical location, and the like. In this and the next two chapters, we will ask under these simplifying assumptions what effects of current actions on future generations are acceptable. In doing so, we will test the three abovementioned principles of intergenerational justice— namely, that our descendants should be as well off as we are, that they should be better off than we are, or that they should be sufficiently well off.

Our descendants should not be worse off than we are

As a first principle of intergenerational justice, in this chapter we will examine the idea that we should not leave "the mountain hut" in a worse condition than we found it and were able to use it. In other words, the well-being of our descendants should be at least as high as our own. Equality between the present and the future is the most intuitively plausible notion of intergenerational justice: The idea of our generation enjoying the party and leaving the mess for others to clean up "the morning after" seems unfair. The call for equality is raised in countless forms— explicitly and implicitly—in the prevailing discussion. Even the term "sustainability" reflects this view. The first part of the word, "sustain," indicates that we should preserve something—in our case, well-being. The notion of equality also often underlies the use of the concept of the so-called *ecological footprint*. For many people, the idea of the current world population leaving a footprint of more than one earth—that is, using ecosystems more intensively than they can regenerate themselves— is problematic. It would be unfair to take greater advantage of these services provided by nature than will be possible for future generations. Our current lifestyle should not entail any disadvantages for future generations that we would not be willing to entertain for ourselves.

But why not? Is it, in fact, unjust if some people are better off than others? After all, we do not find it unjust that the standard of living in the past was lower than it is today. What exactly is supposed to be unjust about the idea of it being lower again in the future? This question is surprisingly difficult to answer—at least if we are looking for explicit arguments. Nevertheless, we would like to present an overview of three strategies for underpinning the intuitive call for equality.

A first attempt starts from a specific version of the relational conception of justice that we already encountered in Chapter 3: the idea that justice is based on reciprocity. We have a duty to care for our children and grandchildren because they will take just as much care of us in return when we are old. But this attempt at justification is beset by the problem already alluded to that the effects of climate mitigation measures will become apparent in part only in the distant future. The people affected will never be able to reciprocate our efforts. Thus the demand that even distant generations should be as well off as we are cannot be justified directly in terms of the idea of reciprocity.

One could respond to this objection by modifying the idea of reciprocity as follows: We do not have a duty toward future generations because they will also take care of us, but rather because *past* generations took care of us. The reciprocity involved is *indirect*: We received a rich inheritance from our ancestors; hence we have a duty to hand down at least as much to our descendants in return. A familiar example of this figure of thought is the intergenerational contract. However, there are a number of problems with it.

(1) Indirect reciprocity is, in fact, not a form of reciprocity at all. If Andy gives something to Beth and Beth gives something to Chuck, then Andy, as the first in the chain, can rightly complain that this is not genuine reciprocity from his perspective. After all, he ended up empty-handed.
(2) If someone gives us an unsolicited gift, then we do not generally have a duty to do the same for someone else. Why should it be any different with what we inherited from our ancestors, which, in a certain sense, is like an unsolicited gift?
(3) What was discussed in Chapter 3 still holds: It is a hopeless endeavor to base all our duties on the foundation of reciprocity. We owe human beings something even when they cannot give us anything comparable in return, as is the case, for example, with small children or severely disabled people—or also future generations.

A second attempt to justify the equality requirement does not advocate the principle of reciprocity, but instead draws on the ideas that inform so-called *libertarian theories*. Libertarian theories take as their starting point the question of how a human being who came into the world naked and propertyless can legitimately acquire private property in the goods of this Earth. I can acquire a piece of land, for example, by purchase, through inheritance, or as a gift. The person who transfers it to me in one of these ways may have purchased it him or herself, or acquired it as an inheritance or a gift. But, at some point in human history, someone must have been the first to appropriate this piece of land as property. Under what conditions is such a first appropriation legitimate? In particular, if the Earth is considered to be initially the common property of all mankind, it is plausible to set certain limits to the private appropriation of this common property. Plausible limits, inspired by the well-known formulations of Locke (1689/1960) and Nozick (1974), are, for example, that the appropriation of natural resources is legitimate only when "enough and as good" is left for others, or when others are not left worse off than they would have been without this appropriation. Such limits can be applied to generations instead of individual human beings. If the current generation wants to appropriate the Earth and its resources, then this is legitimate only if it leaves as much and as good as it enjoys for future generations, or if, in doing so, it does not leave future generations worse off than they would have been without this appropriation. Depending on the precise formulation (cf. Gosseries 2008; Vallentyne 2012), such principles inspired by libertarianism do, in fact, support the duty to leave as much and as good for future generations.

A third approach builds on the second, although it also contradicts it. Like the second attempt, it addresses the issue of property in natural resources. According to this third strategy, the Earth is not the property of all human beings; on the contrary, it is not anybody's property—and neither can it ever become someone's property. Far from being the owners of the Earth, human beings are instead its custodians. They should take care of it as something they hold in trust. This perspective is often inspired by religion, such as when the Earth is understood as God's property or is even accorded a godlike status as "Mother Earth." The fact that we are not its owners, however, does not mean that we may not make use of the Earth. We may live off the fruits that it brings forth. It is just that we should not use up its substance: It does not belong to us, after all. If the use of the Earth is a gift to all human beings, then it is also plausible that everyone enjoys the same rights of use. Applied to generations, this means that the current generation may live off the yield of the Earth—but it has a duty to pass on the "capital" itself intact to future generations.

However, these attempts to justify the equality requirement can easily seem somewhat strained, because they are more an expression, than a justification, of the commitment to equality. We should not be surprised at this. Equality is such a fundamental value that it is difficult to justify it by appealing to even more fundamental premises. Deviations from equality are often considered to be more in need of justification than equality itself, which is regarded as a natural starting point. If the present generation cannot specify any explicit reason why it should enjoy a higher quality of life than future generations, then, from an impartial perspective, the assumption must be that it can claim at most as much as it grants subsequent generations. Thus it follows that, even if the three attempts at justification are not ultimately convincing, it remains open to a proponent of the equality requirement simply to reverse the burden of proof. It is the opponents of equality who must offer arguments, not its proponents. And such arguments are, of course, put forward in the debate.

Next, we will consider an argument for the call to leave not only as much, but more, well-being for future generations. From this perspective, a climate policy that ensured only that our descendants are as well off as we are would be inadequate.

Arguments box 4: equality for our descendants

In this part of the book, we are looking for an answer to the second key question of climate ethics: *How much* climate mitigation do we owe future generations? To begin with, we refer in general to the *level of well-being* of different generations and examine three possible positions—that is, that we owe our descendants:

(1) as much as we have;
(2) more than we have; or
(3) enough.

Insofar as we influence the present and future levels of well-being *through climate mitigation*, we can also capture the extent of our intergenerational duty in terms of other—moreover, more easily quantifiable—measures, such as GDP, the rise in temperature, the atmospheric concentration of greenhouse gases, or the emissions budget.

The first requirement—that future generations should be at least as well off as we are—can appeal to three patterns of justification, as follows.

(1) *Reciprocity*: We have duties toward our descendants because they—or our ancestors—care for us in return.
(2) *Libertarian theories of private property*: If a generation regards the Earth and its resources as its property, then it must do so within certain limits, such as that it leaves enough and as good for future generations.
(3) *Rights of use instead of property rights*: Ultimately, the Earth is never the property of human beings; hence although a generation may enjoy the fruits of the Earth, it may not use up its substance.

If these three justifications are not convincing in every respect, then a proponent of the equality requirement can reverse the burden of proof: Equality can be understood as a natural starting point, so that all deviations from equality are in need of justification.

References

Allen, M., Frame, D., Frieler, K., Hare, W., Huntingford, C., Jones, C., Knutti, R., Lowe, J., Meinshausen, M., Meinshausen, N., and Raper, S. (2009) "The exit strategy," *Nature Reports Climate Change*, 3: 56–8.

Gosseries, A. (2008) "Theories of intergenerational justice: a synopsis," *SAPIENS*, 1(1): 61–71.

Locke, J. (1689/1960) *Two Treatises of Government*, P. Laslett (ed.), Cambridge: Cambridge University Press.

McKibben, W. (2011) *Earth: Making a Life on a Tough New Planet*, New York: Times Books.

Nozick, R. (1974) *Anarchy, State, and Utopia*, Oxford: Blackwell.

Stern, N. (2007) *The Economics of Climate Change: The Stern Review*, Cambridge: Cambridge University Press.

Vallentyne, P. (2012) "Libertarianism," in E. Zalta (ed.) *The Stanford Encyclopedia of Philosophy*, Spring 2012 edition, available online at http://plato.stanford.edu/archives/spr2012/entries/libertarianism/ [accessed April 29, 2016].

Wissenschaftlicher Beirat der Bundesregierung Globale Umweltveränderungen (WBGU) [German Advisory Council on Global Change] (2009) *Solving the Climate Dilemma: The Budget Approach*, Special report, Berlin: WBGU.

6 More for our descendants

We will now go on to examine the position that we must leave our descendants more than we have ourselves. This idea resonates, for example, in the declaration of the groundbreaking United Nations Conference on the Human Environment held in 1972 in Stockholm, which called for us not only to protect the environment, but also to improve it. Such a "duty to improve" or "duty to promote growth" seems to be a demanding requirement that requires justification. A supporting argument can be found in a prominent current in ethics—namely, utilitarianism. More than any other theory, utilitarianism focuses on aggregate well-being. Aggregate well-being is the sum of the well-being of every single—including every future—human being. From a utilitarian perspective, politics should always do what best promotes this aggregate well-being; all other ethical considerations—such as those of distributive justice—are ignored. But why does the utilitarian requirement to maximize aggregate well-being lead to the requirement to increase the level of well-being for future generations?

The reason is that we can often increase aggregate well-being if we sacrifice well-being in the present for the sake of well-being in the future. The underlying mechanism is the positive rate of return: When we deposit US$1 in the bank we earn interest on it, so that $1 invested today will be worth more than $1 tomorrow; if we plant a walnut instead of eating it, then a walnut tree will grow and we can harvest countless nuts. The same holds if we "invest" in medical research or in climate mitigation today: It will yield more in the future than it costs today. Many mitigation measures have a positive balance of benefits, which means that future generations benefit more than we have to sacrifice today for these measures (Posner and Weisbach 2010: 21). Exchanging well-being today for well-being tomorrow, therefore, is not a zero-sum game. And because utilitarianism advocates every measure that ultimately results in an increase in well-being, it also turns saving for the future—whether in the bank or through climate mitigation—into a duty.

However, this means that the well-being of future human beings should be higher from the utilitarian perspective than the well-being of human beings in the present. The reason is not that future generations count for more for utilitarians, but that they are interested only in the whole "well-being pie." And because the whole "well-being pie" is bigger the more the present saves for the future, future generations are simply lucky to be born later.

Thus utilitarians demand that we should tighten our belts and sacrifice ourselves for the generations to come—but that is not all. Applying the same logic, they also demand that the future generations should, in their turn, make sacrifices for the generations that follow them, for it also holds for them that they contribute more to aggregate well-being by saving and gainfully investing what they save than when they devote themselves to their own well-being. In the name of aggregate welfare, therefore, every single generation must yield a great deal to the generations that come after it.

Can utilitarianism avoid this seemingly exaggerated conclusion? Utilitarianism can at least attenuate the problem by according the future less weight than the present. Just as some people believe that the well-being of human beings at the other end of the Earth is justifiably of less concern to them than the well-being of their neighbors, one might take the view that we are justified in according the future less concern than the present. In ethics and economics, this idea is discussed in terms of the so-called *discount rate*. Applying a (positive) discount rate means that future well-being counts for less than present well-being when calculating aggregate well-being. Future well-being is "discounted." At a discount rate of 10 percent, for example, well-being a year from now is weighted at just 90 percent of its actual value. This avoids the problem that utilitarianism calls for continuous growth. For example, if a political measure costs 95 "units of well-being" today and prevents harm amounting to 100 "units of well-being" one year from now, then we would not have a duty to take this measure if we were to apply a discount rate of 10 percent (although, without the discount rate, we would have such a duty). The 100 units in the future would simply count for the same as 90 units in the present, and these 90 units are less than the 95 units that the measure would cost at present. The principle at work here is: The higher the discount rate, the lower the weight accorded future generations; and the lower the weight accorded future generations, the lower is also the expenditure required for future generations.

Attaching a lower weight to the future by applying a discount rate therefore renders utilitarianism more plausible, because the present generation is no longer required to sacrifice itself for the future. But is it plausible to supplement utilitarianism with a discount rate? After all, attaching a lower weight to the future can hardly be regarded as anything other than a bias in favor of the present. The plausibility of the discount rate has major relevance for climate policy: What we have just described in abstract terms as "utilitarianism plus discount rate" is the theory that informs many economic studies on climate change and these represent an important voice in debates over climate policy. If a high discount rate is chosen—if future climate damage is accorded a significantly lower weight than the costs that would be incurred today to avoid it—then these studies end up recommending only moderate measures to mitigate climate change. The effect in question is far from negligible. At a discount rate of 3 percent per year, harm to the climate occurring 100 years from now ultimately features in the calculations of economic studies at a mere 1/20th of its actual value. This is the inverse effect of the compound interest effect: Someone who invests $50,000 today at 3 percent interest will almost be a millionaire 100 years from now.

However, economists generally shy away from asking whether a discount rate is even plausible by arguing that people do, in fact, discount in their everyday calculations. That is no doubt true: We are, by nature, impatient—that is, what lies in the distant future counts less for us than the here and now. But appealing to the psychological fact of impatience has a snag. The fact that human beings behave in a certain way of itself does not necessarily mean that their behavior is also acceptable. This is especially true when their behavior affects others and not only themselves. When people accord less weight to future costs and benefits within their *own* lifetimes, then this is their own decision. But when it is no longer a question of discounting within their own lifetimes, but of discounting the well-being of *others*, then things look different. When we accord less weight to climate damage that will occur decades after our deaths than to the costs that would be needed to prevent it today, we are doing just that: discounting other people's well-being. In that case, our preference for the present can no longer serve as a justification for a discount rate. The fact that we are predisposed to lose less sleep over a risk to the environment ten years from now than over a risk to the environment today—that is, that we discount within our own lifetimes—is not a good reason to take a risk to the environment 100 years from now less seriously than a risk to the environment today. Therefore it is not a good reason for discounting beyond the scope of our own lifetimes.

But if a discount rate cannot be justified from an ethical point of view, then we should not supplement utilitarianism with it. We can also avoid the demand to increase the well-being of our descendants by simply abandoning utilitarianism instead of modifying it. By focusing exclusively on the *sum* of the well-being of all human beings, utilitarianism ignores the decisive question of how this sum *is distributed*. Another plausible theory, however, takes into account not only the size of the "pie," but also whether this pie is divided fairly among the different generations. For example, if the costs of a mitigation measure are incurred by the poor among the present generation, but the benefits are enjoyed by the rich section of the future generation, then this measure is not justified, even if the benefits for the wealthy outweigh the costs for the poor. As a result, the positive cost–benefit balance of many mitigation measures in itself is not a compelling argument for implementing these measures; rather, the decisive question is whether a measure is necessary if the future generations are to be able to achieve the level of well-being to which they are entitled. Conversely, the negative cost–benefit balance of a mitigation measure of itself is not a compelling argument against the measure in question; again, the decisive question is whether the measure is necessary to enable future generations to achieve the level of well-being to which they are entitled. We may also have a duty to implement mitigation measures that are more costly than the harm they prevent. In this sense, our duties are independent of the utilitarian requirement to maximize well-being. Moreover, this assertion does not reflect a radical outsider position, but belongs to the very foundation of our moral sense: For example, a lover of roses may not steal a special specimen from her neighbor's garden even if the theft would cost the latter only a small measure of well-being and bring the former a large increase in well-being. (In the case of climate mitigation, however, when measures with a negative cost–benefit balance are mooted *one* critical question in fact arises: Are more efficient measures possible, measures that achieve the same level of well-being for future generations at a lower cost to the present generation?)

Given that future generations are owed a certain level of well-being regardless of considerations of costs and benefits, the question arises of how high this level is. In the previous chapter, we examined the position that future generations could be entitled to at least as much well-being as we enjoy. This chapter has shown that they are not entitled to *more* well-being than we enjoy—at least not if this is justified in utilitarian terms. In the next chapter, we will examine the idea that they may be entitled to a "sufficient" level of well-being.

Arguments box 5: more for our descendants

The call for an increase in well-being for future generations rests on the following two premises.

(1) *Utilitarianism*: We have a duty to maximize aggregate well-being.

(2) *Positive rate of return*: If we forgo one unit of well-being in the present, then we can increase future well-being by more than one unit, for example through climate mitigation.

However, there is an objection to this call for an increase in well-being: It seems to be unfair to the present generation. The objection could be avoided by supplementing the utilitarian requirement to maximize aggregate well-being with a discount rate. However, the core idea of a discount rate—namely, that future well-being should count for less—is hard to justify. The more plausible option is to abandon premise (1) altogether: By abandoning utilitarianism, with its insensitivity to questions of distributive justice, we can dismiss the call to increase the well-being of future generations.

Reference

Posner, E., and Weisbach, D. (2010) *Climate Change Justice*, Princeton, NJ: Princeton University Press.

7 Enough for our descendants

When we spend the night in a mountain hut, we may encounter a rule for cleaning the hut that makes no reference to the condition in which we found it; it simply requires that the hut be left in a *clean* condition. Depending on how well the previous occupants cleaned the hut, we must or may leave the hut in a less clean, an equally clean, or a cleaner condition than we found it. There is a precise analogy between this example and the sufficiency requirement in intergenerational justice: It calls on us to leave *enough* for future generations. The threshold value in question is independent of the present level of well-being. This is what differentiates the sufficiency requirement from the two requirements discussed previously—namely, the equality requirement and the requirement to improve the condition of future generations. While the latter two requirements call for *equal* or *greater* well-being in the future than in the present, the sufficiency requirement lacks any such reference to the present.

What speaks in favor of the sufficiency requirement? Is the duty to leave "enough" for our descendants a plausible alternative to the requirements to leave equal amounts or more for them? In order to assess this, we first need to know what is meant by saying that a generation is "sufficiently" well-off. If we want to specify the threshold value that future generations must be guaranteed according to the sufficiency requirement in a plausible way, then we can no longer rely on a general notion of well-being. Having "enough" certainly means more than having access to the resources that are absolutely necessary for survival. For example, the idea of a sufficiency threshold could be defined in terms of human *needs*. Needs are more than mere desires. Needs are very similar from one person to the next, while there are substantial differences between their desires. Moreover, needs are satisfied at a certain point, whereas some desires are insatiable. On a literal reading, the most famous definition of sustainability reflects a needs-based sufficientarian perspective: "Sustainable development is development that meets the needs of the present without compromising the ability of future generations to meet their own needs" (Brundtland Commission 1987). This definition does not say that future generations must be just as well off as we are (equality requirement) nor does it say that we must bequeath a better world to our descendants (improvement requirement); rather, it says that future generations must reach a certain threshold—namely, the threshold of needs satisfaction.

An alternative characterization of the sufficiency threshold focuses on *human rights*. On this conception, "sufficient" could mean that we bequeath our descendants a world in which human rights can be fulfilled. In particular, our emissions should not violate the human right to life and should not withhold from our descendants the resources that they need to enjoy the human right to a standard of living adequate for health, food, clothing, and housing. These rights were enshrined in Articles 3 and 25 of the 1948 Universal Declaration of Human Rights (UDHR). But as a result of climate change, we are violating them in a variety of ways (see Caney 2010): Storms, heat waves, dengue fever, and the like are directly responsible for disease, deprivation, and death, but also give rise to them indirectly through food production. Further examples of human rights jeopardized by climate change include the right to property (Article 17 UDHR), the right to return to one's country (Article 13 UDHR), and the right to development proclaimed by the United Nations General Assembly in 1986.

And, of course, the call for "enough" for future generations can also be spelt out in ways other than the satisfaction of needs and human rights. For example, one could call for making possible a "decent" human life, a life in human dignity, or a life that does not inspire pity (see Crisp 2003; Nussbaum 2006). These notions go beyond the bare minimum required to satisfy needs and protect human rights. However, when illustrating the sufficiency requirement in what follows, we will base our arguments on the human rights threshold.

What, if anything, speaks in favor of the sufficiency requirement? What is the basis of our supposed duty to future generations to ensure that things should go "sufficiently" well for them—specifically, that their human rights should be protected? Few people doubt that we owe them *at least* this much. In the eyes of many, human rights obviously have priority over other noble objectives. We should protect them not only for those closest to us, but also for strangers—even at great cost. Moreover, protecting human rights is not merely an end in itself: Many moral objectives that go beyond human rights could not even be achieved unless human rights were protected first. For example, it is difficult for climate refugees or people who are starving to make an active contribution to constructing a stable, democratic community. Such moral ideals require that human rights be protected. Last, but not least, this is also in the interest of the present generation. If we want future generations to honor our memory, and pass on our values and achievements, then we must ensure that they are able to do so, which includes ensuring that they are able to develop their potential without their lives being dominated by concern about their basic rights.

The more difficult question for the sufficiency requirement, however, is why we must leave our descendants *merely* enough: Why not more? In particular, should we not ensure that things will be at least *as good* for them as they are for us? In the first place, it is not as easy as it might initially seem to ensure that future generations will be equally well off as we are. The problem is that, if we were to implement this ideal, we would have to know what it means for our descendants to be equally well off. Our great-great-grandchildren will live in a world that is so different from our world in terms of culture, technology, politics, and religion that we can hardly foresee what their preferences and values will be, and hence what will be conducive or detrimental to their well-being. What, for example, will unspoiled nature, a high GDP, or the opportunity to travel mean to them? It is consequently also difficult to specify what is required to ensure that they will be just as well off as we are. It is much easier to make such an assessment in the case of the sufficiency threshold. The goods protected by human rights will, in all probability, also be important for our descendants. The need for food and health scarcely changes over time, in sharp contrast to more comprehensive conceptions of a "good life." The question, therefore, is not only whether we *ought* to create equality, but whether we are even *able* do so.

But even if it were easy to specify how equality can be achieved, other questions arise. Why is equality even important? Some people regard equality as a means to an end: It is an important factor in ensuring social cohesion. This observation is indeed correct. But it cannot be used as an argument for the equality requirement in the case of intergenerational justice, because distant generations do not coexist and hence do not have any need of equality as a kind of social cement. Other people do not regard equality as a means to an end, but as an end in itself. But does equality really have intrinsic value? What is ultimately important is how well off we are and not how well off we are *in comparison to others*. Assuming that we have everything we need, why should it matter to us whether others have more or less than we have? The sufficiency requirement, by contrast, stresses precisely that—namely, what all human beings need (independently of comparisons with other generations). In addition, the goal of equality requires more comprehensive political control and more extensive interference with our freedom than the more limited sufficiency requirement, which could be considered a negative point against the equality requirement.

Rebutting these objections does not seem to be a hopeless endeavor for proponents of the equality requirement (and they can also continue to emphasize that the equality requirement does not necessarily call for an explicit justification anyway). If the objections are not judged sufficiently strong to force its proponents to abandon the equality requirement, they could nevertheless meet the sufficiency requirement halfway when it comes to the *weight* attached to the equality requirement. They could acknowledge that the sufficiency requirement is one of the most urgent among all of the various moral objectives, whereas the equality requirement—even though it is indeed a moral requirement—ranks far down the list of priorities. Thus the sufficiency requirement can be understood as the most urgent part of the equality requirement.

The conclusion that we draw for the remainder of the book is that the *least* we owe our descendants is to ensure that they should be sufficiently well off and that we may *in addition* have a duty to ensure that they should be as well off as we are. The "sufficiency" comes first. However, it does not necessarily constitute intergenerational justice in its entirety; it may simply be the most important part of the equality requirement.

Arguments box 6: enough for our descendants

In contrast to the equality and the improvement requirements, the sufficiency requirement imposes a duty on us that is independent of our own level of well-being: We should ensure that future generations are *sufficiently* well off. What it means to live above this sufficiency threshold can be spelled out in different ways. The interpretation of the threshold value in terms of *human rights* is especially relevant.

The duty to leave *at least* enough for our descendants is hardly in need of justification. It is more difficult to justify why we do not owe them more—in particular, to ensure that they should be just as well off as we are. Proponents of the sufficiency requirement could pursue three strategies, as follows.

(1) They could criticize the equality requirement on the grounds that it has to compare well-being across extended periods of time and that this makes measurement difficult.
(2) They could question whether equality has intrinsic value at all and whether it can be defended in instrumental terms (as a means for ensuring social cohesion) in the intergenerational case.
(3) They could maintain that the goal of equality requires more far-reaching political interventions than the goal of sufficiency.

However, the sufficiency requirement does not have to be understood as an alternative to the equality requirement; it can also be regarded as the most important component of the equality requirement and the one to which greatest attention should be paid. From this perspective, we at least have a duty to ensure that human rights are fulfilled in the future and possibly also a duty to ensure that the level of well-being is maintained over time.

References

Caney, S. (2010) "Climate change, human rights and moral thresholds," in S. Humphreys (ed.) *Human Rights and Climate Change*, Cambridge: Cambridge University Press, 69–90.

Crisp, R. (2003) "Equality, priority, and compassion," *Ethics*, 113(4): 745–63.

Nussbaum, M. (2006) *Frontiers of Justice: Disability, Nationality, Species Membership*, Cambridge, MA: Harvard University Press.

World Commission on Environment and Development (WCED/Brundtland Commission) (1987) *Our Common Future: Report of the World Commission on Environment and Development*, Oxford: Oxford University Press.

8 Uncertainty and the precautionary principle

The question addressed in the previous three chapters was: How much climate mitigation do we owe future generations? This question is embedded in the more general question: What do we owe to future generations as such? In the light of the various arguments and intuitions, *at least* the sufficiency requirement seemed to be justified. The sufficiency requirement—namely, on the present conception, the requirement to protect the human rights of future generations—can be understood either as an alternative to the equality requirement or as its most important component.

However, one could maintain that we do not need to decide between the equality and sufficiency requirements at all, because we already satisfy them both in the real world anyway. Is it not reasonable to assume that future generations will be better off than we are—not merely as well off or sufficiently well off? If so, then we are more than fulfilling our duty even without having to exert ourselves. Should we not instead do *less* for posterity, therefore, and *more* for ourselves?

It is, in fact, not unrealistic to expect that future generations will be better off than we are. Viewed in global terms, the standard of living has increased sharply in recent decades. There have been massive improvements in areas such as life expectancy, income, education, child mortality, and poverty in recent years and decades (Van Zanden et al. 2014; United Nations 2015). Even though technological progress has brought problems, in the past these were far outstripped by the wealth it created. Why should this change in the coming decades? Circa 1900, no one could imagine the progress that would be achieved by the end of the 20th century; in the same way, we are in danger of underestimating the opportunities that human ingenuity will create by the end of the 21st century. The economic gains in welfare could far outstrip even the losses as a result of climate change. The Stern Review estimates in a pessimistic scenario, for example, that the costs of climate change in the year 2200 could correspond to more than 35 percent of global GDP in that year (Stern 2007: 177; see also Stern 2009: 94). If past trends continue, however, the global economy will grow by more than that amount in a single decade. This would mean that, as a result of climate change, humanity would attain the level of prosperity in 2200 that it would otherwise have attained, for example, by 2190. In either case, however, it would be better off than we are today. Climate change comes at a cost in terms of future well-being—but the costs involved are deductions from a level of well-being that will apparently be much higher than today's level.

Thus neither the equality nor the sufficiency perspective calls for additional climate mitigation: The increase in the standard of living will give rise to intergenerational justice of its own accord. At least, this is how it *appears*. On closer inspection, this line of argument is seriously flawed: It ignores the aspects of uncertainty and inequality, because it is based exclusively on the expected value of the average well-being of future generations.

These flaws can be illustrated using an example. The boss of a company has made a commitment to pay his workers a wage of US$2,000. If the boss then decides to pay half of the workforce chosen at random $1,000 and the other half $3,000, we would not say that this boss had fulfilled his duty. Even if he in fact pays $2,000 per worker *on average*, his generosity toward some does not make up for violating his duty toward the others.

Let us now consider a different case. The boss announces to the workers that the company will win a large order in the following month with a 50 percent probability, but that there is also a 50 percent probability that it will not have any orders. Therefore he has decided (without the consent of the workforce) that, in the former case, he will increase wages to $3,000, but in the latter, he will reduce them to $1,000. In this scenario, the *expected* wage remains $2,000 (given that each worker has a 50 percent probability of receiving a salary either of $1,000 or of $3,000). Nevertheless, we would not say that this boss had fulfilled his duty: The workers have a right to a wage of $2,000. The possibility of generously receiving more than $2,000 does not balance out the possibility of receiving less than $2,000.

In the case of climate change, we encounter two analogous problems. If we have a duty to ensure that things go sufficiently well for future generations, then it is not enough if things go sufficiently well for them merely on average, or if their well-being exceeds the sufficiency level merely on expectation. Even if things turn out to be better for our descendants than for us as regards their *average* well-being, many people will nevertheless be worse off than we are, because of global inequality. Many people will still have to struggle with extreme poverty in the future, whereas others will live in excess. Climate change will even exacerbate global inequality. Intergenerational justice must not be based on the average well-being of future generations. Just as in the case of the company, not only inequality, but also uncertainty, poses a problem.

Even if the *expected value* of our descendants' well-being is higher than ours, the uncertainty surrounding any forecast of the future is such that, with some probability, they may also end up worse off than we are. If one of the pessimistic climate scenarios were, in fact, to become a reality, it would be a poor consolation for our descendants that things could also have turned out better. If predictions of the future are fraught with uncertainty, then intergenerational justice should not take the expected value of different possible future scenarios as its basis for calculation.

Up to now, we have excluded this aspect from our discussion of the equality, improvement, and sufficiency requirements. In this and the following chapter, therefore, we will deal with the uncertainty of climate forecasts (Chapter 8) and global inequality (Chapter 9) as two central reasons for climate mitigation.

The intuition informing the precautionary principle

Let us recall the example in Chapter 3. A colleague has lent you a book that she needs back in two days at the latest in order to prepare for an important lecture, so you have promised to return it to her within this period. You now compare the public postal service with a somewhat more expensive private courier service. If you send it by mail, then the book will probably arrive in two days—but it could very well be that it will take a day less or more. The courier service, by contrast, will deliver the book with certainty in two days, neither earlier nor later. Which service should you opt for in this case? The expected value of the delivery time in both cases is two days. But, because you have promised your colleague to return the book by a certain date, you should choose the courier service even if it is more expensive. With the public postal service, the forecast of the delivery date is uncertain: It exhibits a range around the expected value. This is not the case with the courier service and that is what decides the issue in its favor.

We can apply this intuition to climate change. One of the scenarios of the IPCC predicts an estimated rise in temperature of 2.2°C by the end of the century (IPCC 2013: 23). However, there remains uncertainty on this score: This scenario specifies a likely *range* for the rise in temperature of between 1.4°C and 3.1°C. Do we have equally good reason to mitigate climate change whether we factor this uncertainty into our calculations or not? By analogy with the book example, we seem to have *more* reason to avoid this climate change scenario if we expressly factor the uncertainty into our calculations than if we proceed on the simplifying assumption that it would certainly lead to 2.2°C warming. The spread around the expected value has a negative effect on the ethical evaluation.

Therefore uncertainty constitutes an additional reason for climate mitigation. In political practice, this insight is the driving force behind the so-called *precautionary principle*. Different versions of this principle agree in emphasizing the uncertainty surrounding our forecasts of the future and express the conviction that this uncertainty is not carte blanche for inaction (see Chapter 3); on the contrary, the uncertainty should lead us to be especially cautious in how we act. A well-known field of application of the precautionary principle is, for example, genetic engineering. Many people intuitively believe that we need sounder knowledge of its effects than is available at present in order to justify its wide-scale use. Hans Jonas (1984: x) expressed this in the demand "to give the prophecy of doom priority over the prophecy of bliss." As the 1992 UNFCCC puts it in Article 3.3: "Where there are threats of serious or irreversible damage, lack of full scientific certainty should not be used as a reason for postponing [precautionary measures on climate change]." The core idea of the precautionary principle, therefore, is that there is reason to avert looming harm even when there is scientific uncertainty over whether this harm will occur, and if the uncertainty is not about *whether* the harm will occur (which might be taken to at least diminish the reason to avert the harm compared to a case where the harm occurs with certainty), but rather about its *scale*, then uncertainty even adds to the reason to avert the harm in question.

But, it might be objected, does the precautionary principle not reflect an excessively conservative attitude toward uncertainty? Is not everything we do fraught with risks? And would we not have to forbid even the slightest movement if we were really keen to avoid all risks? Is it not a sign of timidity, or even alarmism, to pay full attention to the possibility of things turning out worse than expected, but not to attach equal weight to the possibility that they could also turn out better than expected? In this chapter, we will argue that these questions should be answered in the negative. The intuitive risk aversion expressed in the different versions of the precautionary principle can indeed be supported with good arguments. In what follows, we will examine three justifications for the thesis that uncertainty provides a reason for additional efforts to mitigate climate change—namely, disproportionate damage, asymmetry of rights, and lack of probability.

In this discussion, we rely on the concept of the *expected value*. Its meaning can be illustrated by an example.

> If you have a 50 percent chance of winning $2 in a lottery, then the expected value of your winnings is $1. If the fine for speeding is $100 and the likelihood of being caught is 1 percent, then the expected value is likewise $1.

The expected value is calculated as the sum of the possible conse-quences, where the consequences are multiplied in each case by their probability. In the example of the fine, there are two possible outcomes, where the outcome "$100 fine" occurs with a probability of 1 percent and the outcome "$0 dollar" with a probability of 99 percent. The result is the expected value of $1: $(1/100 \times \$100) + (99/100 \times \$0) = \$1$.

Disproportionate damage

The more uncertain the extent of the rise in temperature, the more urgent it becomes to limit the rise. If the range of the possible rise in temperature around a given expected value increases, then the threatening character of the situation also increases. This is the intuition that we are assuming here. A first argumentative underpinning of this intuition is based on the assumption that climate damage rises *disproportionately* with increasing temperature (see Fig. 8.1): One additional degree of warming leads to greater additional damage at high temperatures than at low temperatures. (A remark on terminology: Generally speaking, "disproportionate" could mean either that it leads to more or to less additional damage; here, we focus on the former case.) Disproportionate damage means that if we double the increase in temperature, the climate damage will be *more* than double. Climate-related damage—in the sense of loss of well-being or human rights violations—increases faster with every additional degree. Disproportionate damage is also often described in terms of the related expressions "non-linear," "convex," or "exponential" damage.

Let us assume, by way of illustration, that there is an equal probability of the temperature rising by 1°C, 2°C, or 3°C as a result of climate change. Imagine a farmer living near the coast who faces crop losses of 10 tons if the temperature increases by 1°C and losses of 20 tons if it increases by 2°C. In the case of a rise in temperature of 3°C, by contrast,

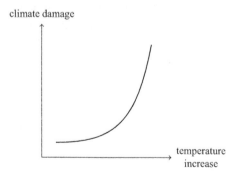

Figure 8.1 Disproportionate damage

the sea level will rise above the protection dams, leading to the destruction of the entire harvest of 60 tons. In such a case of disproportionate damage, it would be a mistake to focus on the *expected value of the rise in temperature* for the sake of simplicity. The expected value is 2°C, which is associated with a loss of 20 tons. However, this expected value "conceals" the fact that the temperature can also increase by 1°C or 3°C. And—this is the crux—these two possibilities do not cancel each other out: The difference between crop failures of 10 tons and 20 tons (in the case of a 1°C rise in temperature vs. one of 2°C) is relatively small, whereas the difference between losses of 20 and 60 tons (given rises of 2°C vs. 3°C) is much greater. Losing 20 tons with certainty is not as bad as losing 10, 20, or 60 tons with equal probability.

This insight can also be expressed as follows: The expected *rise in temperature* is 2°C, whereas the expected crop failure *is not 20 tons, but 30 tons*—that is, $(1/3 \times 10) + (1/3 \times 20) + (1/3 \times 60) = 30$. But what interests us are the crop failures, not the increase in temperature. Thus if we were to want to limit the crop failure to the expected value of 20 tons instead of 30 tons, then we would have no other option—given the uncertainty—than to aim at a rise in temperature the expected value of which is *lower than* 2°C.

As a general rule, for any given expected value of the *rise in temperature*, the expected value of *climate damage* is higher the greater the *uncertainty* surrounding the increase in temperature. But what ultimately interests us is climate damage, not the rise in temperature. The expected value of climate damage depends on the uncertainty surrounding the rise in temperature. Therefore, when speaking of the rise in temperature, we should never take our orientation simply from its expected value, but must always take the associated uncertainty into account as well. Of course, these assertions do not apply only to the increase in temperature and climate damage; strictly speaking, they also apply to any example involving two factors, the second of which is what ultimately interests us, while the first exhibits uncertainty and contributes disproportionately to the second. (A more detailed—and also, in part, more precise—presentation of these general claims can be found in introductions to decision theory such as Mas-Colell et al. 1995: ch. 6; Gilboa 2009; Peterson 2009.)

Is the assumption that the climate damage increases disproportionately plausible? Does climate damage—in the sense of impairments in well-being or of human rights violations—actually increase more rapidly with increasing temperature? The general trend in economic climate models does indeed point in this direction (Deuber et al. 2013: 40). This is also, to a certain extent, intuitively plausible. For example, a farmer who has already lost a large part of his harvest obviously loses more well-being with each additional ton of crop losses than a farmer who has not yet experienced any harvest losses. Those who have already lost a lot as a result of climate damage experience a greater impairment of their well-being with each additional loss. This is just a mirror-image formulation of the more general principle that $1 generates greater utility for a poor person than for a wealthy person (assuming that one is poorer with climate damage than without it).

Positive social feedback effects provide another intuitively understandable reason for disproportionate damage. The general meaning of positive feedback loops is that harm gives rise to further harm as a side effect. This occurs, for example, when our CO_2 and CH_4 emissions contribute to the thawing of permafrost in Siberia, which in turn discharges additional CO_2 and CH_4 into the atmosphere. Of primary relevance in the present context, however, are social feedback loops. For example, when a flood claims lives, the harm is not confined exclusively to the loss of life; additional harm occurs as a "side effect" because, before their deaths, the victims were active members of society who ran hospitals, educated children, or governed cities. But if a hospital were suddenly to lose 100 employees, this would obviously be *more* than 100 times more detrimental than if it were to lose just one employee. Similarly, more than twice as many problems arise when two countries are destabilized simultaneously by climate-related droughts than if only one of them is destabilized. So-called *tipping points* are particularly dramatic examples of disproportionate damage. The climate is a complex system subject to abrupt change. For example, the monsoon in India could exhibit constant incremental change as a result of small rises in temperature, but then suddenly reach a point at which it comes to an abrupt halt. In such cases where a rise in temperature up to a certain threshold causes hardly any damage, but beyond a certain point suddenly leads to a cascade of damage, it would be fatal if we were to pay attention only to the expected value of the rise in temperature—for the expected value could lie within the harmless range before the tipping point is reached.

Special attention should be paid to disproportionate increases in damage not only in the much-discussed area of a rise in temperature of around 2–4°C, but also beyond this, in the domain of worst case scenarios. While an increase in temperature of 2°C will undoubtedly entail serious suffering for many human beings, a planet that is 10°C warmer is scarcely imaginable. Such a rise in temperature is so drastic that not even a 10 percent probability is needed to regard it as just as much a threat as a rise in temperature of 1°C occurring with certainty. The expected value of the damage is much higher in the case of a 10 percent probability of an increase of 10°C than it is in the case of a 100 percent probability of an increase of 1°C, even if the expected value of the increase in temperature is the same in both cases. The underlying intuition is the same as in the case of fire prevention measures: Even if the chance of a blaze breaking out is extremely slight, the loss in the event of a fire would nevertheless be so grave that even a slight chance of such a worst-case scenario is sufficient to justify taking precautionary measures.

The asymmetry of rights

In the previous section, we showed that the uncertainty surrounding the rise in temperature provides an argument for additional climate mitigation, assuming that what ultimately interests us is the expected value of *climate damage*. In this section, we will now question whether we should take our orientation from the *expected value* of climate damage in the first place. A more plausible alternative is to take our orientation from the magnitude of the risk of causing climate damage in ways that violate rights.

The difference between the orientation to the expected value and to the risk of violating rights can be illustrated by an example.

> Imagine you find a wallet lying unattended at a party. The owner has already gone home, but you decide to play a little game for fun. You flip a coin: heads you remove $100 from the wallet; tails you place an additional $100 in the wallet. In so acting, have you respected the owner's rights?

The answer is: "No." In this example, you are taking a 50 percent risk of stealing $100 from the owner. You should not steal—and you should not steal with a 50 percent probability either. That you simultaneously take the risk of donating $100 to the owner is indeed generous. After all, you do not owe him anything. But even if you create a 50 percent chance of the owner making a profit, this in no way justifies simultaneously taking a 50 percent risk of stealing from him. If the owner has a *right* to his money, then a certain probability of theft is not made good by an equal probability of a donation. What is interesting about this example, however, is that the expected value of your game for the owner is $0. Viewed in terms of the expected value, therefore, you do not steal from the owner: He has a right not to have money stolen from him by you, and *in terms of the expected value* you do not do so either. Nevertheless, you violate your duty—for the simple reason that you take a 50 percent risk of stealing from him. This can be called the "asymmetry of rights": The probability of an act of generosity going beyond what is owed does not make up for the probability of a violation of rights.

We are in an analogous position vis-à-vis future generations. They have certain rights against us—in particular, their human rights. Whatever climate policy we adopt, we are in a certain sense tossing a coin. The difference is that there are not only two sides to the coin; rather, the broad spectrum of more and less likely climate impacts is more like a die with many faces.

Let us assume for the moment—and only for the sake of illustration—that the rights of future generations could be translated into a right to have climate damage limited to less than 20 percent of global GDP. If future generations actually had such a *right*, then a climate policy that caused climate damage of between 10 and 30 percent of global GDP with equal probability would be unacceptable. The expected damage caused by this climate policy would indeed be 20 percent. But because we are speaking of a *right* that the damage should not exceed this threshold, we are not interested in the expected value, but instead in the magnitude of the risk of exceeding it—that is, in the magnitude of the risk of violating the right. That there is simultaneously a 50 percent probability of the damage falling *below* 20 percent is indeed welcome. But this does not make up for the probability of violating rights. This "rights-based risk-aversion" implies that if uncertainty about the extent of future climate damage is unavoidable, then one must choose a climate policy that aims at a very low expected value of climate damage. A low expected value ensures that, despite the range of uncertainty around this mean, the likelihood of rights-violating outcomes remains low. If the *range* of potential impacts includes a margin of 20 percent, then climate damage of 11 percent, for example, could be considered an acceptable *expected value*. The spectrum of possible effects would then extend from 1 to 21 percent. Hence there would only be an acceptably low probability of a loss exceeding 20 percent of GDP.

Uncertainty can thus turn the moral evaluation of climate policy on its head. If the *expected* climate damage is slightly higher for political option A than for political option B, we may nevertheless prefer A over B—if option B involves a far higher level of uncertainty. This uncertainty not only means that there is a higher probability of things turning out better than expected and therefore that we will bequeath future generations more well-being than we owe them, but also means that there is a higher probability of things turning out worse than expected and hence that we will violate their rights. And the latter—the risk of violating rights—is especially grave from a moral point of view and is not counterbalanced by the former. This constitutes a second argument for why uncertainty provides a reason for additional climate mitigation.

Lack of probabilities

Thus far, we have asked why climate mitigation is more urgent if we cannot specify the scale of climate change with *certainty*, but merely know the *probabilities* of various future scenarios. But one can also ask what we should do if we cannot even ascribe probabilities to the different scenarios. What should we do if we know only the *range of the possible rise in temperature*, but the underlying climatic processes are so complex that no scientific model can reliably quantify the probabilities within this range? This is not an abstract question. In practice, scientists are often guarded when it comes to attaching probabilities to developments in the distant future. A relevant example from the past is the Third Assessment Report of the IPCC released in 2001: It refrained from ascribing probabilities to one of its core assertions—that the rise in temperature by the year 2100 will be between 1.4 and 5.8°C—as well as to the underlying scenarios (IPCC 2001). Since that time, it has become more common to make statements of probability. But we should not forget that, in some cases, intuitive expert judgments or the assumptions on which they are based are highly controversial from a scientific point of view (see Betz 2007, 2008).

So on what basis should we opt for one climate policy over another if we do not even know what policy has what consequences with what probability? In such cases, where we lack probabilities, it is often proposed that we should take our orientation from the worst possible case. The idea is to choose the policy for which the worst-case scenario is the least bad. This decision-making principle is known as "maximin." The name stems from the fact that the principle calls for choosing from among all the minima (that is, the worst cases) the option that is maximally good (or, more precisely, least bad). For example, one could argue on the basis of the maximin principle that a weak climate policy entails a worst case of global environmental disasters for future generations, whereas an ambitious climate policy entails a worst case of economic losses for the present generation. In this case, the ambitious climate policy should be preferred because its worst case is less bad.

But is such a maximin principle not overly cautious? Imagine that scientists unexpectedly find a climate-engineering solution that solves the problem of climate change cheaply and effectively with a 99.9 percent probability, but with a 0.1 percent probability of a slightly worse worst-case scenario than climate change. A one-sided fixation on the worst case seems exaggerated in this case, for it would mean forgoing the virtually certain success of the cheap and effective solution simply because it involved a very low probability of slightly worse consequences. This criticism misses the real point, however: The maximin principle should be used only if it is not possible to estimate the probabilities. As soon as we know the probabilities—as in the present example—the maximin principle does not apply.

Critics of the maximin principle nevertheless have a hard time dealing with the idea that even the mere *possibility* of a catastrophic worst case should be sufficient to reject a climate policy as unacceptable. Should the doomsayers in the public debate not at least bear the burden of proof and first demonstrate that the catastrophic scenario has a certain basic level of scientific plausibility before such a possibility has to be taken seriously? Would a maximin principle not otherwise be tantamount to a crippling stalemate? After all, *any* policy could, in principle, lead to a catastrophe under more or less bizarre circumstances. Many things are indeed *possible*: An unattended candle can ignite a city fire, which can in turn trigger new elections, in turn triggering a national uprising, and this, in turn, a world war. Therefore the mere possibility of a catastrophe would not only forbid CO_2 emissions, but also, strictly speaking, lighting a candle or any other human action. In response to this criticism, however, defenders of the maximin principle such as Stephen Gardiner (2006: 51) argue that the range of "possible" effects does not include *any* imaginable option; only "realistic" scenarios should be taken into account when determining possible worst cases. Thus the critique of the maximin principle is based on an exaggerated interpretation of the concept of possibility. Any worst case that can be conceived in the abstract need not count as possible in the sense of realistic.

Even a proponent of the maximin principle can concede that defining the realistic worst cases of different climate policy options is a difficult task. For example, it is tempting to pay more attention to some worst cases than to others. Thus a global environmental disaster as a result of a *lack* of climate mitigation is not the only possibility; *excessive* climate mitigation could also lead to economic losses and subsequent delays in the fight against poverty.

If this way of spelling out the maximin principle is convincing, then we have a third argument for why uncertainty provides a reason for additional climate mitigation. Like the first two reasons, this third reason does not rest on irrational, timorous risk aversion; rather, it outlines a plausible way of dealing with situations in which catastrophic worst cases are indeed realistic possibilities, but in which it is not possible to make a scientific estimate of their probability.

Conclusion

Taken together, the three arguments from uncertainty presented in this chapter support the concern underlying the precautionary principle. They show that a policy of caution rests on good grounds and not merely on irrational fear. Anyone who thinks that fire insurance is reasonable should also be open to a risk-averse approach in climate policy. We have sufficient reason to engage in climate mitigation even if current CO_2 emissions violate the rights of future generations neither with certainty nor in the mean. All that is required to justify our duty to mitigate climate change is that the risk of violating rights exceeds a certain limit or—if science does not permit any reliable statements of probability—it is sometimes even sufficient that such a violation is a realistic possibility. In this sense, climate mitigation needs a safety margin: By doing *more* to mitigate climate change than would be necessary if the expected value of the rise in temperature were to occur with certainty, we lower the probability of serious rights violations to an acceptable level—or even banish it altogether from the domain of realistic possibilities. In other words, the rights of future generations must be protected robustly—that is, they must be protected even if the pessimistic scenarios materialize. The uncertainty surrounding the extent of future climate change is thus one of the central reasons why we cannot simply lean back in the face of growth forecasts and wait for general economic progress to relieve us of the need for further action to fulfill our duties toward future generations. If we want to ensure that the rights of future people are protected even under conditions of uncertainty, then we must make additional efforts to mitigate climate change.

Arguments box 7: uncertainty and the precautionary principle

The uncertainty surrounding the extent of future climate change requires us to step up our efforts to mitigate climate change. We have a duty to keep the risk of rights-violating climate change for our descendants low even if their expected well-being is higher than ours.

Three arguments can be cited in support of this risk-averse position.

(1) *Disproportionate damage*: If climate damage increases disproportionately (that is, it increases faster with rising temperatures), then greater uncertainty surrounding the rise in temperature translates into a higher expected value of the resulting climate damage. If we merely focus on the expected value of the rise in temperature while ignoring the associated uncertainty, then we will underestimate the scale of climate damage.

(2) *The asymmetry of rights*: If future generations have a right to a certain level of well-being, then we fail in our duty if we leave them less than they are entitled to with some probability, even if we also leave them more than they are entitled to with some probability. The latter does not make up for the former. Our duty is to keep the risk of rights-violating damage to a sufficiently low level.

(3) *Lack of probabilities*: If science cannot ascribe probabilities to the different possible impacts of climate change, then the appropriate response is to base our orientation on the worst case in accordance with the maximin principle.

References

Betz, G. (2007) "Probabilities in climate policy advice: a critical comment," *Climatic Change*, 85(1–2): 1–9.

—— (2008) "Der Umgang mit Zukunftswissen in der Klimapolitikberatung: Eine Fallstudie zum Stern Review," *Philosophia Naturalis*, 45(1): 95–129.

Deuber, O., Luderer, G., and Edenhofer, O. (2013) "Physico-economic evaluation of climate metrics: a conceptual framework," *Environmental Science & Policy*, 29: 37–45.

Gardiner, S. (2006) "A core precautionary principle," *Journal of Political Philosophy*, 14(1): 33–60.

Gilboa, I. (2009) *Theory of Decision under Uncertainty*, Cambridge: Cambridge University Press.

Intergovernmental Panel on Climate Change (IPCC) (2001) *Climate Change 2001: Third Assessment Reports*, available online at https://www.ipcc.ch/ ipccreports/tar/ [accessed April 29, 2016].

—— (2013) "Summary for policymakers," in *Climate Change 2013: The Physical Science Basis—Contribution of Working Group I to the Fifth Assessment Report of the Intergovernmental Panel on Climate Change*, available online at http://www.ipcc.ch/pdf/assessment-report/ar5/wg1/WG1AR5_SPM_ FINAL.pdf [accessed April 29, 2016].

Jonas, H. (1984) *The Imperative of Responsibility: In Search of an Ethics for the Technological Age*, Chicago, IL: University of Chicago Press.

Mas-Colell, A., Whinston, M. D., and Green, J. R. (1995) *Microeconomic Theory*, New York: Oxford University Press.

Peterson, M. (2009) *An Introduction to Decision Theory*, Cambridge: Cambridge University Press.

Stern, N. (2007) *The Economics of Climate Change: The Stern Review*, Cambridge: Cambridge University Press.

—— (2009) *The Global Deal: Climate Change and the Creation of a New Era of Progress and Prosperity*, New York: PublicAffairs.

United Nations (2015) *The Millennium Development Goals Report 2015*, available online at http://www.un.org/millenniumgoals/2015_MDG_Report/pdf/MDG% 202015%20rev%20(July%201).pdf [accessed April 29, 2016].

Van Zanden, J., Baten, J., d'Ercole, M. M., Rijpma, A., Smith, C., and Timmer, M. (eds.) (2014) *How Was Life? Global Well-Being since 1820*, Paris: OECD, available online at http://www.oecd-ilibrary.org/economics/how-was-life_ 9789264214262-en [accessed April 29, 2016].

9 Inequality and an interim conclusion

The essential point of the foregoing considerations was that people living in the future should be able to achieve at least the threshold of sufficiency, if not even the same level of well-being, as the present generation. More-over, given the uncertainty surrounding predictions of the future impacts of climate change, it is inappropriate to focus only on the *expected value*. But it is equally inappropriate merely to focus on the *average* level of future well-being—for the average does not take into account how well-being is distributed among people living in the future. Recall the boss who has a duty to pay his employees a wage of US$2,000. If he were to transfer $1,000 to half of them and $3,000 to the remainder, then they would, in fact, receive $2,000 on average. But that would clearly be unacceptable, given that each employee has a right to a wage of $2,000. What matters is that this right of *each individual* employee is satisfied. Likewise, in the case of climate change, if future generations have a right to a sufficient level of well-being, then each individual human being within the future generations has this right. If a human being suf-fers under a climate change-induced drought 100 years from now, then it is no comfort to him or her that one of his or her contemporaries is living in abundance and thus that they are both sufficiently well off on average. Inequality means that we must raise future average well-being to a *higher* level than the level owed to each individual. By leaving our descendants more on average than we owe them individually, we ensure that the descendants at the lower end of the income distribution also have enough. The more inequality that prevails in the future, therefore, the more we should do to mitigate climate change. This is one of the most straightforward, but at the same time most important, reasons for climate mitigation.

A critic might object that it is not the fault of the present generation if future generations do not divide up the legacy we bequeath them equally among themselves. Because future inequality is not our responsibility—one could maintain—we do not have a duty to do more for our descen-dants than would be necessary if they were to live in equality.

There are two answers to this objection. First, even if it were true that responsibility for future inequality should not be ascribed to the present generation, it should not be ascribed to those living at the lower end of the income distribution in the future either. We can hardly justify exposing those people to the risk of climate change if—through no fault of their own—their contemporaries fail to share the resources necessary to adapt to climate change with them (see the more detailed discussion in Chapter 17 on the just response to injustice). A characteristic feature of human rights violations is that, in contrast to certain other moral wrongs, they concern us irrespective of the reason for a given violation and of how far removed—in space or time—we are from those affected.

The second, and more important, answer to this objection is that the blame for the unequal standard of living in the future also lies with us, the members of the present generation. We are making an active contribution to future inequality—in particular, through our greenhouse gas emissions. People living in poverty are especially vulnerable because they often live in flood plains, drought zones, and other sensitive regions in which the impacts of climate change are especially rapid and forceful. The economies of developing countries are relatively heavily dependent on agriculture, which is more sensitive to climate change than the service sector, for example. Moreover, the political institutions of developing countries are often more unstable. As a result, scarcity of resources and climate-related migration flows also lead more readily to social unrest. So climate change makes the poor even poorer. Preventing this provides one of the most important reasons for climate mitigation.

An interim conclusion

The foregoing chapters addressed the second key question of climate ethics: How much should we do to mitigate climate change? We have argued that we at least owe it to future generations to safeguard their human rights. In addition, we may have a duty to ensure that future generations are not worse off than we are. These goals must also be fulfilled for those at the lower end of the income distribution and even under pessimistic scenarios. As a result, the duties in question are more extensive than it may initially appear. So much for the general ethical assertion. But how can this requirement be operationalized in practice? What implications does it have for the other elements of the chain of effects depicted in Fig. 5.1, for example with regard to a maximum admissible rise in temperature?

Global warming of 2°C is often treated as an acceptable maximum in the discourse on climate policy. This target did not gain currency because scientific evidence supports a clear distinction between the effects of a rise in temperature of greater as opposed to less than 2°C; rather, it emerged more as a useful point of orientation for structuring the political discussion (see Geden 2013: n. 4). What the 2°C target means in practical terms remains open in many cases, because the probability with which the increase in temperature must be kept below 2°C is not specified. But it obviously makes a difference under the aspect of risk already discussed whether the 2°C target is achieved with 90 percent probability or—also a common interpretation (see Luers et al. 2007; IEA 2010)—with only 50 percent probability.

However, the most vulnerable agents—small island states and the least-developed countries (LDCs)—and a variety of NGOs regard 1.5°C as already the maximum tolerable warming. They highlight the significant climate damage that is to be expected even below the threshold of 2°C (see Hansen et al. 2008; Smith et al. 2009; World Bank 2012). Measured by the criteria, the terms of which we have argued up to now, therefore, the 2°C target would probably not be ambitious enough. This has been acknowledged in the Paris Agreement of 2015 in which nations committed to pursuing efforts to limit the temperature increase to 1.5°C. However, a detailed comparison of the 2°C and 1.5°C targets has scant relevance given the current political realities: As things stand, we are far from adopting a change of course that would confine warming to 2°C. Emissions are still growing quickly—and, in the first decade of the new millennium, they increased at an even faster rate than they did in the previous three decades (IPCC 2014: 5). Even if it is technologically and economically feasible to radically and quickly reduce emissions, such reductions are highly improbable given the hunger for growth of both poor and rich economies, and given how difficult political coordination proves to be. Based on the pledged contributions in Paris, there is about a 90 percent chance of exceeding 2°C and a 50 percent chance of exceeding 2.7°C (Climate Action Tracker 2015: 6). There are even more pessimistic studies that reveal a sizeable probability of ending up with warming of over 4°C: For example, based on the assumption that unconditional pledges in Paris will be implemented fully, the United Nations Environment Programme (UNEP 2015: xviii) estimates a probability of more than 33 percent of exceeding 3–4°C, while two of the three central scenarios of Climate Interactive (2015) estimate a probability of around 5 percent of exceeding 4°C.

What would a world that was on average 4°C warmer look like? Because temperatures will not rise uniformly across the globe, this could mean an increase in the average summer temperature of more than 6°C in some regions, such as North Africa, the Middle East, and the United States. Heat waves, such as that which claimed an estimated 55,000 lives in Russia in 2010, would become normal summer temperatures. The sea level could rise by up to 0.5 meters by 2100 and by several additional meters over the following centuries. There would be significant increases in water shortages. Many animal and plant species would become extinct, and increasing flooding would expose people living in poverty to epidemics and food supply problems (World Bank 2012). It is difficult to imagine these and other consequences without widespread human rights violations. This suffices to qualify the current course as untenable from the perspective of intergenerational justice. If we imagine a world that is, on average, 4°C warmer, it may be possible to justify bequeathing this scenario to our descendants with a tiny probability, but not with any sizeable probability: We do not hesitate to get into a car even though there is always a very slight chance of a serious or fatal accident; very few of us would climb into a car if this were a very serious possibility. However, with our present-day emissions, we are in effect placing future generations—in particular, those from poorer areas—into just such a dangerous vehicle.

In order to evaluate current climate policy from the perspective of intergenerational justice, therefore, we must assess at least two aspects: the possible consequences and (insofar as it is scientifically possible to ascribe probabilities) the probability with which they will occur. We must ask ourselves whether violations of human rights are among the possible consequences of current climate policy and whether the risk of such rights-violating consequences exceeds a maximum acceptable limit. The evaluation of current climate policy just undertaken is sufficiently clear with regard to these two aspects: Emissions must *fall*—and they must fall, specifically, by more than is envisaged by present-day policy. The general nature of the arguments presented in this chapter hardly allows us to specify a precise goal of, say, 1.37°C. But as long as the direction is clear and as long as achieving the targets of 1.5°C or 2°C remain beyond our reach, these marks can serve as milestones to be aimed at, at least as intermediate goals.

However, one might wonder whether the need for extensive reductions in emissions does not in turn impose excessive costs on the *present* generation. If drastic climate mitigation were to prove to be so burdensome that it conflicted with the rights of the present generation, then that would, of course, represent a problem for intergenerational justice: Not only the rights of future generations, but also those of the present generation, should be protected.

However, the fear that ambitious climate mitigation could constitute an injustice to those living today is unfounded. First, we should not

overestimate the costs of climate mitigation. Thus, for example, Edenhofer et al. (2010) assume that the measures required to reach the 2°C
target with a probability of 80 percent would lower GDP by less than
2.5 percent. Even if this conjecture significantly underestimates the
costs, there would still be no question of a "return to the stone age"; on
the contrary, the authors predict significant growth in spite of the costs of
mitigation.

Second, we can situate climate change within the larger picture of
the intergenerational distribution of costs and benefits. We affect the
lives of our descendants not only through the scale of our emission
reductions and the extent of the associated climate change, but also
through countless additional channels. The well-being of future generations depends on how much we invest in basic medical research, on
our savings rate, and on our efforts to expand and stabilize democratic
institutions, as well as on how many schools we build and how much
money we set aside for measures to adapt to climate change. We have
no compelling reason to assume that we are doing too little for our
descendants in these *other* areas. We may even be leaving them more
than we owe them—in contrast to climate mitigation, where the lack of
efforts today means unacceptable risks for our descendants. Taken
together, this opens up the following perspective: If we have a duty to
take measures to mitigate climate change, but consider the necessary
measures to be too costly, then, as the present generation, we could
increase our climate change mitigation efforts, but in return reduce the
provision for our descendants in one of these other areas. What ultimately counts from the intergenerational perspective is the *entire* basket of goods and risks that we bequeath to our descendants. If we
ensure that this basket does not contain any unacceptable climate risks
and if the basket for the rest already contains *more* than enough other
goods, then we would be justified in keeping some of these other goods
for ourselves (see Rendall 2011). In concrete terms, we might be justified in financing climate mitigation by reducing investments in other
future-oriented infrastructure and research projects or by taking on
long-term public debt.

Third, whether the costs of climate mitigation are excessive or not for
the present generation depends, of course, on who bears these costs: For
example, climate mitigation would certainly not be excessively onerous if
the wealthiest were to bear the brunt of the costs. This raises the question
of who among the present generation must assume which burdens—
hence, of how we should distribute our responsibilities toward the future
among ourselves. That is what is at stake in the third key question of
climate ethics, to which we will now turn.

Arguments box 8: intergenerational justice and climate mitigation

In Chapters 5–9, we have discussed the second key question of climate ethics. Given that the costs of climate mitigation and climate change influence how well-being is distributed between the present and the future, we asked what we owe future generations as such. Our conclusion was that, although we do not have a duty to ensure that they are better off than we are, it is our duty to ensure that they are sufficiently well off—in the sense that their human rights are protected. In addition, we may even have a duty to ensure that they are as well off as we are. In fulfilling our duty, it is not enough to take our orientation from the expected value and the average level of future well-being, both of which could easily exceed present-day values; rather, we have a duty to place the protection of the rights of future generations on a robust footing. They must be protected even if things turn out to be worse than expected. Moreover, the rights of those at the lower end of the income distribution must also be protected. The latter requirement is especially relevant because climate change has particularly serious impacts on the poor and hence gives rise to new inequality.

It is indeed difficult to draw precise practical conclusions from these general ethical assertions. Nevertheless, the likelihood that current climate policy violates the rights of future generations seems unacceptably high. Therefore the direction is clear: From the perspective of intergenerational justice, emissions should decrease more rapidly than is envisaged by current policy. That the costs to be borne by the present generation for this purpose are acceptable seems to be beyond question.

References

Climate Action Tracker (2015) "2.7°C is not enough: we can get lower," available online at http://climateactiontracker.org/assets/publications/briefing_papers/CAT_Temp_Update_COP21.pdf [accessed April 29, 2016].

Climate Interactive (2015) "Scoreboard science and data," available online at https://www.climateinteractive.org/tools/scoreboard/scoreboard-science-and-data/ [accessed April 29, 2016].

Edenhofer, O., Knopf, B., Barker, T., Baumstark, L., Bellevrat, E., Chateau, B., Criqui, P., Isaac, M., Kitous, A., Kypreos, S., Leimbach, M., Lessmann, K., Magné, B., Scrieciu, Ş., Turton, H., and van Vuuren, D. P. (2010) "The economics of low stabilization: model comparison of mitigation strategies and costs," *The Energy Journal*, 31(1): 11–48.

Geden, O. (2013) *Modifying the 2°C Target*, SWP Research Paper, available online at http://www.swp-berlin.org/fileadmin/contents/products/research_papers/2013_RP05_gdn.pdf [accessed April 29, 2016].

Hansen, J., Sato, M., Kharecha, P., Beerling, D., Berner, R., Masson-Delmotte, V., Pagani, M., Raymo, M., Royer, D. L., and Zachos, J. C. (2008) "Target atmospheric CO_2: where should humanity aim?" *The Open Atmospheric Science Journal*, 2: 217–31.

Intergovernmental Panel on Climate Change (IPCC) (2014) "Summary for policymakers," in *Climate Change 2014: Synthesis Report—Contribution of Working Groups I, II and III to the Fifth Assessment Report of the Intergovernmental Panel on Climate Change*, available online at http://www.ipcc.ch/pdf/assessment-report/ar5/syr/AR5_SYR_FINAL_SPM.pdf [accessed April 29, 2016].

International Energy Agency (IEA) (2010) *World Energy Outlook 2010*, available online at http://www.worldenergyoutlook.org/media/weo2010.pdf [accessed April 29, 2016].

Luers, A. L., Mastrandrea, M. D., Hayhoe, K., and Frumhoff, P. C. (2007) *How to Avoid Dangerous Climate Change*, available online at http://www.ucsusa.org/assets/documents/global_warming/emissions-target-report.pdf [accessed April 29, 2016].

Rendall, M. (2011) "Climate change and the threat of disaster: the moral case for taking out insurance at our grandchildren's expense," *Political Studies*, 59(4): 884–99.

Smith, J. B., Schneider, S. H., Oppenheimer, M., Yohe, G. W., Hare, W., Mastrandrea, M. D., Patwardhan, A., Burton, I., Corfee-Morlot, J., Magadza, C. H. D., Füssel, H.-M., Pittock, A. B., Rahman, A., Suarez, A., and van Ypersele, J.-P. (2009) "Assessing dangerous climate change through an update of the Intergovernmental Panel on Climate Change (IPCC) 'Reasons for Concern'," *Proceedings of the National Academy of Sciences*, 106(11): 4133–7.

United Nations Environment Programme (UNEP) (2015) *The Emissions Gap Report 2015*, Nairobi: UNEP.

World Bank (2012) *Turn down the Heat: Why a 4 C Warmer World Must Be Avoided*, available online at https://openknowledge.worldbank.org/handle/10986/11860 [accessed April 29, 2016].

Suggested further reading for Part II

Bell, D. (2011) "Does anthropogenic climate change violate human rights?" *Critical Review of International Social and Political Philosophy*, 14(2): 99–124.

This article details and defends the claim that anthropogenic climate change violates human rights.

Gosseries, A. (2008) "Theories of intergenerational justice: a synopsis," *SAPIENS*, 1(1): 61–71.

A short and clear overview of some theories of intergenerational justice.

__ and Meyer, L. H. (2009) *Intergenerational Justice*, Oxford: Oxford University Press.

A collection of articles on various approaches and themes in intergenerational justice.

Hayenhjelm, M., and Wolff, J. (2012) "The moral problem of risk impositions: a survey of the literature," *European Journal of Philosophy*, 20(S1): E26–E51.

This article examines a number of stances in the ethics of risk.

Rendall, M. (2011) "Climate change and the threat of disaster: the moral case for taking out insurance at our grandchildren's expense," *Political Studies*, 59(4): 884–99.

A number of topics from Part II are discussed in this article, including discounting, risk, passing on benefits to our descendants by means other than mitigation measures, and the issue of future generations being better off than the present.

A more comprehensive list of further readings for this part is available at http://climate-justice-references.christianseidel.eu

Part III

HOW SHOULD WE ASSIGN RESPONSIBILITY? GLOBAL JUSTICE

10 The greatest redistribution in human history

Thus far, we have clarified two of the three key questions of climate ethics. In Part I, we saw that we have a fundamental moral obligation to engage in climate mitigation. In Part II, we specified more precisely to what extent we must protect the climate: We should ensure that future generations will be at least sufficiently well off, and perhaps even just as well off, as we are. But anyone who has ever shared an apartment knows that it is not enough to know that the kitchen must always be kept tidy and that it should be clean enough, or maybe even as clean as, at the beginning of a house party. A decisive question remains: Who should do what? When it comes to cleaning up, who should perform which tasks to what extent? We will address this question (as it applies to climate change, of course) in this part of the book: How should we spread the amount of climate mitigation to be performed across different shoulders? At stake in this third key question of climate ethics is what, in fact, constitutes a just distribution of the advantages and disadvantages entailed by climate mitigation among members of the present generation. This can also be called the "question of intragenerational global climate justice."

One might think that we have already answered this question—for, amazingly enough, there is a widely held view within international climate policy circles about the standard according to which the costs of climate mitigation should be distributed. In the 1992 UNFCCC, 154 states committed themselves to protect the climate system "in accordance with their common but differentiated responsibilities and respective capabilities" (Article 3.1). Does that not already sound like a reply to our third key question?

But appearances are deceptive: Even though the slogan "common but differentiated responsibilities and respective capabilities" plays a special role in international climate change negotiations, it is far from clear how this guiding principle should actually be understood. Does the word "responsibility" refer to a country's contribution to causing climate change, or instead to the responsibility arising from the fact that a country has benefited economically from past emissions? Do the respective capabilities refer to the ability to reduce emissions—which depends essentially on technological know-how—or to the ability to pay the costs of climate mitigation—which depends essentially on economic prosperity? The guiding principle "common but differentiated responsibilities and respective capabilities" is open to many different interpretations. This is why answering the third key question of climate ethics calls for a more in-depth ethical analysis.

The following chapters will be devoted to precisely this issue. We will consider different attempts to spell out the widely accepted guiding principle of climate policy in terms of a "principle of distributive justice"—namely, a conception of what a fair distribution of the benefits and burdens of climate change within our generation would look like. We will examine how plausible the individual principles are—that is, what speaks for and against them. Because this can quickly become confusing, in this chapter we will begin by making some distinctions that will help us to arrive at a better understanding of the various distributive principles, their scopes of application, and also their limits. In addition, these distinctions will help us to identify which principles contradict each other, which complement each other, and how several principles can be combined to provide a cogent answer to the third key question of climate ethics.

Climate mitigation as a question of distributive justice

What is meant in general by a principle of distributive justice? Let us first consider a prime example for the issue of distributive justice.

> You are a member of an urban gardening cooperative that has leased a plot of land on which to grow vegetables. In addition to their financial contributions to the lease, the members must also perform work assignments so that the potatoes, carrots, cabbages, and so on can thrive. Throughout the year, the vegetables harvested are distributed among the members.

In such a community, the following question arises immediately: What would constitute a fair distribution of the membership dues, the work assignments, and the harvests? Should everyone—from the baker to the corporate board member—pay the same dues or should the membership fee be tied to income? Should all of the members receive equal shares of the harvest or should they be distributed in proportion to the amount of work performed? And what about the single working mother who has little time to spare for gardening work, but must feed three children from the harvested vegetables?

We will not try to answer these questions; rather, we want to draw attention to three features of the example that make it especially relevant for the issue of distributive justice.

(1) It involves the distribution of something important—namely, food. Not only is food inherently important (without it we could not survive), but also it has special importance for the members of the cooperative (they have decided to take their food supply into their own hands instead of shopping at the supermarket).
(2) There is a group of people who contribute to the good to be distributed—namely, those who pay membership dues and perform work assignments.
(3) There is another group of people who benefit from the good to be distributed—namely, the recipients of the harvested vegetables.

As the example of the children of the single mother illustrates, the two groups (2) and (3) need not be identical (the children have not performed any work assignments, but nevertheless benefit from the proceeds of the work of others). One can therefore say in general that issues of distributive justice become particularly pressing where (a) something important, which (b) is produced by a group ("load bearers"), (c) benefits a—possibly different—group ("benefit recipients").

Avoiding climate change also exhibits precisely these three features and therefore it too is a matter of distributive justice. This becomes clear once we consider the scale of the challenges that go hand-in-hand with climate mitigation and that it undoubtedly involves something important (first feature). If greenhouse gas emissions are to be reduced to the extent required, production processes must become more energy-efficient, our CO_2-intensive energy supply system must be switched over to renewable energy sources such as solar, wind, and hydroelectric energy, and apartments and homes must be modernized and insulated. Changes are also unavoidable in the areas of mobility (think of air travel) and agriculture (meat and feed production generate large amounts of greenhouse gases). All of this comes at a high price in terms of time, patience, and money. Studies in climate economics such as Stern (2009) or Edenhofer et al. (2010) estimate that the costs of moderate-to-ambitious climate mitigation could amount to a very low, single-digit percentage of global GDP. Such numbers are subject to considerable uncertainty and hence must be treated with caution. However, their approximate magnitude suggests that, although these costs would by no means leave us impoverished, there is nevertheless a lot at stake (in absolute terms, some US$1 trillion). Moreover, this money would no longer be available for other things that make life more pleasant (opportunity cost). Therefore, if we want to avoid climate change, we will have to pay for it.

But climate mitigation not only costs something; it also produces something. Among the beneficiaries of the measures required to avoid climate change are, for example, manufacturers of certain energy technologies, who tend to be located in the developed industrial countries. Even so, the developing countries would derive the greatest benefit from avoiding climate change. By comparison with a scenario in which nothing is done to mitigate climate change, they would benefit from the absence of droughts, less extreme desertification, a slower rise in the sea level, and less frequent hurricanes. That is simply the reverse of the fact that unimpeded climate change would mainly affect the "South"— that is, the developing countries. And as already in the case of the costs, here, too, we are undoubtedly dealing with something important (first feature)—namely, the well-being and human rights of a large number of those affected. As for the second and third features, it is important that climate mitigation is a joint task. No individual or state alone can prevent dangerous climate change through its actions. In climate mitigation, therefore, there is a group (comprising those who reduce emissions) that produces an important good (preventing climate damage), which in turn benefits another group that is, at least in part, different. Therefore climate mitigation also raises the question of what constitutes a just distribution of advantages and disadvantages in a particularly acute way: Who must contribute how much to preventing climate change and who may benefit from it to what extent?

Answering the question of distributive justice was already very difficult in the case of the urban gardening cooperative. The problem is that it is controversial which *moral aspect* of the situation should be made the basis for the distribution: Should we distribute according to the idea of equality (should all make the same contribution and receive the same yield?), according to need (should the mother not receive more?), or according to ability (should the wealthy not pay more and the unemployed perform more work?)? The relevant moral aspect is indeed also highly controversial in the case of climate change. But, in addition, it even remains unclear what is supposed to correspond to the vegetables in the case of the gardening cooperative: Which good is distributed when it comes to preventing climate change—money, emissions, or well-being?

Complex redistribution: what is distributed?

In the first place, the talk of "avoiding" climate change can easily obscure the fact that we would have to expect a certain amount of climate change even if we were to stop emitting greenhouse gases overnight. Moreover, it is possible that, despite all attempts to keep climate change below a certain level, more than this level of climate change could nevertheless occur. Accordingly, "the" avoidance of climate change involves two distinct distributional issues: on the one hand, the distribution of the advantages and disadvantages associated with the climate change that is actually *avoided*; on the other, the distribution of advantages and disadvantages associated with the climate change that will nevertheless *occur* (see Fig. 10.1).

To the second group belong, first, beneficial and detrimental effects on the climate. In some regions, it will become unbearably hot; droughts and extreme weather events will become more frequent occurrences, and the sea level will rise. In other regions, the climate will become milder, and it will become possible to grow wine and to pursue new recreational activities. Thus there will be "climate damage" and "climate benefits." In order to avoid causing damage to the climate, people will (have to) adapt to climate change as it occurs: They will build dams and more stable houses, inoculate themselves against widespread tropical diseases, and build water reservoirs. Such adaptation measures have advantages (better security, more well-being, new jobs), but also disadvantages (they cost money, time, and well-being). These disadvantages that will have to be accepted if they are to prevent or mitigate the harms caused by the climate change that actually occurs are called "burdens of adaptation." Those climate-related harms that cannot be prevented or mitigated in this way are sometimes called "loss and damage."

The other group of advantages and disadvantages is somewhat less clear. Successfully avoiding climate change depends, in the first instance, on the amount of emissions that remain in the atmosphere— that is, the so-called *emission balance*. But this can be viewed from three different perspectives and hence we can also distinguish between three distribution problems (see Fig. 10.2). If we are to fulfill our intergenerational obligations, the amount of emissions produced in a certain period of time (say, from 1850 to 2050) must not exceed a certain amount. This is the *total permissible emission balance* ("1" in Fig. 10.2) and this amount can be regarded as the good to be distributed in the case of climate mitigation. But part of this amount has already been emitted in the past (between 1850 and the present day). Thus the difference between these historical emissions incurred to date and the total permissible emissions constitutes the *remaining emissions budget* ("2" in Fig. 10.2). One could also view this as the good to be distributed— namely, the remaining possible emissions that can be used for many desirable purposes (heating, electricity, mobility, etc.). But, third, one can also regard the *emission reduction requirements*—that is, the difference

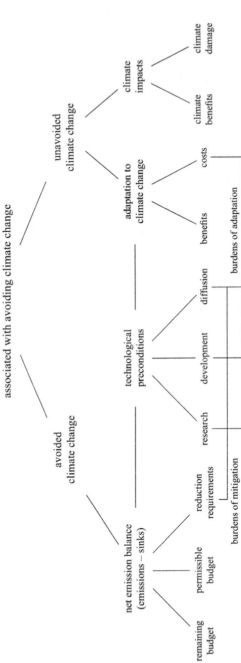

Figure 10.1 Taxonomy of the climate change-related advantages and disadvantages

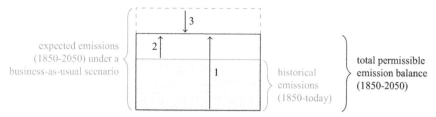

Figure 10.2 Emissions-related advantages and disadvantages

between permissible emissions and the quantity of emissions that we would emit if we were simply to continue as we have done in the past until 2050 ("3" in Fig. 10.2)—as a good. The "good" to be distributed consists in this case of disadvantages or costs: They are the efforts that we must undertake if we are to switch from the emission path that we are on at present to the permissible path. All of these disadvantages that must be accepted in order to prevent climate change are called "mitigation costs." (Strictly speaking, here we should always speak in terms of "net emissions." Natural sinks—above all, forests and oceans—also absorb greenhouse gases before they reach the atmosphere, where they contribute to climate change through the greenhouse effect. Then, net emissions are the emissions *that remain in* the atmosphere—that is, the difference between (a) the total amount of emissions produced and (b) the greenhouse gas storage capacity of the non-atmospheric sinks.)

However, with this we have not yet captured all of the advantages and disadvantages associated with avoiding climate change. There are technological preconditions both for avoiding climate change and for adaptation measures. The corresponding technologies must be studied, developed, and then disseminated and implemented as well. Again, this involves, above all, costs and hence must be regarded as a burden (of mitigation or adaptation, depending on the use to which the efforts and funds are put). These "technological" costs must also be taken into account when it comes to the fair distribution of advantages and disadvantages.

To make matters worse, all of the advantages and disadvantages depicted in Fig. 10.1 can be measured in different ways. First, they can be expressed in terms of a *resource*, for example tons of emissions, a certain amount of wood, lost crop yields, consumption of materials in research, or numbers of workers. But, second, advantages and disadvantages can also be considered in terms of how well or badly off the people who enjoy these advantages and disadvantages are in each case: Think of the cozy warmth of a pleasantly heated room, the harsh deprivations of a crop failure, or the suffering after a hurricane that has destroyed all of a person's worldly possessions. Here, what is distributed is not resources, but the *well-being* that a person derives from using the resources. Finally, advantages and disadvantages are often expressed in terms of money—which, on the one hand, is a resource, but, on the other, is understood primarily as an approximation to well-being.

In contrast to the urban gardening cooperative, therefore, in the case of climate change, there is no single, clearly defined good to be distributed, but a whole "bouquet" of advantages and disadvantages. As will become clear later, it is important not to lose sight of this diversity, because different answers to the third question of climate ethics often concern different elements of this "bouquet."

In search of principles of intragenerational global climate justice

We have already indicated the huge dimensions of the redistribution associated with preventing climate change. The global energy supply system must be transformed, inefficient technologies must be replaced by "clean" ones, and our mobility, transportation, and logistics systems have to be redesigned. We have now seen that, even on an initial consideration, the details of this redistribution seem to be extremely tricky because there is not only one clearly defined good to be distributed, but several related goods that influence each other. This suggests that the redistribution required to prevent climate change is unprecedented. It is the largest and perhaps most difficult redistribution in human history. That is why we cannot rely here on our "moral gut feelings." On the one hand, not everyone has a spontaneous, clear gut feeling on this question; on the other, the gut feelings that different people nevertheless have sometimes seem to be very different. Some favor a per capita equal distribution of the remaining emission rights as the "intuitively" fair answer, whereas others favor the "polluter pays" principle, which stipulates that each state must pay in proportion to its contribution to the problem. In view of what is at stake, we cannot simply leave it up to moral gut feelings to answer the question of distributive justice. But neither can we simply fall back on an—albeit uncontroversial but, for all that, abstract—idea such as the guiding principle of "common but differentiated responsibilities and capabilities" mentioned at the outset of this chapter. This guiding principle is too unspecific as a measure of the fairness of distributions. Instead, we need an informative principle that helps us to evaluate a distribution from the standpoint of justice: a *principle* of distributive justice.

But what *is* a principle of distributive justice? One principle in the context of our example of the urban gardening cooperative might be: "Every member receives the share of the harvest that corresponds to the amount of time he or she spent on gardening work." Such a principle tells us, first, what *the good to be distributed* is—namely, the fruits of the harvest. It tells us, second, who *the recipients* of the distributed good are—namely, all of the members. And it tells us, third, *in accordance with which aspect* the distribution is conducted—namely, it is conducted in proportion to the duration of work assignments. More generally, one can say that principles of distributive justice tell us (a) what is allocated (b) to whom and (c) why. Thus they have three components.

In the following chapters, 11–15, we will proceed to examine more closely the most important principles of distributive justice, discussed in the context of climate mitigation, and to work out their respective components. With regard to the "bouquet of goods" alluded to above, we will pay particular attention to whether a principle distributes costs for mitigation or costs for adaptation and compensation, and to whether or not it refers to historical emissions (and hence to the past). In this way, we can see more clearly where the principles contradict each other and at what points they are, in principle, compatible with each other. Moreover, we will begin by discussing each of the principles separately. This makes it easier to work out what is problematic about the guiding consideration that informs each principle and how serious the objections are in each case. This will be relevant for the "mix of principles" that we would like to propose in Chapter 16 in the context of a comprehensive change in perspective for answering the third key question of climate ethics. The discussion of the different principles of distribution will show that the idea of global climate justice rests on *several* guiding considerations simultaneously. Therefore we will sketch a proposed solution in which:

(1) different normative aspects are combined (whereby the objections against the individual principles discussed determine their weight or role in the mix of principles);
(2) not only emissions, but all of the advantages and disadvantages that arise in the context of climate change are distributed together; and
(3) the avoidance of climate change is not seen in isolation, but instead as closely interconnected with facilitating economic development in poorer countries.

This "holistic" solution is admittedly a complex one—but this is perhaps also to be expected given the complexity of the underlying problem.

At this point, we still need to offer a brief clarification. In the debate on climate change, one often hears it said that "Germany" should do more to reduce its emissions or that "the United States" should finally ratify a binding international climate agreement. Here, moral demands seem to be addressed to collective agents (states). However, this should be understood instead as a simplifying way of speaking: The demand in each case is, in fact, addressed to the individuals living in the respective countries. After all, it is the people who live in Germany who would have to bear the burden of a steeper reduction in emissions. Accordingly, one should also treat the third key question of climate ethics as a problem of the distribution of the advantages and disadvantages among individuals. When we nevertheless apply principles of distribution to states in what follows, this is always meant as a simplification. If the burdens are distributed according to the ability to pay, for example, and Germans are on average better off than people in India, then we say that Germany must bear more costs than India, even if some Indians are better off than some Germans. As long as one keeps such deviations in the distribution of individual claims and costs within a country in mind, there is nothing to be said against a simplifying "collectivist" way of speaking.

References

Edenhofer, O., Knopf, B., Barker, T., Baumstark, L., Bellevrat, E., Chateau, B., Criqui, P., Isaac, M., Kitous, A., Kypreos, S., Leimbach, M., Lessmann, K., Magné, B., Scrieciu, Ş., Turton, H., and van Vuuren, D. P. (2010) "The economics of low stabilization: model comparison of mitigation strategies and costs," *The Energy Journal*, 31(1): 11–48.

Stern, N. (2009) *The Global Deal: Climate Change and the Creation of a New Era of Progress and Prosperity*, New York: PublicAffairs.

11 Grandfathering

To those who have, more shall be given

There is an intuitively comprehensible answer to the question of the just distribution of climate mitigation duties: Climate change affects all human beings and hence its prevention is a joint task of all mankind. Therefore it is tempting to say that, to begin with, all countries should reduce their emissions equally. From the fact that climate change is a problem that affects *us all*, therefore, a call for *equal obligations to reduce emissions* seems to follow directly.

But this requirement can be interpreted in different ways. On a first reading, the requirement that "all must reduce equally" means equal *absolute* emission reductions. If meeting our intergenerational obligations means that global greenhouse gas emissions must fall by—let us say—500 billion tons by 2050, then these 500 billion tons must simply be distributed equally among all human beings. Given a global population of roughly 10 billion human beings, this would work out at 50 tons per person for this period. This proposal is so manifestly unjust (some people in developing countries do not even produce 50 tons of emissions in their whole lifetimes, so for them this reduction obligation would be tantamount to a prohibition on emissions) that we will not discuss this interpretation further in what follows.

According to a second reading, it is a matter of equally high *relative* emission reductions. On this reading, if fulfilling our intergenerational obligations means that global greenhouse gas emissions must fall by—let us say—50 percent by 2050, then each country must simply reduce *its* emissions by 50 percent. That would mean that the shares in the emission cake would ultimately remain unchanged, only that the whole cake would have become smaller. A country that previously accounted for 17 percent of total global emissions will also receive 17 percent of the total permissible global emissions in the future, and since total permissible future emissions will be lower than total present emissions, the 17 percent will represent less emissions in absolute terms (that is, expressed in tons) than before (see Fig. 11.1).

The requirement that emissions should be reduced equally relative to the status quo is known in the expert discussion in climate ethics as

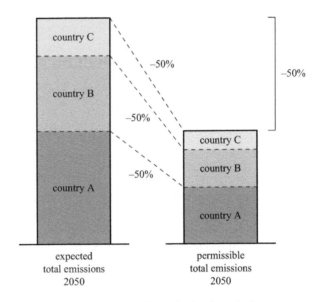

Figure 11.1 Grandfathering as equal relative reduction in emissions

"grandfathering." This term is explained by the fact that the distribution of *future* emissions is derived from the distribution of *past* emissions. If one stipulates equal relative reduction obligations for all, then, starting from the previous level of emissions (the status quo), one can calculate the magnitude of the permissible future emissions. What one may emit in future follows directly from the stipulation of the reduction obligations—*based on* past emissions. Therefore the grandfathering principle treats emission reductions as the burden to be distributed and it ultimately determines the fair distribution of these burdens based on past emissions. In this, it resembles a series of proposals in current climate policy. The Kyoto Protocol, for example, likewise focuses on the distribution of emission reductions and specifies concrete (although, in contrast to grandfathering, unequal) obligations for individual countries to reduce emissions by a certain percentage compared to a base year (1990). Here, the guiding assumption is also that the just distribution of the remaining emissions should be determined on the basis of past emissions.

The grandfathering principle claims to provide an answer to the third key question of climate ethics. Thus it is supposed to tell us what is a *just* or *fair* distribution of the burdens of climate change prevention. (It differs from the Kyoto Protocol in this respect, since the latter can also be understood as merely claiming to specify a viable or workable, but not necessarily fair, distribution of burdens.) In this chapter, we would now like to argue that the grandfathering principle proves to be untenable on closer inspection. To this end, we will first explain what normative considerations support the grandfathering principle and then subject it to critical examination.

Normative foundations

What considerations speak in favor of grandfathering? There are a total of three justification strategies. We have already mentioned the first, which starts from the notion that averting climate change is a joint task of humankind, which as a result should also be shouldered by humankind as a whole. The burdens to be shouldered, it is claimed, are first and foremost emission reductions, and they must be distributed equally among all human beings—precisely because it is a joint task.

On closer inspection, however, it becomes apparent that this argument has two weaknesses. First, the assumption that the relevant costs should be measured exclusively in terms of the emission reductions represents a gross simplification. For one thing, if one is poor, then the burdens of reducing emissions weigh much more heavily than if one is starting from a high level of economic development. A solvent and technologically highly developed state can cope easily with emission reductions; in such countries, the costs to be paid for climate mitigation do not pose a threat to subsistence. In poorer countries, by contrast, the money that would have to be spent on climate mitigation and emission reductions is badly needed elsewhere. Simply imposing the same reduction burdens on all without regard to their respective abilities to cope with a reduction represents an unjust imposition on the poorer countries.

A second weakness is that this first strategy for justifying grandfathering rests on a hidden, but implausible, premise. The consideration cited—avoiding climate change is a joint task and hence the burdens should be shouldered by all—supports the conclusion only with the aid of a further assumption: that the burdens not only must be shouldered by *all*, but also must be shouldered by all *equally*. Only then does it follow from the fact that a task must be performed jointly that the individual contributions to performing it (the reductions in emissions) must also be equal. However, the assumption that the burdens must be shouldered by all equally is not plausible. It completely ignores that other factors are morally relevant for burden-sharing when performing a joint or communal task: A problem may be caused primarily by individual members of the community; some members are not in a position to perform certain tasks; others are predestined to perform certain tasks or have special needs that must be taken into consideration. In the context of climate change, distributing the relative reductions in emissions equally ignores all of these factors. It ignores the facts that some countries have contributed more to the problem than others, that some countries do not have the financial or economic resources to implement the corresponding changes, and that some countries, because of geographical or demographic peculiarities, have special needs that justify a higher level of emissions. Clearly, the bare fact that the problem affects a community and, in addition, can be only solved jointly does not automatically entail that all must do the same thing.

Thus the first justification strategy makes things too easy for itself. But, in addition, it does not even rest on the basic idea that is characteristic of the grandfathering principle. This basic idea comes to light instead in the second and third justification strategies. According to the second justification strategy, equal relative emission reductions are defensible because the individual countries appropriated a certain part of the atmosphere by using it in the past and thereby acquired a *right* to continue to make use of this share of the sink capacity of the atmosphere. If avoiding climate change now requires that all countries taken together must make lower demands on the atmosphere, then this right guarantees the same share even under conditions of the new, lower demands of the atmosphere—and this implies that the reduction in the use of the atmosphere (the emission reductions) should be the same for all. Thus the underlying idea is that the de facto and unchallenged use of a good gives rise to a kind of "customary right" to continue to use it accordingly.

The third justification strategy also starts from past usage behavior and derives claims on the distribution of future emissions on this basis. However, this does not occur via the idea of the appropriation of a good, but is instead based on the following consideration. The denizens of the industrialized countries pursue certain life plans: They want to work in the city, but live in a big house in the country; they want to be individually mobile by driving a car, to travel the world by air, to eat meat, and to consume products that are relatively cheap thanks to a global production and logistics chain. Some would like to be pilots; others, to build cars. All of these life plans are part of their individuality and autonomy. People in the industrialized countries have organized their lives on this basis, have projected their lives accordingly, and have become accustomed to their life plans. Therefore they have a *legitimate expectation* that they can pursue them in future as well. As a general rule, however, this necessitates high levels of emissions under the current technological conditions of an economy based on fossil energy sources. But if one can legitimately expect to continue to pursue something that one has already pursued in the past and that necessitates a high level of emissions, then one also seems to have a right to high future emissions—and a drastic reduction in emissions seems to be too demanding insofar as it would frustrate the legitimate expectations of people who live in the industrialized countries.

The second and third justification strategies have something in common: they take the given de facto use behavior in the past as a basis for deducing distribution entitlements—either via the idea of appropriation or via the idea of legitimate expectations. This is exactly the basic moral idea of grandfathering: Entitlements to future emissions can be deduced from past emission behavior. In this context, those who accounted for a large portion of the emissions in the past will also be accorded a large portion of emissions in the future—precisely *because of* their past emissions. Therefore the basic idea of grandfathering can be captured by the following—somewhat exaggerated, but nevertheless apt—formula: "To those who have, more shall be given—precisely *because* they had."

Critical discussion

The grandfathering principle will strike most of us as suspect. This is because this principle tries to deduce *normative* claims (who has a legitimate claim to how much and who has which duties?) from *descriptive* premises (who emitted how much in the past?). However, it seems to be impossible in principle to make a direct inference of this kind: From the fact that the things *are* such and such, nothing follows when taken in isolation about how they *ought to* be. This can be illustrated by a series of examples: From the fact that a tree has some yellow leaves, it does not follow that it ought to have yellow leaves or that it ought not to have any yellow leaves; from the fact that people are often suspicious of each other, it does not follow that they ought to be suspicious of each other. Philosophers speak in this context of an "is–ought gap." Applied to grandfathering, this means that from descriptive statements about how emissions *are* in fact distributed, one cannot derive any normative statement about how the emissions *ought* to be distributed. But is that not precisely what the grandfathering principle does when it takes the historical emissions and the status quo as a basis for distributing the entitlements to future emissions? After all, historical emissions and the status quo merely describe a factual state and hence do not have any normative relevance as such.

However, the grandfathering principle cannot be dismissed quite so easily. This is because the is–ought gap merely states that no normative statement follows from a descriptive statement *alone*. With the aid of further normative "bridging statements," however, we can indeed make inferences from descriptive to normative statements. If one assumes, for example, that one *should* take special care to maintain trees with yellow leaves, then from the fact that a tree has a few yellow leaves, one can indeed draw a normative conclusion—namely, that one should tend to the tree. The proponent of the grandfathering principle can make use of precisely this strategy by pointing out that the derivation of the distribution entitlements is not based exclusively on past emissions, but includes further—normative—assumptions. In the case of the second argumentative strategy, for example, this was the notion that one can legitimately acquire a resource through unchallenged, habitual use. The third argumentative strategy brought a further normative assumption into play in the guise of the idea of legitimate expectations: "If one may *legitimately* expect to pursue a specific life plan, and if this leads to a relatively high level of emissions, then one is *entitled* to the high emissions."

By appealing to the notion of legitimate appropriation or of legitimate expectations, therefore, the proponent of grandfathering has something with which to oppose the is–ought objection. If he or she is to be successful, however, that proponent must show that the status quo is normatively relevant in the way described—that is, precisely because thereby a legitimate appropriation has occurred or because it supports legitimate expectations. However, this maneuver raises the question of what the conditions for a legitimate appropriation or for legitimate expectations are in general, and in particular whether these conditions of legitimacy are, in fact, fulfilled in the case of past emissions. Is it, in fact, the case that (as the second justification strategy maintains) the industrialized nations acquired a *legitimate* share in the use of the atmosphere through their habitual use of it in the past? And is it, in fact, the case that (as the third justification strategy maintains) the expectation that one can continue to pursue an emissions-intensive lifestyle is *legitimate* and that an ambitious emission reduction target would frustrate this expectation?

Let us begin with the third justification strategy. First, it is unclear what follows precisely from the reference to legitimate expectations—for the argument can be understood in such a way that it speaks against *any* reduction in emissions. If, based on past use behavior, one develops a legitimate expectation to continue pursuing a certain way of life, then one has a right to this way of life and to all of the emissions needed to pursue it. Here, there can no longer be any question of emission reductions (in particular, of equal relative reductions); hence it is not even clear how far the argument can support the call for equal relative emission reductions. And assuming that it could do so, it must be observed that the scope of this consideration is limited, for even if we presuppose that *in the past* the formation of legitimate expectations justified an entitlement to higher future emissions, it is nevertheless clear that *now*—that is, now that the causes and consequences of climate change have become common knowledge—one can no longer legitimately expect to realize emissions-intensive life plans. If the third argument has any application at all, therefore, then it applies only to part of the population of the industrialized countries—namely, that part which formed its life plans before knowledge of climate change became sufficiently widespread. Moreover, one can also question whether extensive emission reductions would even frustrate the supposedly legitimate expectations. Without a doubt, an abrupt reduction in emissions from one day to the next would be a painful, and perhaps even unacceptable, step for the industrialized countries. But no such scenario is being entertained; instead, all of the scenarios under discussion involve reducing the level of emissions *step by step* to a fair level. In this context, the instrument of emissions trading, in particular, also plays a role (see Chapter 19): If the industrialized countries buy up unused emission rights from developing or newly industrializing countries, then they can even continue their emissions-intensive lifestyle to a certain extent. Thus if the transition from the status quo to just distribution is managed carefully (here, one can also speak of "transitional" justice), then an ambitious climate policy need not necessarily frustrate legitimate expectations. And with this the third justification strategy for the grandfathering principle loses its persuasiveness.

A similar criticism also applies to the second justification strategy: The proponent of grandfathering must show that the many emitting industrialized countries appropriated their part of the atmosphere through habitual use in the past *in a legitimate way*. Two main criteria for the legitimate appropriation of a good are discussed in ethics: first, the criterion (which we already encountered in Chapter 5) that one must leave "enough and as good" for others after the appropriation; and second, the criterion that the appropriation benefits others in some way, or at least does not cause them any harm. Neither criterion is fulfilled in the case of climate change (see Singer 2002: 27–31), for up to now the appropriation of the atmosphere by the industrialized countries has, in fact, *harmed* other countries—in particular, developing and newly industrializing countries—owing to the climate change it causes. And because the remaining capacity of the atmosphere to absorb greenhouse gases without causing dangerous climate change is limited and the industrialized countries appropriated the lion's share of this limited capacity in the past, there can be no question of leaving "enough and as good" for others. Since neither of the two criteria for legitimate appropriation is fulfilled, the industrialized countries have *not* appropriated "their" part of the atmosphere legitimately—and this is also why the second justification strategy fails to render the normative relevance of the status quo intelligible, and to bridge the gap between "is" and "ought."

Conclusion

In this chapter, we have examined a—*prima facie* plausible—answer to the third key question of climate ethics. According to the grandfathering principle, the distribution of the costs involved in tackling climate change is fair if the relative emission reductions compared to the status quo turn out to be equal for all concerned. One can argue for this principle in three ways: with the argument from the joint task of humankind as a whole, with the argument from appropriation through customary use, or with the argument from legitimate expectations. The normative idea at the heart of the grandfathering principle is captured by the second and third argumentative strategies, because in them entitlements to future emissions are derived directly from past emissions. The underlying assumption is that those who produced more emissions than others in the past may, for this reason, also produce more emissions in future. In a critical examination of the three arguments, we have shown that the grandfathering principle, contrary to initial appearances, is by no means plausible (see Arguments box 9): on the one hand, the principle ignores a series of relevant normative considerations—in particular, the differences in responsibility for causing climate change; on the other hand, the fundamental problem of grandfathering resides in rendering intelligible the normative binding power of the status quo—on the basis of which future entitlements are ascertained. Therefore grandfathering can scarcely be justified from the perspective of justice.

Arguments box 9: the grandfathering principle

The grandfathering principle is a principle of distribution which tells us (a) what is owed (b) to whom and (c) why: (a) The emission reductions required to prevent climate change are distributed (b) among all countries (c) equally (relative to the status quo), because high past emissions create an entitlement to high future emissions.

There are three strategies for justifying grandfathering, all of which fail, however.

(1) *Strategy*: "Eliminating climate change is a joint task, which must therefore be shouldered equally by all."
    Reply: This ignores other normatively relevant considerations—in particular, the fact that countries are responsible in varying degrees for the problem to be solved.

---

(2) *Strategy*: "The industrialized countries acquired their part of the atmosphere in the past through customary, unchallenged use and thereby acquired a right to their part of the emissions."
Reply: The appropriation has to be *legitimate*—but the conditions for legitimate appropriation are not satisfied. The appropriation is neither beneficial to others nor does it leave "as much and as good" for others.

(3) *Strategy*: "The denizens of the industrialized countries have a legitimate expectation that they can continue to pursue their emissions-intensive life plans; drastic reductions in emissions would frustrate this expectation."
Reply: Expectations formed *after* climate change became common knowledge are not legitimate; moreover, the transition to a low-emissions way of life can be managed in a tolerable way through prudent measures, so that the expectations in question are not frustrated.

The grandfathering principle does not ultimately succeed in deriving a normative claim about how emissions *ought* to be distributed from the descriptive fact that they *are* distributed in a certain way; hence the principle "To those who have, more shall be given—precisely *because* they had" is morally untenable.

Reference

Singer, P. (2002) *One World: The Ethics of Globalization*, New Haven, CT/ London: Yale University Press.

12 The "polluter pays" principle

Taking responsibility for one's actions

Let us return once again to the commitment made by the state parties to the UNFCCC to protect the climate "in accordance with their common but differentiated responsibilities and respective capabilities." In the light of the problems with grandfathering discussed, it seems plausible to place particular emphasis on the "differentiated responsibilities" part of this principle. If different states contributed—to different extents—to *causing* climate change and thus have different levels of responsibility, then it would seem that they should also contribute—precisely to this extent—to *coping* with climate change. This is exactly what the so-called *"polluter pays" principle* affirms. It thereby takes up an intuition that every child learns early in life—namely, that one must take responsibility for one's own actions: "You destroyed the tower, so see that you rebuild it."

Like the grandfathering principle, the "polluter pays" principle is a "historical" principle of distribution: It posits that the distribution of costs depend on what happened in the *past*. In comparison to grandfathering, however, this dependency is "biased" in precisely the opposite direction. Whereas, in the case of grandfathering, higher past emissions are supposed to lead to higher relative *advantages*—that is, shares in the remaining emissions—the polluter pays principle states specifically that higher past emissions should lead to greater *disadvantages*—that is, shares of the costs of coping with climate change. In this way, the polluter pays principle links up with a central moral aspect of the UNFCCC that grandfathering ignored: the different responsibilities. As will become apparent in what follows, however, the basic intuition that "the one who caused a problem must also make a special contribution to meeting the costs of addressing it" is ambiguous. We would like to distinguish two different versions of the polluter pays principle and of the moral intuitions that inform it before subjecting them to a critical examination.

Versions and normative foundations

That one must bear the costs of addressing a problem in proportion to one's role in causing it can mean two things, depending on what one regards as the problem to be dealt with. This can be best illustrated by an example:

> You and your two roommates are celebrating the five-year anniversary of your shared apartment. The landlord has donated a cake (comprising 24 pieces) as a gift, with which you want to hold a small celebration in the afternoon, with three further guests. When you enter the kitchen, you find, however, that your two roommates have already eaten half of the cake for lunch and have left the kitchen behind littered with crumbs.

In this example, you are facing several problems: on the one hand, the kitchen has to be cleaned up; on the other, there is now less cake left over for your guests. Both problems have the same cause—namely, your two roommates. Thus the requirement that those who caused the problem now have special responsibility for dealing with it can mean, first, that the two of them should tidy up the kitchen; second, it can also mean that the remainder of the cake (12 pieces) should not be simply divided up "fairly"—which, let us assume, would simply mean "equally"—among the six persons, but that the 12 pieces should instead be divided up between you and the three guests alone. The two gluttons would then have to make do without cake at the celebration, and you and the three guests would at least receive three pieces of cake each instead of, as originally planned, four pieces each (or, if the remaining pieces were to be distributed among six persons, two pieces each). On the first interpretation, your roommates contribute to dealing with the problem of the dirty kitchen; on the second, to alleviating the problem of the shortage of cake created by their taking more than their fair share.

Therefore, if someone takes more than his or her fair share and in addition harms others, then, on one reading, the polluter pays principle specifies who must rectify the damage; on another reading, it specifies how the remaining benefits should be distributed among the perpetrators and the others involved. In an analogous way, in the case of climate change one can also distinguish between two readings of the principle that those who caused the problem should also bear the costs of coping with the problem in proportion to their share in causing it—simply because the problem has two aspects. On the one hand, because of the long retention period of most greenhouse gases in the atmosphere, some climate damage would occur even if we were to stop producing emissions immediately. This unavoidable climate damage corresponds to the cake crumbs littering the kitchen. Taking responsibility *for this* as the polluter and contributing to addressing *this* problem would mean financing adaptation measures for those affected and, if necessary, paying compensation (if adaptation measures to prevent or reduce the damage are no longer possible—the situation occasionally discussed today under the heading "loss and damage"). Then, the burdens to be distributed under this aspect of the problem are the adaptation and compensation costs for the portion of climate change that actually occurs.

On the other hand, one can also consider the industrialized countries by analogy with the gluttonous roommates: By claiming the lion's share of past emissions, the industrialized countries have taken more than they were entitled to and the remaining emission cake is now smaller than it would have been if they had produced only the level of emissions to which they were entitled (just as each guest would have received four pieces of cake if your two roommates had been able to curb their appetites). Taking responsibility *for this* as the polluter and contributing to addressing *this* problem would then mean receiving a smaller share of the remaining emissions budget than the others (just as the gluttons also have to make do without a share of the remaining cake at the afternoon celebration). Then, the costs to be distributed under this second aspect of the problem are mitigation costs for the portion of climate change that is avoided.

Thus the polluter pays principle features in the discussion in climate ethics in two versions. Common to both is that the costs to be borne are distributed in proportion to the contributions to *causing* the problem. However, the two versions differ in terms of the nature of the costs to be borne and the justification for the distribution. The first reading deals with the distribution of the costs for *adapting* to climate change and the underlying idea is that of "putting one's moral house in order": One must rectify the damage for which one is responsible as best one can. In the context of climate change, this means reducing vulnerability to climate change; hence, paying for adaptation measures, or at any rate compensating those who were harmed (which can also be accomplished, for example, through development aid or technology transfer). The second reading deals with the distribution of the remaining emissions, which can also be understood as the distribution of the costs for *mitigating* climate change. The underlying idea is that of "failing to show appropriate moral restraint": Someone has helped him or herself to more than he or she was entitled to, which is unfair and demands counterbalance. On this second reading, it is not a matter of repairing the damage as far as possible, but of correcting an unfairness. The two readings of the polluter pays principle are, however, not mutually exclusive. In the case of climate change, the two dimensions of the problem are even closely interrelated, because they can be traced back to the same fact (a certain amount and distribution of emissions in the past). Nevertheless, the two readings can be discussed separately, because the two aspects of the problem are separable in principle: If your roommates had simply eaten the pieces of cake to which they were entitled beforehand (hence four, instead of six, pieces) and had created a mess in the process, then they would have only had to tidy up the kitchen. Thus there can be harm without unfairness and there can also be unfairness without harm—for example if your roommates had eaten half of the cake without strewing cake crumbs around the kitchen.

Critical discussion

How persuasive are the two versions of the polluter pays principle and the respective underlying moral intuitions? Let us begin with the second version: "lack of moral restraint." This is problematic in two respects (on which, see the article by Caney 2005). First, it already presupposes an independent standard of fairness—after all, part of the problem in the cake example and in the case of climate change was that someone had taken more than he or she was *entitled* to. But the distribution principle was supposed to explain what everyone is entitled to in the first place. We *first* need to know what a fair division of the cake would look like and only *then* does the second reading of the polluter pays principle come into play (if someone takes more than his or her fair share). In the cake example, we simply assumed that the fair distribution is an equal distribution of the pieces of cake. In an analogous way, it is often assumed in the context of climate ethics that the fair shares of the total emissions to which all are entitled are *equal* shares. But *that* is already an answer to the third key question of climate ethics—namely, the question of the just distribution of emissions (on which, more discussion appears in Chapter 15)—and the polluter pays principle merely supplements this answer: It tells us something about how the remaining available emissions should be allocated *if* someone has taken more than he or she was entitled to. As such, it does not itself provide an answer to the third key question, but instead presupposes it. (This does not rule out the possibility that the polluter pays principle may nevertheless be applied *in conjunction with* some other principle(s) to cover the distribution of mitigation costs. We might, for instance, think that—disregarding past unfairness—the remaining available emissions should be allocated on an equal per capita basis, but that that these equal shares should be topped up or off depending on whether someone took less or more than his her equal share in the past. The polluter pays principle would then be used to "adjust" the otherwise specified just distribution. In this way, although it would not, in itself, provide a complete solution to the problem of distributing mitigation costs, it might still be part of that solution.)

Second, the polluter pays principle on the second reading seems to boil down to the claim that one does not have to take responsibility for *one's own* actions, but for those of one's *past fellow countrymen*. In the context of climate change, this reading states that, for example, *Germany* or the *United States* should bear higher mitigation costs because, in the past, they produced more emissions than they were entitled to—and to say that a country has to bear higher costs ultimately means that the *individuals* who live in these countries must bear these costs and reduce their emissions. However, these individuals who are supposed to forgo emissions in the present are *not* the same individuals as those who produced more emissions in the past: Some of our ancestors are already dead. Therefore the guiding intuition behind the polluter pays principle—that one must take responsibility for *one's own* actions—does not fully apply in the context of climate change, because some of those who failed to show moral restraint are no longer alive. If one nevertheless wants to insist by appeal to the polluter pays principle (in its second reading) that the industrialized countries must now bear higher mitigation costs in order to compensate for a historical unfairness, then one must presuppose a kind of "individual inheritance" of duties—namely, that the citizens of a state who are alive today have inherited duties from those who lived in the past. It is true that something like this is familiar from some contexts, for example when financial debts are inherited or duties to compensate for war crimes, expulsions, and expropriation are "bequeathed." But it is important to recognize that many duties, and among them duties to compensate for unfairness, *cannot* be inherited. Compare family Minion with family Goldinger:

> Some 150 years ago, great-great-grandfather Goldinger and great-great-grandfather Minion grew up side-by-side in the same impoverished circumstances. But then great-great-grandfather Goldinger, through the—undeserved, random—favor of a prince, received an extended private education, which enabled him to achieve a high income as counselor to the prince, while great-great-grandfather Minion, after a short period of schooling, had to hire himself out as a day laborer.

This is a case of past unfairness. Today, let us assume, this unfairness no longer has any effects: The members of both families belong to the middle class and live in exactly the same conditions. It would be peculiar to demand that the present-day Goldingers should forgo part of their prosperity and hand it over to the present-day Minions. Duties arising from historical unfairness simply do not seem to be bequeathed from one individual to another in this way. It is a matter of taking responsibility for *one's own* actions and, because the action in question is a past unfairness, one cannot apply the polluter pays principle in its second reading to the distribution of the mitigation costs.

Now, one could point out in defense that something crucial was overlooked in the example of the two families: The reason why the duties may be bequeathed after all is that the Goldinger descendants *benefit* from the unfairness (the preferential treatment of great-great-grandfather Goldinger over great-great-grandfather Minion)—for example through a large fortune that Counselor Goldinger was able to build thanks to his preferential treatment. This reasoning could also be applied to climate change: The present-day descendants of those who caused climate change in the past benefit from their mothers' and fathers' emissions—for example, they enjoy the benefits of the infrastructure that was developed and built decades ago at a high cost in emissions. If one focuses on the benefits arising from the unfairness, therefore, then individual inheritance of costs and duties is no longer problematic.

However, this reply is not convincing because it introduces a completely different distribution principle—namely, the principle that the costs of avoiding climate change should be distributed in proportion to the *benefits* derived from the actions that caused climate change. This principle imposes costs on someone even if he or she contributed nothing to causing a problem, but has benefited from the fact that others caused the problem. We will discuss this so-called *"beneficiary pays" principle* in detail in the next chapter. At this point, suffice it to say that the attempt to defend the second version of the polluter pays principle ultimately leads to abandoning it. If the costs to be borne are distributed in proportion to the benefits derived from the cause of a problem, then this no longer has anything to do with the basic moral intuition that informs the polluter pays principle—namely, that one must take responsibility for one's own actions.

In the end, therefore, the polluter pays principle in its second version (compensation for unfairness) is not convincing. Let us therefore consider the first version: "putting one's moral house in order" after one has caused some harm. Is the proposal to distribute the costs of adaptation and compensation measures in accordance with the contributions to causing climate damage more convincing? In our opinion, the answer to this question is: "Yes and no." Here, too, it holds in the first instance that duties to pay compensation are not simply bequeathed between individuals. If great-great-grandfather Goldinger had harmed great-great-grandfather Minion, for example by abusing his position as a counselor to dispossess great-great-grandfather Minion, then *he* would have had a duty to compensate Minion—but the present-day Goldingers would not have a duty to compensate the Minions living today. One could indeed justify such a transfer of duties again by appealing to the advantages derived from the expropriation—but that would again be to abandon the polluter pays principle in its first reading in favor of the beneficiary pays principle.

In the case of climate change, however, we are dealing with a cumulative harm caused over a period of time. This opens up the possibility of circumventing the problem of inherited duties by taking into account only the climate damage caused by emissions during a limited period of time in which there is no need for duties to be bequeathed. The fact is that a large proportion of emissions has been produced over the past 35 years—that is, approximately since 1980 (see Boden et al. 2012)—and most of the people who were alive during that time—that is, the majority of the polluters—are still alive today. Therefore the costs incurred by adaptation to the climate damage that can be traced back to emissions produced since 1980 can indeed be distributed in proportion to the emissions that each individual contributed to causing this damage. Thus the polluter pays principle in its first reading can be applied to the problem of distributing the costs of adaptation that have arisen from the emissions produced since 1980. (This move of restricting the principle's scope is also available to defend the second reading against the second objection discussed above: In the case of distributing mitigation costs, one could also argue that there is no need to bequeath the duty to compensate for past unfairness if we consider a limited period of time only. But note that, given the first objection—that is, that the polluter pays principle in its second reading presupposes an independent answer to the third key question and might, at most, supplement this answer—the principle will make even less difference if we restrict its scope in this way.)

However, some complications remain. One problem is that it is not at all clear what exactly should count as causing a harm. This can be illustrated by so-called *grey emissions*. Many products are not manufactured in the country in which they are ultimately consumed: To whom should the emissions be credited that are generated by the manufacture and transportation of a product produced in China, but consumed in Germany—China or Germany? This is a difficult, but also a very relevant, question. Given the magnitude of the worldwide flows of goods, the answer has major implications for the distribution of the costs among the countries concerned. Underlying this is the question of what exactly counts on the first version of the polluter pays principle as "causing damage": the action of the producers that directly gives rise to a certain amount of emissions, or the action of the consumers for whom the action of the producers is necessary? One could divide up the emissions between producers and consumers in proportion to the bene-fits that both parties derive from the trade, but again that would be to go beyond the framework of the polluter pays principle and bring the beneficiary pays principle into play. Of course, this does not show that there is no answer to the difficult question of what exactly counts as a cause of the damage; rather, it shows only that one plausible answer leads away from the polluter pays principle and that a different answer must be sought. Viewed in this light, this first difficulty is just that: a difficulty, not an insurmountable objection.

The first version of the polluter pays principle does, however, encounter another difficulty: It is open to question how far those who produced greenhouse gas emissions in the past could have known anything about the harmfulness of their actions. It hardly dawned on someone who was driving an automobile at the beginning of the 20th century that its exhaust fumes could cause damage in the distant future. And would it not be unfair to make someone pay for damage that he or she knew nothing about—and *could know nothing about*? The last addition (that one *could not have known*) is crucial. This is because the bare fact that you did not know about the harmful effects of your action does not automatically release you from the obligation to pay for the damage: Perhaps you did not, in fact, know that one should not leave the gas valve open over an extended period—but you still have to foot the bill for the explosion, because you *should have* known. We generally distin-guish between "excusable" and "culpable" ignorance. On the one hand, there are things that one should know and someone who does not know them is guilty of culpable ignorance; on the other hand, there are things that one does not need to know and the ignorance of someone who does not know them is excusable.

This raises the question of the point in time after which someone should have known that he or she was causing climate damage by emit-ting greenhouse gases. This is a controversial question, the answer to which is relevant because one can be held responsible for emissions only after this point in time. The first scientific evidence of the greenhouse effect is often attributed to the Swede Svante Arrhenius—in 1896—but this remained a minority scientific opinion for long afterwards. The first sci-entifically well-founded and publicized models of the greenhouse effect date from the 1970s. Therefore one might speak of culpable ignorance only from that point onwards. In climate policy practice, the year 1990 is often cited as the point in time from which it should have been obvious to a wider public and the relevant decision-makers—based on existing scientific evidence—that greenhouse gas emissions lead to climate change: This was the year of the first report of the IPCC. From this point onward at the latest, therefore, one can apply the second version of the polluter pays principle. But this also means that a significant portion of all emissions that have ever been produced goes by the board and that nobody would have to take responsibility for the climate damage that can be attributed to emissions prior to 1990. And it also entails a shift in the relations between the industrialized and the developing countries: The developing countries produced around 48 percent of all emissions between 1850 and 2010, but almost 57 percent of the emissions between 1990 and 2010 (see den Elzen et al. 2013: 403); accordingly, the developing countries would also have to bear relatively more costs. Thus the "appropriate" point in time from which the polluter pays principle should take into account emissions and the resulting damage in distributing the costs of adaptation seems to lie somewhere between 1970 and 1990. We pointed out earlier, in the context of the inheritability of duties, that one can assume that a large proportion of total emissions for the period of the last 35 years will be taken into account and, thus, that a large proportion of the polluters are still alive. Therefore, in what follows, we would like to propose 1980 as the year from which the polluter pays principle applies.

Taken as a whole, then, we are left with a mixed picture. The polluter pays principle cannot be conclusively refuted in its first version, which refers exclusively to the distribution of the adaptation and compensation costs. But it has to wrestle with difficulties (grey emissions and excusable ignorance) that restrict its practical applicability. Anyone who wants to use the polluter pays principle to distribute the costs of adaptation and compensation must extend it in two ways to (a) explain more precisely what it means to cause damage and (b) specify more precisely at what point in time ignorance becomes culpable. And there are further pressing reasons for such extensions: One must ensure that the costs imposed on a country by the polluter pays principle are not *too* onerous; high levels of emissions are not always reflected in high levels of prosperity (witness some former Eastern bloc countries); and, moreover, to require that a poor country should also foot the bill for the damage in proportion to its contribution to causing it could mean exacerbating poverty—which seems to be morally unacceptable. If we follow this argument, we would have to build a kind of "ability-to-pay" limit into the polluter pays principle. Further, emissions that are necessary in order to meet basic needs should not even fall under the polluter pays principle; then, one would not have to take responsibility for climate damage that can be traced back to emissions that are necessary in order to satisfy vital needs. All of this already suggests that the polluter pays principle, taken in isolation, leaves some of the morally relevant factors (ability to pay, needs) out of account and that a satisfactory answer to the third key question of climate ethics may have to draw on several principles. We will return to this topic in Chapter 16.

Conclusion

In this chapter, we examined a strong intuition concerning the third key question of climate ethics—namely, that the costs should be distributed in such a way that they correspond to contributions to causing the problem. We distinguished two versions of this polluter pays principle. In the first, the costs for adapting to climate change and for compensating climate damage are distributed among those primarily responsible for climate change in proportion to their past emissions. This version of the principle is informed by the idea of "putting one's moral house in order." In the second version, a state receives a smaller share of the remaining emission cake the larger the piece of the cake it "consumed" in the past and hence the greater its contribution to causing climate change. Underlying this version is the idea of compensating for past unfairness. The discussion of the two proposals has shown that the polluter pays principle is plausible, at most, for distributing adaptation costs (that is, in its first version)—and even then only with qualifications (see Arguments box 10).

Arguments box 10: the polluter pays principle

The polluter pays principle can answer the third key question of climate ethics "(a) What is due (b) to whom and (c) why?" in two ways, as follows.

(1) (a) The costs of adapting to climate change and for compensating disadvantages are distributed (b) among those responsible for climate change (c) in proportion to their contributions to causing climate change—in order to rectify a *wrong*.
(2) (a) The remaining emissions are distributed (b) among all states (c) in inverse proportion to their contributions to causing climate change—in order to compensate for *unfairness*.

The second version is questionable for two reasons.

(i) It already presupposes a yardstick for measuring a fair distribution of the costs of climate policy—hence an answer to the third key question—that can be specified independently of the polluter pays principle. Thus the second version of the principle cannot, in itself, provide a complete answer to the third key question of climate ethics.

(ii) Because some of the individual polluters are no longer alive, the polluter pays principle depends on the idea of "inherited" duties (unless the principle's scope is restricted to a certain period of time)—but the idea that duties to eliminate past unfairness can be bequeathed from one individual to another is not plausible.

The polluter pays principle is quite tenable on the first version—for distributing costs of adaptations and compensation—if it is restricted to a certain period of time. But it faces the challenge of explaining more precisely (a) what counts as a contribution to causing damage and (b) from what point in time ignorance of the harmful effects of emissions is culpable (here, we have proposed 1980). In addition, it needs to be supplemented with further morally relevant aspects and must specify, for example, a ceiling above which damage becomes too onerous. Thus the principle of "taking responsibility for one's own actions"—on the first reading—has only limited applicability in climate ethics.

Because the first version of the polluter pays principle focuses exclusively on the distribution of adaptation and compensation costs, a principle for distributing the costs of preventing climate change is still needed in order to provide a complete answer to the third key question of climate ethics. The foregoing discussion has nevertheless provided a clue. In the course of the discussion, a completely different principle cropped up several times: the beneficiary pays principle, according to which the distribution of the costs of climate change should be made not in accordance with the *cause* of the problem, but according to the *advantages* resulting from it. Could this principle provide a satisfactory answer to the third key question of climate ethics?

References

Boden, T., Marland, G., and Andres, R. (2012) *Global, Regional, and National Fossil-Fuel CO$_2$ Emissions*, Oak Ridge, TN: Carbon Dioxide Information Analysis Center, Oak Ridge National Laboratory, U.S. Department of Energy.

Caney, S. (2005) "Cosmopolitan justice, responsibility, and global climate change," *Leiden Journal of International Law*, 18(4): 747–75.

den Elzen, M. G. J., Olivier, J. G. J., Höhne, N., and Janssens-Mænhout, G. (2013) "Countries' contributions to climate change: effect of accounting for all greenhouse gases, recent trends, basic needs and technological progress," *Climatic Change*, 121(2): 397–412.

13 The "beneficiary pays" principle

Those who benefit must pay

Unfortunately, there is injustice in the world. If this injustice cannot be prevented, then the perpetrators should at least have to take responsibility for their offences and compensate the victims: That was the intuition behind the polluter pays principle. But, in reality, our world is more complicated. The problem is that, sometimes, the perpetrators cannot compensate their victims because the perpetrator has died, cannot be brought to justice, or has, in the meantime, become destitute. And sometimes third parties benefit from the injustice that the perpetrators have inflicted on their victims: You may derive benefits from the cheap bicycle that you acquired yesterday in an online auction, but which, a week ago, was locked away in someone's basement. Even if you did not know that it was stolen goods, if you are caught with the stolen bicycle, you can hardly claim that it is none of your concern and that you have no obligations to the rightful owner; rather, you seem to be under an obligation to return the bicycle. Thus our moral practice involves the notion that benefiting from wrongdoing gives rise to moral obligations. If an offender wrongs someone and a third person benefits from the wrongdoing, then the third party seems to have a duty to the victim to make amends for the wrong—at least when the perpetrator is no longer in a position to do so.

This idea can also be applied to climate change. The 200-year history of increasing prosperity in the "North" is, above all, a history of rising emissions. These two phenomena are closely connected in our "greenhouse gas economy," for without the past emissions we would not be so well off today. The rapid economic growth that has taken place since the Industrial Revolution is based on the use of cheap fossil fuels (especially coal and oil); the improved food supply is based on CH_4-intensive, large-scale livestock farming, and the high agricultural yields obtained with oil-driven machinery and oil-based fertilization technology; the structural development of living, working, and mobility spaces was possible only through deforestation and the destruction of natural greenhouse gas sinks. That we are so well off, well nourished, and "well housed" today, therefore, is a consequence in no small part of past greenhouse gas emissions that are now leading to the climate change under which others will have to suffer. We are something like "intergenerational free riders" (Gosseries 2004): While we derive benefits from the actions of our ancestors, others are suffering as a result of them. Just as the benefit you derive from the stolen bicycle is morally "tainted," from this perspective all of our prosperity is tarnished with a moral blemish. It is based on injustice toward others.

What could be more obvious than to make the beneficiaries liable for rectifying the injustice? This is exactly what the "beneficiary pays" principle does. It states that everyone must bear the costs for rectifying a moral problem to the extent that he or she benefits from what caused this problem—in our case, from the past emissions. The beneficiary pays principle—as in the case of grandfathering and the polluter pays principle—is a "historical" principle of distributive justice, because it distributes the costs on the basis of the past. However, it does not focus on the *cause* of a harm or an injustice, but on its *effects*—that is, the fact that third parties benefit from it. In this way, the beneficiary pays principle is fundamentally different from the polluter pays principle: The beneficiary has a duty regardless of whether he or she is also a contributor. Even someone who does not currently produce any emissions derives benefits from past emissions and this justifies imposing costs on him or her for dealing with climate change. Therefore a distribution based on benefiting differs from a distribution based on contribution to causation. Russia and Ukraine, for example, account historically for a significant portion of the total emissions, but have benefited less from them in terms of levels of prosperity than a country with lower emissions such as Italy.

We will first explain the beneficiary pays principle in greater detail and then subject it to a critical examination.

Versions and normative foundation

The beneficiary pays principle also comes in different versions. For this, it is initially helpful to call to mind the exact structure of the moral linkages that the beneficiary pays principle takes as its starting point (see Fig. 13.1).

Past emissions represent a wrong involving four aspects:

(1) The total scale of the emissions produced is such that primarily developing countries are threatened with forms of climate damage. This is the damage aspect of the wrong ("wrong 1" in Fig. 13.1).
(2) The industrialized countries claimed the lion's share of past emissions—more than they were entitled to—so that the remaining emission cake

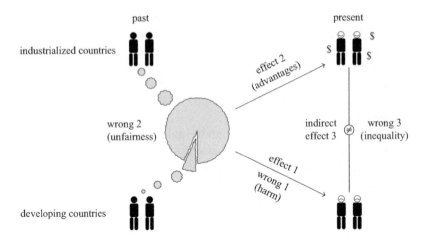

Figure 13.1 Moral linkages in the beneficiary pays principle

is less than it should be. This is the unfairness aspect of the wrong ("wrong 2" in Fig. 13.1).

(3) These unjust past emissions not only lead to the aforementioned climate damage for present and future developing countries ("effect 1"), but also bring the industrialized countries the advantages described above ("effect 2").

(4) The final aspect is that, as a result, the inequality between the industrialized and the developing countries is increasing ("effect 3"), which itself constitutes a wrong ("wrong 3").

Thus there is a chain of actions (past emissions), which gives rise to two direct effects (climate damage and advantages) and one indirect effect (inequality), and which are morally problematic in three respects (as harm, as past unfairness, and as inequality).

Keeping this structure in mind, the general formulation of the beneficiary pays principle—"Everyone must bear the costs of rectifying a wrong in proportion to the benefits he or she has derived from this wrong"—admits of three different readings, depending on what exactly is regarded as a wrong. According to the first reading, the wrong consists in the fact that past emissions harm people in developing countries ("wrong 1" in Fig. 13.1). Rectifying this wrong then means compensating those affected and ensuring—by financing adaptation measures and compensation payments—that they enjoy the best possible protection against climate change or are compensated for climate damage. On this first reading, therefore, the *adaptation and compensation costs* are distributed among the beneficiaries in proportion to their respective advantages. Underlying this is, of course, the basic intuition of "putting one's moral house in order" from the previous chapter. This time, though, the duty to put things in order follows from the fact that someone derives benefits from the harm suffered by others (and not from the fact that he or she caused the harm).

But the beneficiary pays principle can also be used to distribute the costs for *mitigating* climate change. According to this second reading, the wrong consists in the unfairness that the industrialized countries helped themselves to more emissions than they were entitled to ("wrong 2"), so that they must accept smaller shares in the impending distribution of the remaining emissions. Rectifying the wrong then consists precisely in the fact that you receive a smaller share of the remaining emissions budget in proportion to the benefits you derived from the past unfairness. Here, the guiding moral basic intuition is again that failure to show appropriate moral restraint must be counterbalanced and that this duty to pay compensation is a result of the fact that you enjoy benefits from the fact that someone showed insufficient restraint.

There is still a third reading of the beneficiary pays principle. According to this reading, the wrong consists in the indirect effect that past emissions have increased *inequality* between industrialized and developing countries ("wrong 3"). Eliminating this wrong would mean dividing up the advantages and disadvantages of past emissions equally. The advantaged industrialized countries would have to pay the disadvantaged developing countries an amount such that they both derive equal benefits from the historical emissions. In this version of the beneficiary pays principle, the *climate-change-related advantages and disadvantages as a whole* are distributed, not only adaptation or compensation costs or mitigation costs. The guiding underlying idea here is an intuition about equality: If a wrong is unavoidable, then everyone should benefit equally from it. Accordingly, those who benefit unduly have a duty to pay compensation in virtue of this fact alone.

Common to the three readings is the idea that the duty to rectify or alleviate a wrong is grounded in the fact that one enjoys benefits from this wrong (where the wrong, and hence the content of the duty, are defined differently in each case). Strictly speaking, it is the *undeserved* benefits that are decisive here. This is shown by the following example.

> David has stolen a lot of cash from Beth and makes a present of it to his friend, Anna. Anna invests it successfully in a flourishing business and, being an energetic entrepreneur, quickly becomes rich. One day, David gets caught and the police comes knocking on Anna's door: Beth wants her money back.

In this case, Anna has a duty to repay Beth the stolen money, but hardly to hand over her entire wealth (for which this stolen money was a necessary condition). The difference is that while Anna did not earn the stolen money, her wealth can be attributed to her entrepreneurial skill and therefore is earned. The guiding idea underlying the beneficiary pays principle is thus that *undeserved* advantages that result from a wrong should be compensated—and the precise form that the compensation takes depends on what one regards as the wrong. Is this moral basic intuition, and hence the beneficiary pays principle, convincing in one of its three versions?

Critical discussion

The second version need not detain us very long. In this version, the beneficiary pays principle states that a country that has taken more than it is *entitled* to must now also bear more reduction costs in proportion to the resulting advantages. However, for this to be effected, one must already know to what someone is entitled. Just like the second version of the polluter pays principle, therefore, the second version of the beneficiary pays principle already presupposes a different principle of distributive justice.

What about the third version of the beneficiary pays principle? According to this version, the real reason for the distribution is the inequality that arises as an indirect effect of the harm to the developing countries and the undeserved advantages of the industrialized countries (see Fig. 13.1). This means that the inequality *in itself*—that is, independently of its specific history—already gives rise to claims to redistribution. If the third version of the beneficiary pays principle is understood in this way, then it is no longer a beneficiary pays principle; on this reading, the bare fact of inequality would be decisive for the distribution of the costs—that is, the fact that one country is wealthier than another—and that would amount to a completely different principle of distribution: the so-called *"ability-to-pay" principle* (see Chapter 14). In this case, everyone would have to bear costs according to their economic possibilities, regardless of whether there was a causal connection between these economic possibilities and the past emissions. This has nothing more to do with the basic intuition of the beneficiary pays principle, according to which one must bear costs *because* one has benefited from past emissions.

Let us turn therefore to the first version of the beneficiary pays principle. According to this version, everyone must limit the impending damage (hence bear adaptation and compensation costs) to the extent that he or she has benefited from past emissions. We should first recall that, when it comes to adaptation and compensation costs, we have already endorsed the polluter pays principle with some qualifications (see Chapter 12). However, its field of application was limited, because some of the polluters no longer exist or can be excused on account of ignorance. The beneficiary pays principle can be interpreted at best as complementing the polluter pays principle—that is, it applies where forms of damage to the climate are not already captured by the polluter pays principle—for in a case in which one can sue the polluter for eliminating the damage, it would be very implausible to hold the beneficiaries liable *instead* of the polluters. Once again, this indicates that a complete answer to the third key question of climate ethics must fall back on several principles of distribution—assuming that the beneficiary pays principle is, in fact, convincing on the first reading.

There are, however, four reasons why it is not. First, the beneficiary pays principle is affected by the nonidentity problem. Strictly speaking, one cannot say that the people living today in the industrialized countries have *benefited from* past emissions, because that seems to imply that *these* people would have been worse off if these past emissions had not been produced. Yet this is wrong, because if the past emissions had not been produced, then completely *different* people would be living in the industrialized countries today. In Chapter 3, we dispelled the problem of nonidentity as a fundamental objection against the possibility of future-oriented duties by replacing the concept of harming with that of infringements of rights. But this maneuver is not open to a defender of the beneficiary pays principle, because if he or she replaces the idea of enjoying a benefit in an analogous way with another idea, then he or she is no longer defending, but instead abandoning, the beneficiary pays principle.

Now, one could object that the nonidentity problem is not so relevant for the beneficiary pays principle: A large proportion of the emissions and the prosperity (hence the benefits from the emissions) have occurred over the past three decades (Boden et al. 2012) and, in this short period of time, the nonidentity problem does not apply. This, in fact, weakens the first objection. But, at this point, a second reason why the beneficiary pays principle on the first reading is not very convincing comes into play: It is simply not true that all undeserved benefits from a wrong also obligate the beneficiary to pay compensation (see Anwander 2005). The additional construction workers who were hired to clean up the debris of the World Trade Center after the September 11, 2001, terrorist attacks benefited from a wrong, just as, in an X-ray examination, we benefit from the knowledge about the correct dosage of radiation that stems from studies of the victims of the atomic bombings of Hiroshima and Nagasaki. But it would be absurd to assert that the construction workers or any patient who has undergone an X-ray examination has a duty to compensate the victims. What makes benefiting from a wrong such as the bicycle theft mentioned at the beginning morally problematic in a way that gives rise to duties to compensate someone is instead only the fact that we sometimes *perpetuate* wrongdoing already committed (for example by refusing to return the bicycle to its rightful owner), or *enable* such wrong in the first place (by buying a cheap bike, we provide the thief with a guarantee that he or she can fence stolen goods), or *exploit* the wrong at the expense of those affected (perhaps by proposing to the rightful owner that he or she should "buy back" the bicycle he or she cherishes above all else at a grossly overinflated price).

So although enjoying benefits from wrongdoing may be morally problematic in some sense, it does not necessarily in and of itself imply a duty to compensate the victims; it does so only when enjoying the benefits contributes to perpetuating, enabling, or exploiting a wrong. But this is not the case in the context of climate change. After all, the benefit that the industrialized countries derive from past emissions is their high standard of living and, according to the first reading of the beneficiary pays principle, the wrong from which this benefit results consists in the climate damage suffered by the developing countries. However, the high standard of living does not perpetuate this wrong: It is at most the further—*present-day*—emissions that perpetuate this injustice, but not the *past* emissions that led to the high standard of living. The high standard of living does not enable this wrong either: In the case of the implicit guarantee of being able to fence stolen goods, the advantage enjoyed by the beneficiary provides an incentive for the perpetrator to commit the wrong. Yet, in the case of the past emissions of our ancestors, the incentive for the emissions was not *our* present-day prosperity (the advantage of the beneficiary), but *their* prosperity (the advantage of the offender). Our predecessors did not produce emissions so that *we* would be better off, but so that *they* would be better off. And, finally, although it is unfortunately true that the industrialized countries exploit the developing countries in many ways, most of these are not cases of directly taking advantage of the vulnerability of the South to climate change: For example, the industrialized countries do not sell the technologies required to adapt to climate change to the developing countries affected at overinflated prices.

A third problem with the first version of the beneficiary pays principle is that, like the polluter pays principle, it must be supplemented with a kind of "ability-to-pay" limit. It is unfair to require someone to pay back the benefits resulting from wrongdoing if this would impoverish him or her (for example because he or she has now exhausted the benefit and is destitute). This shows once again that what is required is an interplay of different distribution principles—and that the ability to pay plays a role here.

A fourth objection to the beneficiary pays principle (in all versions) is that it is difficult to apply. On the one hand, one would have to imagine what the world would look like today *without* emissions-intensive industrialization in order to determine who derived what benefits from past emissions. One would even have to be able to separate the part of our prosperity attributable to past emissions from that part which is based, for example, on hard work and that part which is based on other historical wrongs (such as wars, slavery, or colonization). This is far from easy. On the other hand, the example of grey emissions shows—as in the case of the polluter pays principle—that it is not so easy to translate the central moral concept of the beneficiary pays principle into practice: Who benefits, for example, from the emissions that are produced when China manufactures goods that are consumed in other countries—the consumer countries or China or both? And if both benefit, in what proportions? A mirror-image problem is that of spillover effects: Do not even those who are harmed by climate change derive some benefit from past emissions? Does it not also benefit the low-emitting, but climate-vulnerable, states of the poorer South when Western countries grow economically because of their emissions? After all, with rising prosperity, the latter can (or could) provide more development aid to, and import more goods, from the South. Granted, it is highly contentious whether and to what extent the structure of world trade really benefits low-emitting developing countries. However, we do not have to commit ourselves to any answer to this controversial question in order to conclude that, when it comes to the crucial question "How does one measure the extent to which someone benefits?", the devil is in the detail.

Conclusion

In this chapter, we have examined the view that the costs for coping with climate change should be divided up in accordance with the benefits derived from past emissions. We distinguished three versions of this beneficiary pays principle, each of which is based on a different element of the moral linkages existing in the case of benefits from past emissions. The first version—which states that the adaptation and compensation costs should be divided up among the beneficiaries in proportion to their respective benefits—accords central importance to the aspect of damage; the second version—remaining emissions should be distributed in inverse proportion to the benefits from past emissions—focuses on compensating for unfairness; the third version—the benefits from past emissions should be divided up equally—is geared toward eliminating undeserved inequality. The critical discussion of the different versions has shown that none of the three is ultimately convincing (see Arguments box 11).

It became apparent in the discussion that, time and again, there is argumentative pressure to supplement the beneficiary pays principle with additional morally relevant aspects—in particular, the aspect of the ability to pay crops up here, for example, in connection with limits beyond which compensation payments become too demanding or in connection with the third interpretation of the beneficiary pays principle. Underlying this is the notion that a country's wealth (as the sum of all of the benefits it enjoys) *in itself* should serve as a basis for the distribution of the costs of climate policy; the sources from which a state derives its ability to pay would then be irrelevant. We will turn to this notion next.

Arguments box 11: the beneficiary pays principle

The beneficiary pays principle can answer the third key question of climate ethics "(a) What is due (b) to whom and (c) why?" in three different ways, as follows.

(1) (a) The costs for adapting to climate change and for compensating disadvantages are distributed (b) among those who benefited from the past emissions (c) in proportion to their respective benefits from the emissions—in order to rectify a *wrong*.

(2) (a) The remaining emissions are distributed (b) among all states (c) in an inverse proportion to the benefits that each country has derived from the past emissions—in order to compensate for *unfairness*.

(3) (a) The benefits deriving from past emissions are divided up (b) among all states (c) equally—in order to rectify an undeserved *inequality*.

Version (2) faces the same problem as the corresponding version of the polluter pays principle: It already presupposes a principle of distributive justice because it must specify when the past emissions were *(un)fairly* distributed. Version (3) mutates into the "ability-to-pay" principle, which states that inequalities per se (and not the benefits derived from them) are morally decisive.

In version (1), the beneficiary pays principle meets with several objections that render it untenable. The two most important are the following:

---

(1) *The nonidentity problem*: A person living today does not derive any benefit from past emissions because he or she would have to be better off today than *he or she* would have been without past emissions—but, without the past emissions, he or she would not even exist.

(2) *The wrong basic intuition*: As the examples of benefits from terrorist attacks or atomic bombings show, the simple fact that one enjoys benefits from a harm does not necessarily imply that one has a duty to compensate anybody—and the conditions under which such a duty in fact exists (perpetuating, enabling, or exploiting wrongdoing) do not hold in the case of climate change.

This is why the beneficiary pays principle is not a convincing answer to the third key question of climate ethics.

References

Anwander, N. (2005) "Contributing and benefiting: two grounds for duties to the victims of injustice," *Ethics and International Affairs*, 19(1): 39–45.

Boden, T., Marland, G., and Andres, R. (2012) *Global, Regional, and National Fossil-Fuel CO2 Emissions*, Oak Ridge, TN: Carbon Dioxide Information Analysis Center, Oak Ridge National Laboratory, U.S. Department of Energy.

Gosseries, A. (2004) "Historical emissions and free-riding," *Ethical Perspectives*, 11(1): 36–60.

14 The "ability-to-pay" principle

To each according to his or her means

The principles discussed in the three foregoing chapters have a "historical" orientation: They answer the third key question of climate ethics with reference to the past and they determine the just distribution of the costs of tackling climate change *within the present generation* in terms of past emissions. They can be understood as attempts to "bequeath" moral duties and claims across generations. The assumption is that because certain things were (not) the case in the past, other things should (not) be the case in the present. As we have seen, however, this intergenerational "inheritance" of moral claims and duties is not convincing. This is reason enough to look for an "ahistorical" answer to the third key question of climate ethics that makes fair burden-sharing depend exclusively on aspects of the present.

Our reflections in the previous chapter already pointed us toward a possible candidate. The current prosperity of a country *in itself*—regardless of whether it is based on wrongdoing or not—could be taken as a basis for allocating costs. The guiding idea would then be that, given one's prosperity, one is in an especially privileged position to help to rectify a moral problem. This seems to be a good moral rule of thumb: The more one earns, the more one should also donate to combating poverty, starvation, and other forms of misery—just as, the stronger a removals man is, the more of the heavy moving boxes he should carry. When it comes to climate mitigation, the especially privileged position is held by those who enjoy a high standard of living (since the burdens to be borne are not literally heavy, but costly). In the context of climate change, therefore, the moral rule of thumb leads to the principle that everyone must contribute to averting climate change in accordance with his or her economic capacity—"everyone according to his or her means."

This "ability-to-pay" principle does not refer to the past; instead, it is geared to current economic capacity and hence is ahistorical. At the same time, it links up with the UNFCCC. This affirms that state parties should protect the climate "in accordance with their common but differentiated responsibilities and *respective capabilities*" (Article 3.1, emphasis added), and the principle of distribution under consideration distributes the costs specifically in accordance with the countries' respective abilities (to pay). These two points mean that the ability-to-pay principle initially seems a very promising approach. Whether this initial impression can withstand closer analysis will be assessed in what follows.

Versions and normative foundation

The ability-to-pay principle can be understood in two ways. On the one hand, "each according to his or her means" can mean that individuals or states should bear more of the costs for coping with climate change the more capable they are in economic terms. This is compatible with the claim that even a very poor player should also make a contribution, if only a small one. On a second reading of the ability-to-pay principle, this claim is ruled out. According to this reading, someone who has *too much* must also bear more costs to the extent that he or she has too much; by contrast, someone who is poor and has *too little* does not have to make *any* contribution to climate mitigation. We have already pointed out in a number of places that the various principles discussed must be supplemented with an ability-to-pay limit. It is simply morally inappropriate to require someone who already has too little (to survive or to live in dignity) to make additional contributions. Nobody would require poverty-stricken people in Ethiopia to make a contribution—even a small one—to combating poverty in Somalia. This is why the second reading of the ability-to-pay principle is more plausible: Those who can afford it must contribute to climate mitigation according to their ability to pay and those who cannot afford it are exempted—that is, "those who have have to do something, but those who do not have do not have to do anything."

Which arguments support this principle? An initial argument deals with two pragmatic advantages. Unlike the polluter pays or the beneficiary pays principles (which were convincing at most for the adaptation and compensation costs), the ability-to-pay principle can be plausibly applied in the first instance to *all* kinds of costs. Adaptation and compensation costs, as well as mitigation costs, can be distributed according to the ability to pay: For example, the remaining emissions budget can be divided up among the countries in such a way that countries receive fewer emissions the more prosperous they are. A further advantage is that there are hardly any problems with measurability. A country's economic capacity can be operationalized, for example, through its GDP adjusted for purchasing power. In this respect, too, the ability-to-pay principle differs from the beneficiary pays principle, because, as we have seen, it was quite difficult to determine the benefits resulting from past emissions.

Although these considerations are not unimportant, they are more of the order of pragmatic advantages rather than solid moral arguments for the ability-to-pay principle. However, we are not looking for a pragmatic principle ("Everyone should contribute whatever he or she likes" would also be pragmatic), but for a *just* one (which ideally also has pragmatic advantages). For the same reason, pointing out that the ability-to-pay principle has certain efficiency advantages is also unsuited to lend it moral support. Even if it were true that it is more efficient to have the wealthy countries pay for emission reductions, such a consideration would justify the ability-to-pay principle only from an economic point of view. We are looking instead for an argument that makes it intelligible to us why prosperity or the ability to pay in itself is supposed to be a decisive *moral* factor in distributing the costs associated with climate policy. How can this be explained in greater detail?

The moral basis of the ability-to-pay principle becomes apparent when we contrast it with a different principle of distribution. Let us imagine three people (Alf, Beth, and Sid) who enjoy different levels of prosperity: Alf has US$60 per day, Beth has $40, and Sid has $20 (see Table 14.1). These three people must jointly finance a small wind power plant, which costs $60 per day. How should the financial costs be distributed? If the costs are simply divided up equally in *absolute* terms (distribution D-1 in Table 14.1), then each of them would have to pay $20 per day—and that would be manifestly unjust, because Sid would then have nothing left over on which to live. Alternatively, one could divide up the *relative* financial costs equally (distribution D-2 in Table 14.1). If the three-person community taken together has an income of $120 per day and must contribute $60 per day—hence 50 per cent of its income—for the wind power plant, then everyone could simply contribute 50 per cent of his or her income. But even this could be unfair: If you need exactly $10 per day in order to have enough to survive, then on this distribution Sid would be forced to eke out his existence at exactly this limit.

It would seem to be fairer to distribute the costs according to Alf's, Beth's, and Sid's respective abilities to pay and to ensure that none of them falls below the threshold mentioned—namely, that each of them has *enough*. This formulation is reminiscent of the sufficiency requirement in Chapter 7: There, it was a question of a principle of intergenerational justice, according to which we have a duty to future generations to ensure that they are "sufficiently well off." Naturally, this notion of a morally significant "threshold" of well-being can also be applied to questions of *intra*generational justice. The ability-to-pay principle does just that: "Those who have have to do something, but those who do not have do not have to do anything" means that everyone must bear costs to the extent that he or she has more than enough and that nobody must

Table 14.1 Example of the distributive effects of the ability-to-pay principle

person	income ($/day)	D-1		D-2		D-3		D-4	
		burden	remainder	burden	remainder	burden	remainder	burden	remainder
Alf	60	20	40	30	30	$2/3 \times (60 - 10) = 33$	27	$20 + (2/3 \times 10)$	33
Beth	40	20	20	20	20	$2/3 \times (40 - 10) = 20$	20	$20 + (1/3 \times 10)$	17
Sid	20	20	0	10	10	$2/3 \times (20 - 10) = 7$	13	$20 - 10$	10
	120	**60**	**60**	**60**	**60**		**60**	**60**	**60**

contribute so much that he or she has less than enough left over. A distribution of the costs associated with climate policy is just, therefore, when everyone is sufficiently well off and when everyone also contributes more the more he or she lives above the threshold.

Of course, this raises the question of how exactly to determine the sufficiency threshold: When does one have enough? When it comes to preventing climate change and allocating the remaining emissions budget, one can draw, for example, on the idea of so-called *subsistence emissions* (see Shue 1993). These are the emissions required for survival, for a minimally decent life, for meeting the most important basic human needs, and to ensure that human dignity and human rights are respected (emissions that go beyond these would be "luxury emissions"). The distribution of the emissions budget is then a matter of ensuring that all are granted their subsistence emissions. One can also express the threshold in financial terms—that is, as the income that is necessary in order to lead a decent life in which the most important basic human needs are satisfied. Of course, in neither case is it easy to express this threshold exactly in tons of greenhouse gases or in monetary terms (which is already an indication that, after all, the ability-to-pay principle may not be as easy to implement in practice as initially suspected). The value specified by the so-called *Greenhouse Development Rights (GDRs)* approach—which advocates the ability-to-pay principle—can perhaps serve as a point of orientation: $7,500 per person per year (Baer et al. 2008: 41*ff.*).

But what would a distribution in accordance with the ability-to-pay principle that took this threshold into account actually look like? For the sake of simplicity, in our example we assume that the sufficiency threshold for Alf, Beth, and Sid is $10 each per day. One could then distribute the relative costs equally with reference to the income that lies *above* the sufficiency threshold. The income of each of the three individuals that lies above the sufficiency threshold, taken together, amounts to $90 ($50 + $30 + $10) per day; a total of $60 per day—hence two-thirds of this sum—must be spent on the wind power plant. Therefore if we were to deduct two-thirds from each of the incomes above the sufficiency threshold, each person would still have the remaining third plus his or her sufficiency threshold (distribution D-3 in Table 14.1). One *could* distribute in this way if one wanted to do justice to the sufficientarian element in accordance with the ability-to-pay principle.

But doing justice to sufficientarianism by no means *necessitates* making such a distribution. We could also first collect the same absolute financial contribution (that is, $20 per day) from all, provided that this would not force them beneath the sufficiency threshold; in a second step, we could increase the income of those who would otherwise slip below the sufficiency threshold up to the sufficiency threshold through additional contributions from the others (in proportion to their respective levels of prosperity). Therefore, in the first step, we would end up with distribution D-1; in the second step, Sid's excessively low income would be topped up by $10 per day to the sufficiency threshold. On the basis of this arrangement, Alf—who has twice as much income after the first step as Beth—would also have to pay twice as much of the topping-up payment of $10 as Beth (distribution D-4 in Table 14.1). Such a distribution would also ensure that no one falls below the sufficiency threshold.

Therefore the sufficientarianism included in the ability-to-pay principle is compatible with different distributions. Nevertheless, distribution D-3 seems to correspond better with the "spirit" of this principle. This is because, by comparison with distribution D-4, it is marked by less *inequality* between the richest and the poorest person. As a result, the ability-to-pay principle seems to contain in addition an egalitarian element. Above the sufficiency threshold, the relative costs should be distributed equally as in distribution D-3; although wealth as a whole would not be completely equal as a result, it is less unequally distributed. Viewed in this context, the ability-to-pay principle actually expresses a combination of *two* moral guiding ideas: sufficiency, on the one hand; and equality, on the other. How convincing is this combination?

Critical discussion

An initial complication comes to light when one recalls that the distribution is ultimately supposed to be made between *individuals* and therefore that the morally relevant criterion is the individual's ability to pay. If one were simply to consider *states'* ability to pay (for example based on average per capita income), one would still have to allocate a country's burdens among its citizens in a way that accounts for how wealth is distributed within this country. Otherwise the resulting distribution could be unfair. A wealthy Chinese person may very well be richer than a poor Italian and hence, if we take the guiding consideration behind the ability-to-pay principle seriously, the former should bear more costs than the latter. But if one were to go exclusively by the average income of each country and determine each person's burdens by his or her country's ability to pay, then the rich Chinese person would have to contribute less to climate mitigation than the poor Italian (since average per capita income is lower in China), and that seems unfair. Therefore the ability-to-pay principle is plausible only if it refers to individuals—and so the principle immediately loses much of its practical applicability. In order to apply it successfully, we would have to have precise information about each individual's level of prosperity.

A second complication concerns the status of the principle. Moral philosophers sometimes say that "ought" implies "can," by which they mean that we can have a duty to do only what we are also able to do. If you cannot run, for example, then you cannot have a duty to run to fetch help in an emergency either. But, conversely, "can" does not necessarily imply "ought": Being able to do something does not always imply that one has a duty to do it. Just because you *can* play the piano or cook well does not mean that you also *ought* to do these things; it is up to you whether you do them or not. This even holds true in the case of providing assistance. The bare fact that someone is particularly well placed to help someone else does not of itself mean that he or she is morally required to do so—at least not in the sense that the person in need is entitled to this assistance (see Thomson 1971). If you own a postage stamp and a Spaniard who is unknown to you has become depressed because he wants to own *your* postage stamp in particular, then you are in a particularly privileged position to help him—and, without a doubt, it would be generous and nice of you if you did so, but this cannot be required of you: The Spaniard simply has no claim on you that you should make him a gift of your postage stamp. If you help him in this way, this action goes beyond what you are obligated to do: It is a so-called *supererogatory action*. And if the fact that one is able do something does not necessarily imply that one ought to do it, but can instead reflect a supererogatory demand, then we can also ask, in the context of climate policy, whether a distribution of the associated costs based on economic capacity is not also a supererogatory requirement rather than a duty of justice: Are the wealthy really *obligated* to contribute to climate mitigation in proportion to their wealth, or would it simply be decent and nice of them to do so? Do we really do something wrong if we do not comply with the requirement of the ability-to-pay principle, or is it simply a matter of doing less than we ideally could do? The latter would be regrettable, but not objectionable. It is not clear, therefore, what status should be attached to the requirement expressed by the ability-to-pay principle.

A third complication concerns the distribution of the costs of climate policy *among* the prosperous countries (Page 2011: 418*ff*). If a country's ability to pay is the *only* decisive factor, then the principle does not distinguish between rich "climate offenders" and rich "climate protectors." For example, Germany and Australia have a similar per capita GDP, but their per capita emissions in the recent past and their total historical emissions since 1900 are significantly different (with Germany's being higher than Australia's, in both absolute and per capita terms). There is a mirror-image problem in the case of poorer countries: Here, too, the principle cannot distinguish between poor countries with a responsible climate policy and poor countries with an irresponsible climate policy.

But it seems unfair to lump all countries with equally well-filled coffers together and, in the process, ignore differences in responsibilities.

This third complication points toward a more fundamental problem: The ability-to-pay principle is an ahistorical principle of distribution and hence it is in tension from the outset with a historical consideration such as responsibility for the problem of climate change. Perhaps, given the failure of our attempts to render the historical "inheritance" of duties and entitlements plausible, one might be inclined to abandon the idea of responsibility altogether. But that would be to throw the baby out with the bathwater, because one cannot dismiss out of hand that differences in the responsibility of different countries should play *some* role in the distribution of the costs. It would be ideal, therefore, if the ability-to-pay principle could be combined with the aspect of responsibility, for example in the form of the polluter pays principle. Actually, this is a key point of controversy in climate negotiations of the past years. While most parties agree that the ability-to-pay aspect should play some role, certain parties (in particular, countries from the developing world such as India) are keen to complement ability-to-pay considerations with a reference to historical emissions.

So what might a more balanced combination of both aspects look like? One possibility is to hold fast to distributing the costs in proportion to prosperity, but to increase or decrease these shares according to degrees of responsibility—that is, depending on how emissions-intensive the process of wealth creation was in a given country (see Caney 2010: 215). However, this proposal inherits some of the problems of the beneficiary pays principle, because it brings the *sources* of present-day prosperity into play (via the concept of the "process of wealth creation"), and this raises several questions that we have already encountered: Which portion of present-day prosperity is based on past emissions, which on hard work, and which on other historical wrongs (such as slavery)? Was the wealth created in China through grey emissions generated in an emissions-intensive way, or did the countries that imported Chinese goods benefit instead? And was part of the present-day prosperity in the South not created through an "indirectly emissions-intensive" process because of spillover effects from the economic activity of the industrialized countries? In attempting to reconcile the polluter pays principle with the ability-to-pay principle, the devil is thus presumably in the details.

Conclusion

In this chapter, we have examined the ability-to-pay principle in greater detail. It states that the costs (of whatever kind) associated with climate policy should be distributed among all individuals in such a way that they are proportionate to the ability of each to pay—or rather, to that part of their ability to pay above the sufficiency threshold—and hence that well-being will become less unequally distributed as a result. This answer to the third key question of climate ethics is thus based on two major moral ideas: sufficiency and equality.

The ability-to-pay principle is ahistorical insofar as it disregards considerations of the past. It has some pragmatic advantages and is hardly susceptible to any fundamental objections. For the most part, the worries presented are more a matter of complications, for example in applying the principle to individuals or as to whether it expresses something more than a supererogatory requirement (see Arguments box 12). But a remaining major difficulty seems to be a function of the ahistorical character of the principle: The example of the distribution of costs among the wealthy countries (and, in a mirror-image sense, also among poor countries) made clear that it does not take adequate account of the aspect of the responsibility for the problem. And it is not immediately apparent how this aspect of responsibility can be integrated into the principle.

As we have seen, the ability-to-pay principle involves, in addition to the sufficientarian element, an egalitarian aspect. Surprisingly enough, the idea of equality has not even been touched upon in the principles hitherto considered. In the next chapter, we want to examine whether this idea can provide the basis for a satisfactory answer to the third key question of climate ethics.

Arguments box 12: the ability-to-pay principle

The ability-to-pay principle answers the third key question of climate ethics "(a) What is due (b) to whom and (c) why?" as follows: (a) Both the adaptation and compensation costs, as well as the mitigation costs, should be distributed (b) among all individuals in such a way that (c) each person bears costs in proportion to his or her prosperity above the sufficiency threshold.

This ahistorical answer faces three difficulties, as follows.

(1) In its application to individuals, the principle is reliant on very detailed information about an individual's economic situation and on a controversial specification of the sufficiency threshold (whether expressed in tons of greenhouse gases or in monetary terms).

(2) It is not ultimately clear whether the principle really expresses a duty of justice or merely a supererogatory requirement.

(3) The ability-to-pay principle does not take into account responsibility for causing the problem, and therefore cannot differentiate between climate protectors and climate offenders within the prosperous states or within the poor states. On the one hand, it seems necessary to extend the ability-to-pay principle by the polluter pays principle; on the other hand, the obvious way of doing so seems to invite objections that beset a previously discussed principle (that is, the beneficiary pays principle).

All in all, the ability-to-pay principle is thus relatively convincing, even if it remains unclear whether—and, if so, how—to combine it with the aspect of responsibility.

References

Baer, P., Athanasiou, T., Kartha, S., and Kemp-Benedict, E. (2008) *The Greenhouse Development Rights Framework: The Right to Development in a Climate-Constrained World*, Berlin: Heinrich-Böll-Stiftung.

Caney, S. (2010) "Climate change and the duties of the advantaged," *Critical Review of International Social and Political Philosophy*, 13(1): 203–28.

Page, E. A. (2011) "Climatic justice and the fair distribution of atmospheric burdens," *The Monist*, 94(3): 412–32.

Shue, H. (1993) "Subsistence emissions and luxury emissions," *Law & Policy*, 15(1): 39–59.

Thomson, J. J. (1971) "A defense of abortion," *Philosophy and Public Affairs*, 1(1): 47–66.

15 Emissions egalitarianism

Dividing up the cake equally

One concern with our previous argument is that perhaps the most straightforward answer to the third key question of climate ethics has not yet even been brought into play: Should we not simply divide up the remaining emissions budget *equally* among all human beings living at present? Everyone would receive an equally large piece of the "emissions cake," as it were—a small child from Calcutta, as well as the manager from New York. Would this equal division not be the easiest and fairest solution? This proposal does, in fact, have a range of supporters among experts in ethics and in international climate policy. The so-called *contraction and convergence* approach, for example, pursues the aim of aligning the currently glaring differences in per capita emissions between the different states over a certain period of time (see Meyer 2000). In addition, a range of policy advisory institutes—for example the German Advisory Council on Global Change (Wissenschaftlicher Beirat der Bundesregierung Globale Umweltveränderungen, or WBGU) with its so-called *budget approach* (WBGU 2009)—are proponents of this kind of "emissions egalitarianism."

Emissions egalitarianism, more than any of the proposals discussed thus far, seems appealingly easy to implement: You have only to calculate the budget of greenhouse gas emissions that remains for avoiding dangerous climate change by, for example, the middle of this century and then divide it by the number of people living on Earth. If we follow the calculations of the WBGU, for example, then circa 2050 every person may emit around 1 ton of CO_2 per year. Is that a lot or a little? It is about as much as an average Pakistani currently emits annually—but only around one-ninth of what the average German currently discharges into the atmosphere every year (World Bank 2015). If one considers that a return flight from Frankfurt to San Francisco accounts for 3–4 tons of CO_2, one can imagine what reducing emissions to the same level of 1 ton for all human beings would mean for our lifestyles. Presumably, it would necessitate drastic changes—and this is reason enough to ask ourselves how plausible emissions egalitarianism really is.

Normative foundations

There are three main reasons for the attractiveness of emissions egalitarianism. First of all, as already stated, it seems to be unbeatable from a pragmatic point of view because it is so easy to calculate the exact level of the distributive entitlements: You simply divide the remaining emissions budget by the number of inhabitants of the Earth. Unlike the proposals previously discussed, you do not first have to ask how many or how few emissions were produced in the past, whether someone is solvent or poor, or to what extent someone has benefited from past emissions, and so on. The distributive principle of emissions egalitarianism gets by with relatively little information—information that is, moreover, easily available. Admittedly, it is not so easy for climate scientists to calculate the size of the remaining emissions budget—but that is a problem shared by *all* distributive principles in which the resource to be distributed is the remaining emissions budget.

At this point, one could object that these practical benefits of emissions egalitarianism are all well and good, but ultimately provide the wrong kind of reasons: We are looking for a *just* principle of distribution, not a practical one. It may be the case that a just solution should also be practically feasible, but not every practical solution to a distribution problem is also just: For example, if you divide up a cake at a child's birthday party in such a way that one child gets the whole cake, then that would be very straightforward from a practical point of view—but, of course, in the normal run of things, not fair. That the practical benefits of emissions egalitarianism are also attractive from the standpoint of justice becomes apparent, however, if we include emissions trading (see Chapter 19). In emissions trading, someone who needs additional emission permits to pursue his or her lifestyle has the option of purchasing them from someone who does not need them and is willing to sell them. If we now factor into the equation that current per capita emissions in the industrialized countries are much higher than those in the developing countries and if we were to accord all human beings equal emission rights, then the residents of the industrialized countries would have to buy up emission permits on a large scale if they were to be able to continue to pursue anything close to their current lifestyles. Thus emissions egalitarianism coupled with emissions trading would lead to a major transfer of wealth from the industrialized to the developing countries—which seems only fair.

This second reason for emissions egalitarianism is indeed the right kind of reason: It aims at justice and not merely at practical feasibility. However, this reason does not follow from the proposed principle of distribution (emissions egalitarianism) *itself*, but instead from emissions trading. *Every* distribution principle that accords the industrialized countries less and the developing countries more than their current per capita emissions would lead to a large transfer of wealth from the "North" to the "South" in combination with emissions trading. And, as we have seen, all of the principles discussed—with the exception of the grandfathering principle—in fact imply just that. The fact that emissions egalitarianism (in combination with emissions trading) entails a transfer of wealth certainly does not speak against it from the perspective of justice—but it is not a conclusive reason *for* it either.

The true moral core of emissions egalitarianism resides neither in its supposedly attractive simplicity nor in the resulting transfer of wealth; rather, the basic idea of emissions egalitarianism resides in the fact that the atmosphere, which is used as a sink for emissions, is the common property of *all human beings* and nobody has an overriding claim to make use of it—so that all human beings may use the atmosphere *to the same extent*. And this is why the remaining emissions should be distributed equally among all human beings. Perhaps this idea can be made more concrete with an example.

> Imagine a small town with a population of 200 situated on a beautiful lake that is suitable for bathing. The lake becomes unfit for bathing when it is used too intensively. If people swim in the lake more than 2,000 times during the summer, the water becomes cloudy and dirty, and there is a risk of damage to the water quality. Would it not be fair if access to the lake were to be restricted and everyone in the town to receive a permit to swim ten times during the bathing season (which he or she could use as he or she pleased)? Would that not be fair precisely *because* the lake belongs to everyone in the town?

Someone who argues for such "bathing egalitarianism" is making a number of assertions. First, he or she is saying that the lake, in fact, belongs to everyone—but that on its own is not enough. It may be that the lake formerly belonged to a rancher and that the townspeople purchased it from him, with each resident contributing a different amount to the purchase price and receiving a corresponding share in the lake in return. Then, the lake would be more like a joint stock company: There are several owners with different shares. Therefore someone who wants to support the proposal with the permits must say instead that the lake belongs to everyone *equally* and that this equal ownership should now also entail equal usage. Therefore, second, one must also assert that something that belongs to everyone equally should also be used equally—and if usage in this context means "bathing" (and not, for example, "washing"), then it seems to follow that the remaining bathing opportunities should be distributed equally among all, so that everyone receives a permit to swim ten times.

If we apply this line of reasoning to the atmosphere, then the argument for emissions egalitarianism goes as follows.

(1) The atmosphere belongs to everyone equally.
(2) If something belongs to everyone equally, then its use should be distributed equally.
(3) The use of the atmosphere is distributed equally when the remaining emissions are distributed equally.

Is this argument for emissions egalitarianism convincing?

Critical discussion

A first complication arises when one asks *among whom exactly* the emissions are supposed to be distributed. The problem is that the bathing lake example was drastically simplified in several respects. In the first instance, it ignored the fact that the world's population is constantly changing: Every day many people are born, others die, and on balance the global population is growing. Let us assume, accordingly, that the population of the town increases from 200 to 400 during the bathing season. Then, the share in the bathing opportunities to which each inhabitant is entitled in fact decreases (from ten opportunities at the beginning of the season to five at the end). This temporal aspect gives rise to a further complication. Let us assume that Al spends 40 years in the town from birth to his early death, whereas Betty, by contrast, lives in the town for 80 years. If both have ten bathing opportunities per bathing season, then Al could use the lake 400 times in his life, but Betty, by contrast, twice as often. Things become even more complicated if we factor in that the bathing capacity of the lake also varies over the time (just as the capacity of the atmosphere to absorb greenhouse gases without morally problematic climate change varies over time depending on the emissions produced to date). Depending on weather conditions, and on how the plant and animal populations in the lake develop, in some years the lake can cope with only 1,000 bathing sessions, but in other years, by contrast, it can cope with 3,000. Assuming that the population remains constant, then in some years everyone could bathe just five times; in others, 15 times. The distribution of bathing sessions across lifetimes would then be even more unequal. Would that still do justice to the intuition that the lake belongs to the townspeople *equally* and hence that they should be able to use it equally? Or would one not instead have to distribute the bathing opportunities equally over the expected lifetimes (instead of on an annual basis)?

If we apply these considerations to the atmosphere, then the "equal" share to which every human being is entitled would be extremely difficult to calculate. We would require a lot more information about the past and future level of the world population, the life expectancy of human beings, and how the absorption capacity of the atmosphere develops. There would then be little left of the supposed simplicity and practical feasibility of emissions egalitarianism. These complications arise not only from a practical point of view, but are also an expression of a problem with the central moral intuition behind emissions egalitarianism— namely, the notion that the atmosphere belongs *to everyone equally*. The point is that one could also take the view that the atmosphere (like the world's oceans) does not belong to all, but in fact belongs to *nobody*. Then, the argument for emissions egalitarianism would have to be a different one.

A second problem with emissions egalitarianism is bound up with the second step in the argument presented above. It states that the ownership structure in itself already provides an answer to the question of the fair distribution of the resource. But that does not seem to be the case even in the bathing lake example. Presumably, the townspeople are very different from one another in morally relevant ways. First, there may have been differences in how the lake was used in the past that are relevant for allocating bathing rights. The fact that, on average, the lake can cope with "only" 2,000 bathing sessions per year may be a result of the fact that the owners of the surrounding mansions regularly discharged their waste water into the lake, leading to an increase in phosphate concentrations. Should these individuals also receive the same usage rights as the townspeople who directed their waste water into the town's septic tank? It would instead seem more just that the mansion dwellers should accept a small "deduction" (perhaps an eight-session instead of a ten-session permit) for their past use of the lake.

Second, the townspeople also differ in the extent to which they benefit from the bathing lake. Suppose that the people living in the surrounding mansions rent out umbrellas and adjacent parking spaces during the summer months, and sell ice cream and cold beverages; in this way, they make good money from the usage of the lake by the other townspeople who do not benefit to the same extent. Would it not be fair as a result to downgrade the eight-session permits of the mansion dwellers to six-session permits?

Third, the townspeople also have different needs: Perhaps some of them have no running water and, for them, the bathing lake is one of the few opportunities to wash; others may have jobs (as garbage collectors, auto mechanics, or miners) that mean that they have to wash themselves more often. The rich mansion dwellers, by contrast, have water and showers in abundance—some of them even have swimming pools in their backyards—and they rarely get their hands dirty. And even if they did not have showers or swimming pools of their own, the mansion dwellers, in contrast to the poorer townspeople, are wealthy enough to be able to drive regularly to an expensive swimming pool in the next town. This represents a fourth difference: The mansion dwellers do not even need a ten-, eight-, or six-session permit, while others need one very urgently. A more differentiated approach therefore suggests that the bathing rights should be distributed unequally from the perspective of justice in spite of equal joint ownership.

Something similar also holds for the distribution of rights to use the atmosphere. A straightforward equal distribution of the emission rights does not take into account that human beings are unequal in a variety of relevant respects.

(1) They have contributed in varying degrees to causing the problem of climate change. In the past, people in the industrialized countries produced far more emissions than people in developing countries.
(2) But people from different countries have also benefited in varying degrees from the past emissions. The achievements and gains in prosperity of the North through increasing industrialization, electrification, and digitalization are based crucially on a high level of emissions; thus present-day human beings are still benefiting from the past emissions.
(3) Needs are also different from one country to another, because some are more reliant on emissions than others: In the far North and in the mountains, people have to heat their homes more in order to ensure a certain standard of living; in equatorial regions, they have to cool more to achieve the same standard. For a certain level of mobility, people in countries with a poorly developed infrastructure have to fall back on emissions-intensive means of transport, whereas in other countries people can use solar-powered electric cars.
(4) Finally, the different countries are also able to avoid using the atmosphere in varying degrees. By virtue of their prosperity, people from Western countries have, on average, more means at their disposal to adopt less emissions-intensive mobility technologies or to use more expensive, but (from a climate perspective) "cleaner," power.

If we take all of these factors into account, then it no longer seems just that someone living in the Sahara, in Siberia, or in Bangladesh should be entitled to the same volume of emissions as a central European or an American. People from the Western industrialized countries seem to be entitled to much *less* than the 1 ton of CO_2 per person per year mentioned at the beginning. Therefore, even if emissions egalitarianism were a "simple" solution from a practical point of view (which, as we have seen, proves to be questionable on closer examination), the reverse side of simplicity is a simplification—and emissions egalitarianism makes things *too* easy for itself, because it takes only one consideration (that is, ownership relations) into account in the distribution of the emissions budget, while ignoring many other morally relevant considerations.

Conclusion

This chapter has examined in greater detail what appeared at first sight to be an attractively simple and practical answer to the third key question of climate ethics. According to emissions egalitarianism, a fair distribution of the remaining emissions budget consists in all human beings having equal per capita emission rights. This idea is based primarily on the notion of equal common ownership of the atmosphere—that is, the idea that the atmosphere (the use of which is at stake in the distribution of the remaining emissions budget) belongs equally to all human beings. A closer inspection has shown, however, that emissions egalitarianism, implemented consistently, is hardly more workable than other principles, because the annual emission rights of every person would have to be established through a very elaborate calculation based on a variety of data. In addition, the central three-step argument for emissions egalitarianism did not withstand closer examination (see Arguments box 13). The discussion suggested that emissions egalitarianism is grossly simplified in several respects: It fails to take account of differences in responsibility for the problem, of advantages resulting from the causation of the problem, of capabilities for dealing with the problem, or of differences between the needs of various people—and, in particular, the principle does not include historical emissions. As a result, emissions egalitarianism also loses plausibility from a moral point of view.

Arguments box 13: emissions egalitarianism

Emissions egalitarianism answers the third key question of climate ethics "(a) What is due (b) to whom and (c) why?" as follows: (a) The remaining emissions should be distributed (b) among all human beings equally because (c) the atmosphere belongs to all human beings equally.

Three reasons seem to speak in favor of this principle, although all of them can be refuted.

(1) *Reason*: "Emissions egalitarianism is easy and hence practicable."
Reply: On the one hand, practicability is the wrong kind of reason if you are looking for a *just* solution to a distribution problem; on the other hand, it becomes apparent on closer inspection that the equal shares are not so easy to calculate after all, because the population and the emissions budget to be distributed change over time.

(2) *Reason*: "Emissions egalitarianism, in combination with emissions trading, leads to a major transfer of wealth from the rich North to the poor South."
Reply: This is not the result of emissions egalitarianism, but of emissions trading. *Every* principle of distribution that awards the industrialized countries less than the developing countries by comparison with the status quo would have this effect once we include emissions trading.

(3) *Reason*: The atmosphere belongs to everyone equally. Therefore its utilization (that is, the emission rights) should also be distributed equally."
Reply: Perhaps the atmosphere belongs to nobody instead of everybody. And even if it does belong to everyone, equal ownership does not necessarily entail equal rights of use. A series of further relevant considerations (responsibility, needs, capabilities, benefits) actually support an unequal distribution of usage despite equal ownership.

Ultimately, therefore, few reasons speak in favor of, and many reasons speak against, emissions egalitarianism. Thus the principle of "dividing up the emissions cake equally" is likewise untenable.

References

Meyer, A. (2000) *Contraction and Convergence*, Schumacher Briefings, Totnes: Green Books.

Wissenschaftlicher Beirat der Bundesregierung Globale Umweltveränderungen (WBGU) [German Advisory Council on Global Change] (2009) *Solving the Climate Dilemma: The Budget Approach, Special report*, Berlin: WBGU.

World Bank (2015) *World Development Indicators 2015*, available online at http://data.worldbank.org/products/wdi [accessed April 29, 2016].

16 A far-reaching proposal

Let us briefly review the argument thus far. As an answer to the third key question of climate ethics, we sought a principle of distribution that tells us what is due to whom and why, when it comes to distributing the advantages and disadvantages associated with climate change. We have discussed five principles in all: Three of them were historically oriented, and two of them were plausible only for distributing adaptation and compensation costs. Each of the principles proposed very different considerations. Table 16.1 summarizes the essential features of each the principles discussed (in their respective most plausible readings).

A number of points stand out in this review. First, the different principles of distribution are informed by very different guiding considerations, such as responsibility, equality, sufficiency, or benefiting from wrongdoing. At the same time, all of the principles seem to enjoy a certain initial plausibility: All of them can appeal to moral intuitions about what a just distribution would be in this context. However, if the moral core ideas that inform the respective principles are so different and if, at the same time, each core idea has a certain intuitive appeal, then it seems obvious that a satisfactory answer to the third key question of climate ethics cannot rely on a single principle—on a single moral core idea—but must instead combine different considerations in the right way; otherwise, we cannot do justice to the intuitions on which the other principles are founded. A convincing answer must, it would seem, place global intragenerational climate justice on several "moral feet." In other words, it must allow a plurality of distribution principles.

A second point that stands out on reviewing Table 16.1 is that the principles refer to different goods: Some distribute adaptation costs; others, mitigation costs, in the form of physical emission reductions or financial mitigation costs. This suggests that a pluralism of principles is indeed possible, for principles that stipulate different distributions do not necessarily contradict each other if they distribute *different things*.

Table 16.1 Overview of the five principles of distribution discussed

principle	historical?	good to be distributed	guiding consideration
grandfathering	yes	emission reductions (mitigation costs)	customary rights; protecting legitimate expectations
polluter pays principle	yes	adaptation and compensation costs	responsibility for a problem
beneficiary pays principle	yes	adaptation and compensation costs	benefiting from wrongdoing
ability-to-pay principle	no	adaptation costs and financial mitigation costs	sufficiency (and equality)
emissions egalitarianism	no	remaining budget (mitigation costs)	equality

After all, there is nothing contradictory about asserting that health-care services should be distributed according to need, wages according to merit, and basic rights equally. One could therefore separate different domains, or "spheres," of climate justice and make allocations within each sphere according to its own principle. Things are not quite so simple, however, because some spheres can be converted into each other. We saw in Chapter 10 that there is a close connection between, for example, how the remaining budget is distributed and how emission reductions are allocated (that is, if you know the shares in the remaining budget and what the estimated emissions will be if we continue with "business as usual," then you can deduce the required emission reductions). Likewise, the distribution of financial mitigation costs and of emission reductions are also connected. After all, reductions cost something, so every distribution of emission reductions is *also* a distribution of the mitigation costs. Two domains that are not affected by such a "possibility of conversion," and which can therefore always be separated, are the domains of mitigation costs and of adaptation and compensation costs. When you distribute the financial contributions for measures to adapt to climate change, you are not thereby also automatically distributing the costs of preventing climate change—and vice versa. Granted the first point (pluralism of principles), this suggests that we should look for a satisfactory answer to the third key question of climate ethics in the form of a combination of two principles, each of which governs the distribution in one of these two "spheres" of climate justice: one principle for the adaptation and compensation costs, and another principle for the mitigation costs.

A third conspicuous feature is that—with the exception of grandfathering, which is not tenable in any respect—all distribution principles would impose a majority of the costs on the industrialized countries. In spite of all of their differences, therefore, all of the principles more or less agree on how the costs should be divided up between the prosperous, industrialized North and the poorer, still-developing South: The North must do more. And if we are honest with ourselves, we must admit that this also accords with our moral gut feeling regarding the third key question of climate ethics.

But, beyond our gut feelings, what would a more precise answer that heeds these three conspicuous features look like? Keeping in mind that there are many possible ways of developing a pluralism of distribution principles in more detail, we will now outline one approach that is suggested by our previous discussion: First, it must be remembered that the grandfathering principle cannot be justified from a moral point of view, and that the beneficiary pays principle and emissions egalitarianism face serious objections. Therefore they do not belong in the inner circle of candidates for the combination of principles that we are seeking. The polluter pays principle, by contrast, can indeed be applied to a certain part of the adaptation and compensation costs, taking into account a threshold of what can be reasonably demanded. Since a large proportion of all emissions ever produced have been incurred in the past 30–35 years (Boden et al. 2012), the majority of the polluters living during that time are still alive today and, from around 30 years ago onward, one could no longer in good conscience claim that one knew nothing about climate change. Therefore polluters from around 1980 must also contribute to meeting the costs of climate adaptation in proportion to their respective emissions—at any rate, insofar as this would not impose overly demanding burdens on them, so that they would slip under a (still to be determined) sufficiency threshold. In the distribution of the remaining adaptation and compensation costs, and of the financial mitigation costs, the ability-to-pay principle has proved to be quite plausible. All that remains open is how exactly this principle should be combined with the polluter pays principle.

Here, another point is important: We have discussed the problem of the distribution of the mitigation costs above all as a problem of the distribution of *emissions*—but one can ask oneself whether this is really the correct focus. After all, emissions are not an end in themselves; what is morally relevant is instead what one can do with them. Unlike goods such as status, recognition, well-being, or health, we do not strive for emissions for their own sake, but because we need emissions in order to satisfy our basic needs for heat, food, protection, and mobility, and to derive certain benefits from them. In point of fact, we are less concerned with the just distribution of the emissions themselves than with the just distribution of the *benefits derived from emissions*. This can be seen in the fact that emissions can easily be replaced by other goods that bring the same benefits without making any difference as regards justice (Caney 2012). If Al produces 0.5 ton of CO_2 per year, but Betty 1 ton, then this need not be unfair: If Al has access to energy-efficient technologies, then he can generate *the same and as many benefits* for himself with 0.5 ton of CO_2 as Betty can with 1 ton. It would be extremely odd to assume that there is an injustice here, because the unequal distribution of emissions does not make a difference for either of the two parties affected: Each has the exact same benefits.

This consideration hints at a comprehensive shift in perspective in relation to the third key question of climate ethics. If, instead of goods such as emissions, it is more a matter of human well-being (what people can do with the goods), then there is nothing really to be said for dealing with the question of the just distribution of climate change-related advantages and disadvantages in isolation from other questions of justice, for human well-being is influenced by a range of other distributions, for example the distribution of food, work, technologies, or property. When it comes to human well-being, therefore, different distributive issues—and hence also different issues of distributive justice—*overlap*. This is why the third key question of climate ethics should be addressed in combination with other questions of global, intragenerational distributive justice—in particular, questions concerning the distribution of the costs of combating hunger and poverty, questions concerning the distribution of contributions to economic development, and questions concerning the distribution of water, food, medicines, technologies, seeds, and patents. Instead of inquiring only into the just distribution of emissions or climate-change-related advantages and disadvantages in isolation, we should instead address the question of the distribution of all of these goods together—which means that we should integrate the third key question of climate ethics more closely with other distributive issues.

Climate policy is particularly well suited to such an integrating linkage with development issues and the fight against poverty: For example, development aid and technology transfer can now concentrate much more strongly than it could in the past on "clean" production techniques and on constructing an energy supply based on renewable energy sources. In this way, combating climate change and the fight against poverty would be cleverly combined, and two evils could be alleviated at a single stroke. Viewed in this way, climate policy would be just one piece of a larger mosaic in which what was actually at stake would be a fair distribution of global prosperity, as well as "clean development" leading out of poverty and starvation. Such reflections lead to a proposal in which (a) the just distribution of climate-change-related advantages and disadvantages is closely intermeshed with promoting clean development, and in which (b) the polluter pays and the ability-to-pay principles are combined in the right way. The ability-to-pay principle is particularly well suited to meeting the imperative of "clean development": It ultimately supports payment flows from the North to the South, which would help the South to develop in climate-friendly ways.

But how does this shift in perspective provide an answer to the still-open question of how to combine the polluter pays principle with the ability-to-pay principle in the right way? Our two-part proposal is to limit the moral core idea of responsibility initially to a single specific domain—namely, the domain of climate damage that was knowingly caused by living human beings (or was caused under conditions of no longer excusable ignorance). For this area, the polluters should pay adaptation and compensation costs in accordance with their contributions—in the sense of "putting one's moral house in order"—as long as they do not thereby fall below the threshold that the imperative of "clean development" specifically aims to meet—namely, the sufficiency threshold. This is the previously introduced polluter pays principle for emissions from around 1980, supplemented with the limit on what can be reasonably demanded. Then, in a further step, the issue is to distribute all other climate-change-related advantages and disadvantages in accordance with the ability to pay. This includes all mitigation costs (however they are expressed), as well as the adaptation and compensation costs that can be traced back to emissions prior to 1980 and which are not covered by the first step. The ability-to-pay principle applied in this second step also includes a limit on what can be reasonably demanded: Someone who would fall below the sufficiency threshold as a result of the payments need not do anything, but may leave the costs to others; these others should then meet these costs in proportion to their overall well-being (their ability to pay).

If we want to apply this answer to the third key question of climate ethics practice, then a lot of work needs to be done. The following is a recipe for the concrete calculation of the distribution that results from our proposal.

(1) We must first determine the estimated level of the adaptation and compensation costs A and the emissions budget B that still remains, for example for meeting the 2°C target.

(2) We must then ask where the sufficiency threshold S for the limit of the ability to pay lies (i.e. when human beings are sufficiently well-off) and which emissions are pure subsistence emissions.

(3) Allowing for the human life span and the criteria for excusable ignorance, we must then determine some point in time t after which

human beings can be made directly responsible for their emissions by means of the polluter pays principle (for example 1980).

(4) Then, we must determine—as a whole, as well as for each country—the emissions *E-before-t* that were produced before *t* and the emissions *E-after-t* that were produced after *t* (taking into account only nonsubsistence emissions).

(5) *Distribution according to the polluter pays principle*: The part of the adaptation and compensation costs caused by the emissions produced after *t* (*A-after-t*) are now distributed in proportion to the respective shares of the emissions after *t* (where each country must assume costs up to a maximum of the sufficiency threshold *S*).

(6) Then, we must determine each country's ability to pay, for example in terms of GDP above the sufficiency threshold.

(7) *Distribution according to the ability-to-pay principle*: (a) That part of the adaptation and compensation costs caused by emissions produced before *t* (*A-before-t*), (b) that part of *A-after-t* which, under certain circumstances, could not be borne by countries because otherwise they would have fallen below *S*, and (c) the remaining emissions budget converted into reduction costs, finally, are distributed according to the ability to pay (whereby each country must, in turn, assume costs up to a maximum of the sufficiency threshold *S*). This distribution in accordance with the ability-to-pay principle enables synergies with other issues of global distributive justice (in particular, the fight against starvation, poverty, and water shortages, as well as of access to technologies, health-care services, and patents).

Admittedly, such a calculation is difficult to make in practice. (In fact, the calculation is even more complicated because some numbers are fraught with uncertainty. Thus the approach would also have to be supplemented with "margins of safety" that ensure compliance with the sufficiency threshold with a morally acceptable level of probability.) Although complicated, however, it is not impossible to put this recipe into practice; this is shown by the so-called *GDRs* approach, which, with a similar thrust, comes up with a sophisticated operationalization of concrete distribution proposals for climate policy practice (Baer et al. 2008). Within this approach, countries with high average incomes (industrialized countries) must pay a total of around 75 percent of the costs related to climate change, countries with medium average incomes (emerging countries) together bear around 25 percent of the costs, and the countries with extremely low average incomes pay almost nothing. For example, Germany would bear a significant portion of the costs with 5.5 percent—almost exactly as large as the Chinese share, but considerably less than the American share, which would be around 33 percent. Thus, in this possible concretization of our proposal, the industrialized countries would in fact bear the lion's share of all costs relating to climate change.

There are therefore reasons for hope that the concrete implementation will also do justice to the guiding idea behind our answer to the third key question of climate ethics—namely, that the richer countries, according to their responsibility, will assist those affected by climate change to adapt and, according to their ability to pay, will enable the poorer countries to develop along a climate-friendly path to greater prosperity. To sum up this idea in a slogan, we might say: "Those who caused the damage must pay for it; otherwise, development takes priority."

References

Baer, P., Athanasiou, T., Kartha, S., and Kemp-Benedict, E. (2008) *The Greenhouse Development Rights Framework: The Right to Development in a Climate-Constrained World*, Berlin: Heinrich-Böll-Stiftung.

Boden, T., Marland, G., and Andres, R. (2012) *Global, Regional, and National Fossil-Fuel CO_2 Emissions*, Oak Ridge, TN: Carbon Dioxide Information Analysis Center, Oak Ridge National Laboratory, U.S. Department of Energy.

Caney, S. (2012) "Just emissions," *Philosophy & Public Affairs*, 40(4): 255–300.

Suggested further reading for Part III

Baer, P., Athanasiou, T., Kartha, S., and Kemp-Benedict, E. (2010) "Greenhouse development rights: a framework for climate protection that is 'more fair' than equal per capita emissions rights," in S. M. Gardiner et al. (eds.) *Climate Ethics: Essential Readings*, Oxford/New York: Oxford University Press, 215–30.

An attempt to put a hybrid account (which is based on several normative considerations) into practice.

Caney, S. (2009) "Justice and the distribution of greenhouse gas emissions," *Journal of Global Ethics*, 5(2): 125–46.

Presents powerful arguments against grandfathering, emissions egalitarianism, and the "polluter pays" principle, and goes on to develop the idea of an integrationist and holistic hybrid approach to the third key question of climate ethics.

Okereke, C. (2010) "Climate justice and the international regime," *Wiley Interdisciplinary Reviews: Climate Change*, 1(3): 462–74.

A review of climate justice in international politics that pulls into focus further questions that need to be asked beyond a comparison of burden-sharing principles.

Page, E. (2012) "Give it up for climate change: a defence of the beneficiary pays principle," *International Theory*, 4(2): 300–30.

Exactly what it says on the tin: a sophisticated attempt to defend a particular version of the "beneficiary pays" principle.

Shue, H. (2010) "Global environment and international inequality," in S. M. Gardiner et al. (eds.) *Climate Ethics: Essential Readings*, Oxford/New York: Oxford University Press, 101–11.

Argues that three commonsense principles of fairness (roughly corresponding to the guiding considerations of the "polluter pays" principle, the "ability-to-pay" principle, and sufficiency) converge in their practical implications.

Singer, P. (2002) *One World: The Ethics of Globalization*, New Haven, CT/London: Yale University Press.

Chapter 2 is a prominent exposition and ethical motivation of emissions egalitarianism.

A more comprehensive list of further readings for this part is available at http://climate-justice-references.christianseidel.eu

Part IV

FROM ETHICAL THEORY TO POLITICAL PRACTICE

Part IV

FROM ETHICAL THEORY TO POLITICAL PRACTICE

17 Nonideal theory

What should we do when others fail to do their fair share?

The preceding chapters have answered the general key questions of climate ethics: Do we have to do anything at all? If so, how much? And who must bear the costs? However, the basic principles of inter- and intragenerational justice taken in isolation leave ample room for speculation concerning the next steps to be taken in the real world. In what follows, therefore, we will forge a connection to political practice. In the present chapter, we deal with the just response to the injustices of prevailing climate policy. Chapter 18 will discuss a variety of strategies for reducing emissions. In Chapter 19, we will evaluate a prominent policy instrument—namely, emissions trading. Finally, in Chapter 20, we will shift the focus from just climate policies to just procedures for deciding on climate policies.

One of the greatest challenges in real-world climate policy is the lack of motivation of the agents involved to comply with the requirements of intergenerational and global justice. The lack of progress on climate action can seem depressing—but it should not come as a surprise. First of all, tackling climate change involves significant costs for some, and thus plain and simple self-interest explains inaction to a large extent. Second, given how various challenges—such as the intergenerational character of climate change, its global character, the associated uncertainty, and so on—coincide and reinforce each other in complex ways, we are prone to what Stephen Gardiner (2006) analyzed as moral corruption. The features of climate change incentivize and enable our moral debate to be clouded and distorted. It is one question how we can get out of this predicament in the long term, both by having sounder views of the moral case for climate action and by increasing our willingness to act on these views; it is another question how we ought to respond to this predicament in the meantime. In particular, if some countries are not willing to assume their responsibilities within the framework of a just distribution of the costs, what does this mean for the remaining countries? For example, do the excessive emissions of the United States give the European Union the right to loosen the reins as well? Or might it not be precisely the other way around? Should the European Union reduce its emissions even more aggressively in order to compensate for the failure of the United States to do its fair share to mitigate climate change? In practice, in recent years, the European Union has, in fact, tied its emission reductions to the behavior of other countries: Depending on whether or not other countries do their share, it has pledged to reduce emissions either by 30 percent or by 20 percent by 2020. Such questions not only arise between countries, but also at an individual level: How should you react if you spend your holidays cycling close to home so as to contribute to climate mitigation while your neighbor raves about his regular diving expeditions in distant countries? Is it worthwhile mobilizing one's own climate conscience as an individual and acting as a role model if the majority of society does not play along?

These questions belong to a nonideal theory of justice. A nonideal theory does not ask what a perfectly just world would look like; instead, it asks how we should respond if others do not act in a completely just manner. What is a just response to injustice? Basically, there are three positions on this issue. If one agent does not fulfil his or her duties, this could either increase or reduce the duties of the other agents or leave them unchanged. Let us imagine, for the sake of simplicity, that justice requires the United States and the European Union to reduce their emissions of CO_2 to 1 ton per capita. Let us assume further that the United States is not prepared to comply with this requirement, whereas the European Union is.

(1) According to the first of the three possible positions, the European Union would have to reduce its emissions to *even less* than 1 ton per capita.
(2) According to the second position, the reluctance of the United States to comply means that the European Union may also emit more than 1 ton per capita.
(3) According to the third position, the behavior of the United States has no relevance for the European Union's emissions reduction.

Should we bear one another's burdens?

Let us first examine two examples of unjust behavior from other contexts in order to determine the plausibility of these three positions. Imagine that, in your household, it is your task to clean the bathroom, while it is up to your partner to clean the kitchen. If your partner fails to fulfil his or her duty, you may, of course, continue to clean the bathroom out of a spirit of generosity, but you hardly have a *duty* to do so any longer. In this "nonideal" situation, we would not blame you if you were likewise to fail to clean the bathroom. If the other party does not do his or her bit, then you may also do less.

Now imagine a second scenario. You and your partner happen upon a pond in which two drowning children are crying out for help. Each of you could save one child. But your partner does not want to get his or her clothes dirty and remains standing by the shore. In this "nonideal" situation, your duty is increased: If your partner shirks his or her duty, then you have to rescue not one, but both, children.

Thus our judgments of the two situations are diametrically opposed. In the first case, your duty is weakened in the face of unjust behavior on the part of others; in the second case, it is increased. Why are the two cases so different? Two factors seem to account for this. First, in the example of the pond, *third parties* are affected: The ones who suffer are not, as in the case of the household tasks, only the two parties whose fair or unfair division of labor is up for debate, but innocent children. Second, *goods of different importance* are at stake in the two examples: In the one case, it is a matter of a clean bathroom; in the other, of life and death. These two factors account for the difference. And in the case of climate change, these two factors prompt a specific response. Climate change is much closer to the pond example than to the household example. In the case of climate change, third parties are affected and important matters are at stake. This is why our duties to mitigate climate change become more urgent when others fail to fulfil their duties.

If present-day Americans and Europeans were those mainly affected by climate change, then it would be up to Europeans whether or not they fulfilled their share of the duty to mitigate climate change. But, as it happens, those affected are primarily third parties: The well-being of *future generations* is jeopardized if people living today do not do their fair share to mitigate climate change. As soon as third parties are involved, however, we have to strike a balance between two aspects of justice in nonideal situations: on the one hand, the harm to third parties (in this case, future generations); on the other, fair burden-sharing among those who should protect third parties from harm (in this case, present-day Europeans, Americans, etc.). If the European Union presses ahead alone in response to US inaction, then that is indeed unjust in one respect (namely, regarding the distribution of costs between the European Union and the United States), and the European Union would avoid this aspect of injustice if it were likewise to produce excessive emissions. But in doing so it would also weaken the protection of future generations against climate-related risks and thus contribute to a new injustice— namely, injustice between present and future generations. Therefore, the European Union must assess whether it should attach greater weight to justice in dividing up the task (between it and the United States) or to fulfilling the task (that is, protecting future generations from climate-related risks). In other words, the European Union must strike a balance between intragenerational and intergenerational justice.

The argument for unilateral emission reductions on the part of the European Union would not be so strong if future generations, as third parties, experience only minimal effects. If climate mitigation were merely a matter of making prosperous descendants even more prosperous, then it would not be so bad if the task were performed only in part, but in return the costs associated with this partial fulfillment were distributed fairly. There is more at stake in climate policy, however—namely, the human rights of future generations. Weighty goods such as human lives, health, food security, and water reserves are at stake, and that is why climate mitigation is more like rescuing the drowning children than performing household chores. Therefore, if the United States refuses to contribute its fair share to climate mitigation, then the European Union has a duty to do even more to mitigate climate change.

Is individual climate mitigation ineffective?

In reality, of course, it is far from true that the Americans are the sinners and the Europeans, the saints. The United States and the European Union simply served as a schematic illustration of the moral constellation characteristic of nonideal contexts. The same constellation can also be found at the individual level: Is it acceptable that I, as an individual, should make my efforts to mitigate climate change dependent on the conduct of others?

At the individual level, however, one objection against the conclusion reached in the previous section is particularly relevant—namely, the ineffectiveness objection. Is it of any use if I increase my solitary efforts to reduce my carbon footprint while the rest of society stands by and does nothing? Does it really make a difference if I spend my vacation on the bicycle while everyone else is jetting around the world? *This* will hardly prevent the climate catastrophe—or will it?

But before examining the strength of this objection, we should ask why we are interested in the *effects* of our individual climate mitigation efforts in the first place. Should we view forgoing air travel in a positive light only if it makes a difference to climate protection? After all, in everyday life, our ethical attention is not focused exclusively on the effects of our actions; we often also take the agent's *character* into account. Thus, from a so-called *virtue-ethical perspective*, we can ask, for example, whether an action is informed by a sense of moderation and is in harmony with nature. Of course, such a virtuous attitude often produces the desired effects. But if what ultimately matters is what is manifested in the execution of an action—namely, character—and not its effects, then environmentally conscious conduct can have a positive value independently of its effectiveness. Another example can be found in so-called *rule utilitarianism*. We often look for rules of conduct the observance of which has positive effects *in general*, even if adhering to them may be ineffective in particular cases. For example, adhering for the most part to the *rule* "Avoid emissions-intensive means of transport" may have positive consequences, even though this cannot be said of every single *act* of travelling by emissions-intensive means of transportation (for example when its purpose is to attend a climate conference). In addition, we often judge the harmful effects of our actions according to whether we intend these effects or "merely" accept them—as in the case of climate damage—as a side effect (on which aspect deontological theories focus, for example). In a variety of ethical perspectives, therefore, the effects of our individual actions are at least not the *only* thing that counts.

Of course, this does not mean that the effectiveness of our actions is completely irrelevant. If individual climate mitigation in the midst of widespread inaction were completely ineffective, then the corresponding duty would at least be greatly weakened in most ethical perspectives. However, at this point, there is no need to examine the relevance of the issue of effectiveness in greater detail, because in the case of climate mitigation this question presumably has a positive answer anyway. It can be assumed, in principle, that every emission reduction, however minor, does in fact make some difference to the climate, at least with some probability. To see this more clearly, imagine that humanity emits every single ounce of CO_2 one after the other; it cannot be true that the climate would have changed as a result of 1 trillion tons of CO_2 without any of these single ounces of CO_2 emitted one after the other having made any difference. Of course, it is not the case that *each and every* one of these ounces of CO_2 must have made a difference—but since we do not know *which* of them makes a difference (and might even make a large difference by being the straw that breaks the camel's back and triggers, for example, an additional hurricane), we must assume that every single ounce causes damage with some probability.

Why, then, is skepticism about the effectiveness of personal efforts to mitigate climate change nevertheless so pervasive? One reason is certainly that we often consider the effect of our own contribution to climate mitigation only *in relation to climate mitigation efforts as a whole*. Our contribution appears so minute by comparison that we are tempted to dismiss it as nonexistent. But how great is this effect considered in isolation? One of the few—and, in its interpretation, admittedly highly controversial—estimates concludes that the lifetime emissions of an average American could be responsible for the suffering and/or death of one or two future people (Nolt 2011). However, doubts about the effectiveness of individual emission reductions can also stem from different understandings of the effect at stake. If the only effect that interests us is *whether* there is (dangerous) climate change—and not its *extent*—then it is, of course, true that personal climate mitigation (almost certainly) is not "effective." If we take the plane instead of the bicycle for our vacation, then it will hardly be precisely this choice that triggers the crossing of the threshold to (dangerous) climate change; however, it may very well have the effect of causing *more* climate change. From an ethical point of view, the relevant effects of our actions should include not only *whether* (dangerous) climate change occurs, but also *how much* (dangerous) climate change occurs. A further confusion regarding effectiveness becomes apparent if we take uncertainty into account. As we saw in Chapter 8, an action need not cause a specific harm with certainty in order to be ethically relevant; some probability, or even a realistic possibility, of a harmful effect is sufficient. If we raise the question of the efficacy of our emissions, therefore, we are not interested in whether a specific flight booking will, in fact, aggravate climate change (because this is something that we cannot know), but whether there is a certain probability that it—just like any other flight booking—will aggravate climate change (and we do know that there is such a probability).

However, there is a further more plausible argument against the effectiveness of unilateral climate mitigation efforts—one based on social feedback effects. If Anna increases her efforts to mitigate climate change, this could lead Bert to lower his climate mitigation efforts in response. As a freerider, Bert might think that his contribution is no longer necessary because, as he sees it, Anna is stepping into the breach for him. As a result, of course, Anna's efforts ultimately have no impact. Such social feedback effects also operate—sometimes in indirect ways—at the international level and are often discussed under the heading of "carbon leakage." For example, if Germany introduces a carbon tax, this does not necessarily reduce carbon emissions; instead, it may simply lead German industry to relocate production abroad. If German demand for fossil fuels declines as a result of the tax, this can have the effect of lowering the price of oil on global markets and thus lead to an increase in the demand for fossil fuels in other countries. The end result would be that the German tax would have done nothing to protect the climate.

However, this argument about feedback effects should not be taken to cast radical doubt on the effectiveness of a single individual's, or a single country's, efforts to mitigate climate change; rather, it should be seen as questioning the *extent* of the effectiveness of such efforts. After all, feedback effects are not exclusively negative, but can also be positive. If Anna intensifies her climate mitigation efforts, her example might induce

Bert to step up his efforts. Another example of a positive feedback effect is when a country takes a pioneering role in reducing the cost of clean technologies and thereby makes climate mitigation more attractive for other countries. It should also be noted that an agent can influence whether his or her efforts trigger positive or negative social feedback effects by carefully selecting specific climate mitigation methods and communicating them strategically. In order to be able to criticize an agent's unilateral climate mitigation as ineffective, or even harmful, the negative feedback effects would have to outweigh both the direct effect of this agent's climate mitigation measures and the positive feedback effects. This is very unlikely and hence the ineffectiveness objection can scarcely discharge us from responsibility.

Is individual climate mitigation too demanding?

In this chapter, we have argued that our duty to mitigate climate change increases if others fail to comply with their duty to mitigate climate change. Even if this position were convincing in theory, it seems to many people that it asks too much of us in practice. Regardless of how much we do for the climate, we could always do even more. If the major global players fail to comply with their duty to mitigate climate change, then environmentally conscious people could sacrifice themselves day and night—give up their worldly possessions, and family and friends— and they would still not have exhausted all of the pressing measures that need to be taken. Is there a limit to the efforts that we must make? Or is it really the case that morality can demand even radical self-sacrifice?

In everyday life, we often have a sense of how far morality may go and at which points we may reject its demands as excessive. Intuitively, we feel that morality may sometimes require us to make an effort even if it hurts a bit. But if it requires us to turn our life completely upside-down, then very special circumstances would need to obtain. Others would not deny that morality can indeed demand radical changes in behavior even in "everyday" circumstances, but then acknowledge through the back door that our intuitive feeling is nevertheless right, by conceding that it would be a mistake to heed only the voice of morality in how we conduct our lives. To deny that personal visions and projects, self-interest, aesthetic preferences, or religious values may also inform our actions would be excessively moralistic.

Alas, our intuitive gut feelings are not always a reliable compass. This is especially true for questions relating to climate change. As we saw in Chapter 1, our intuitions concerning cause–effect were not created for the novel kind of challenge posed by climate change, in which billions of people together cause damage on an uncertain scale, the effects of which occur decades later and impact on billions of people. Our sense of right and wrong was calibrated on the basis of much more small-scale, everyday situations. Therefore we cannot appeal to our intuitions about the limits of morality in order to dismiss certain climate mitigation efforts as excessively demanding.

However, this does not mean that there are no such limits. One plausible limit follows in particular from the rights of those who have to shoulder the burdens of climate mitigation. Exaggerated climate mitigation efforts could violate rights if, for example, developing countries were to step into the breach for the inadequate efforts of the West and, as a result, lack the means to combat poverty. After all, climate mitigation ultimately serves to protect the human rights of future generations; hence it would not be convincing if, by contrast, the human rights of those who have to achieve this goal were accorded no weight. This insight is reflected in the position defended in Chapter 16 that no country must assume climate mitigation burdens that would push it beneath the sufficiency threshold.

But which of our rights have sufficient weight to "immunize us" against radical climate mitigation duties? No one will disagree, for example, that the emissions of a bus ride to the capital are justified if it is undertaken by a person in extreme poverty in search of work or by a democratically elected Member of Parliament in order to fulfill his or her responsibilities there. But what about a Greenlander's need to heat his or her home? Or the need to maintain family relationships if this involves an intercontinental flight to celebrate a brother's wedding? What weight do we accord the right to freely choose certain life projects and does that include the freedom to cultivate emissions-intensive hobbies (see Chapter 11)? The boundary between subsistence and luxury emissions is less clear than it may appear at first sight. The reference to the rights of the current generation could also be misused to dismiss too many climate mitigation duties as excessively demanding.

Even if one can indeed deflect some demands to reduce emissions as excessively demanding by appeal to the rights of the present generation, in practice there is ample scope for emission reductions that clearly do *not* infringe the rights of the present generation. Some climate mitigation measures cost very little and others even have economic benefits (see Nauclér and Enkvist 2009). Although some measures cost considerable sums, they nevertheless have scarcely any tangible impact on everyday life, especially if they are implemented *by the state*. If climate mitigation is implemented in a very cost-effective way, achieving the 2°C goal might entail a loss of, say, 0.06 percent of annual economic growth in the coming decades (so that our consumption, for example, would increase annually by 1.94 percent instead by 2 percent—see IPCC 2014). This does not seem excessively burdensome at all. Such figures are admittedly speculative, but they cast considerable doubt on the notion that at least the next steps—at any rate, in Western countries—could seriously conflict with basic rights.

In the case of *personal* measures, things initially look somewhat different. If one allows oneself only cold showers and heeds the voice of one's climate conscience in all other aspects of daily life in an effort to reduce emissions to an absolute minimum, then that *is* burdensome. But even in the individual case, strong climate action is not necessarily burdensome. We could also reduce emissions radically by financing additional climate mitigation measures for others as an alternative to drastic changes in our own behavior. Admittedly, this offsetting of emissions—which we will discuss in Chapter 19—is controversial. But if the objections against it do not withstand scrutiny, then a citizen of an industrialized country could at present presumably reduce "his or her" emissions to zero for about US\$1 per day (see Dhanda and Hartman 2012: 124; EEA 2012: 92).

Arguments box 14: what to do if others do not pull their weight?

We have argued that if part of the present-day generation does not do its fair share to mitigate climate change, then the remaining individuals and states have to step into the breach and perform *more* climate mitigation than they would have to within an equitable burden-sharing scheme.

The reason that speaks in favor of this position is that, without additional climate mitigation efforts, *third parties*—namely, future generations—will be affected, and indeed *seriously* affected. Therefore protecting future generations has priority over fair burden-sharing within the present generation.

Two objections speak against this position, although both of them can be rebutted.

(1) *Objection*: "Isolated emission reductions by individual persons or states have no effect."

Reply: This assertion overlooks the fact that, with a certain probability, individual emission reductions do indeed make a difference for the extent of climate change. Furthermore, it is not empirically plausible that negative social feedback effects outweigh the effect of unilateral emission reductions and their positive feedback effects.

(2) *Objection*: "Making up for the lack of climate mitigation efforts by others would entail excessively high costs."
Reply: The rights of the present generation do, in fact, set certain limits on their duties to mitigate climate change. However, many emission reduction measures have scarcely any effect on these limits.

References

Dhanda, K. K., and Hartman, L. (2012) "Carbon offset markets: a viable instrument?" in S. Rebennack et al. (eds.) *Handbook of CO_2 in Power Systems*, Berlin: Springer, 107–29.

European Environment Agency (EEA) (2012) *Greenhouse Gas Emission Trends and Projections in Europe 2012*, EEA Report 6/2012, Luxembourg: Publications Office of the European Union.

Gardiner, S. (2006) "A perfect moral storm: climate change, intergenerational ethics and the problem of moral corruption," *Environmental Values*, 15(3): 397–413.

Intergovernmental Panel on Climate Change (IPCC) (2014) "Summary for policymakers," in *Climate Change 2014: Synthesis Report—Contribution of Working Groups I, II and III to the Fifth Assessment Report of the Intergovernmental Panel on Climate Change*, available online at http://www.ipcc.ch/pdf/assessment-report/ar5/syr/AR5_SYR_FINAL_SPM.pdf [accessed April 29, 2016].

Nauclér, T., and Enkvist, P.-A. (2009) *Pathways to a Low-Carbon Economy: Version 2 of the Global Greenhouse Gas Abatement Cost Curve*, New York: McKinsey & Company.

Nolt, J. (2011) "How harmful are the average American's greenhouse gas emissions?" *Ethics, Policy & Environment*, 14(1): 3–10.

18 Population, technology, and affluence

Three strategies for reducing emissions

When it comes to the practical implementation of the ethically ideal climate policy, it remains an open question what means should be employed. Thus we must ask not only by *how much* we should reduce emissions, but also *what means* we should employ to do so.

Here, it is advisable to begin by examining the factors that determine the global volume of emissions. Global emissions are higher the more people there are, the more affluent these people are, and the more emissions-intensive the technologies used to create this affluence. Correspondingly, there are also three possible strategies for reducing emissions: reduce the population, reduce affluence, or reduce the emission intensity of technologies. We use the three catchphrases "population," "affluence," and "technology" to refer to these strategies. "Affluence" is used here in the sense of the material standard of living, which can be measured, for example, by GDP. When we speak of the "technology" strategy for climate mitigation, we are referring to the reduction of the intensity of emissions. By "emission intensity," we understand the volume of emissions required to create one unit of affluence. Emission intensity is a function of which goods go to make up our affluence and of the technologies we use to produce these goods; hence the label "technology strategy."

In this chapter, we will examine whether these three strategies are ethically equivalent, or whether one of them can be singled out as the royal road to climate mitigation. It makes a difference for this evaluation whether the implementation of the strategies in question is a matter of political or personal initiative. For example, it matters a lot for the population strategy whether parents decide to have a small family voluntarily or because of legal constraints. Before we evaluate the three strategies, therefore, we will first address the question of whether climate mitigation is a political or personal task. Personal tasks here by no means refer only to tasks for individuals (even if, in what follows, we use individuals as examples); they can also be tasks for private associations such as NGOs, companies, or churches.

Political regulation or personal initiative?

The state can coordinate individual climate mitigation efforts and—if there is lack of motivation on the personal level—ultimately also enforce them. Legal prohibitions and incentives serve this purpose. Many people consider a political solution to the climate problem to be the only possible course. A widely held view is that, although personal initiative may indeed be noble, it will never achieve the goal of a massive reduction in emissions, let alone a fair distribution of the associated costs.

This view does not entirely hit the nail on the head. In theory, the climate problem *could* be solved without political action. After all, it is not logically impossible that every individual would do the right thing of his or her own free will. However, climate mitigation would become extremely arduous if it were based on personal commitment alone; political instruments, by contrast, achieve more climate mitigation with less effort.

There are a variety of reasons why climate mitigation by means of political regulation saves costs and effort. First, there is the fact that some climate mitigation measures would be very cumbersome without the *coordination* of many individuals. Thus constructing a public transport system calls for complicated coordination between countless agents, which is difficult to accomplish without public management. In addition, gathering the necessary *information* about sensible climate mitigation measures would be enormously burdensome for individuals: Does it cause more climate damage to fly from Zurich to Paris or to drive the distance alone by car? Of course, one could assemble the relevant facts through laborious research. But if the state were to tax greenhouse gases, this information would simply be included in the price; a given travel option would then be more expensive depending on how much climate damage it causes. Even more importantly, if the state were to impose a tax on goods that are harmful to the climate, or prohibit them altogether, this would relieve us of the burden of having to constantly motivate ourselves to choose the ethically correct course of action in countless small everyday decisions. If harmful behavior incurs a price or a sanction, then we need only attend to what is in our *own interest*. Depending on how expensive the trip from Zurich to Paris becomes, it may no longer be worth it for us. In particular, it is less strenuous to do the right thing based on rules laid down by the state because this ensures that we are *not alone* in doing the right thing. For most of us, our ethical motivation is not sufficient for protecting the climate if we cannot assume that others abide by the same rules. Without legal coercion, it would not be reasonable to assume that everyone does their fair share of mitigating climate change, with the result that climate mitigation would become much more onerous for the remaining "do-gooders" (see Chapter 17).

But even if political regulation is more cost-effective than individual initiative, this *alone* is not sufficient to justify climate legislation. The fact that action on the part of the state makes climate mitigation easier may well be an advantage for those who are willing to engage in climate mitigation anyway—but what about those who are not willing do so voluntarily? Laws ultimately involve restriction, or even coercion. On a liberal understanding of the state, restrictions and coercion require a stronger justification than just cost savings. Imagine a society in which the majority attaches great importance to physical exercise and may even regard an unhealthy diet as morally blameworthy. Not unlike climate mitigation, in this case it might also be efficient to use the state to prohibit unhealthy food, to create tax incentives for sport, and the like. It would be easier for the majority to achieve its goal of a healthy life than if everything were left up to personal motivation. Nevertheless, it would be wrong to enforce a healthy lifestyle by political means. It would be illiberal to coerce a minority with different preferences to spend their evenings in the fitness studio rather than in a fast-food restaurant. Such issues are matters for personal decision. But why does the same not hold for the decision for or against climate mitigation? What could justify the state enforcing climate mitigation, but not a healthy lifestyle?

The answer lies in the basic liberal idea that the limits of one person's freedom are given by the freedom of others—or, to be more precise, by the *rights* of others. Thus we may do whatever we like as long as we do not interfere with the rights of others. Our freedom to live an unhealthy life should be respected, because this does not harm others in ways that infringe their rights (albeit it is not *exactly* true that pursuing an unhealthy lifestyle does not harm others at all—which is why it is often more difficult to apply the basic liberal idea in practice than it seems). However, as we showed in Part II, excessive emissions can violate the rights of future generations. And this is precisely why placing restrictions on our freedom to emit and enforcing climate mitigation measures by law are also justified.

Thus political action on climate change is justifiable in principle from a liberal perspective. However, it should be noted here that measures taken by the state interfere more or less extensively with individual liberty. From a liberal perspective, politically enforced climate mitigation should infringe as little as possible on individual liberty, and should mainly ensure *that* emissions are reduced and less *how* they are reduced. In this regard, there is a whole spectrum of options. At one end of the spectrum are *prohibitions and standards* that lay down direct regulations governing specific activities, technologies, and goods. *Incentives* such as taxes on goods that are harmful to the climate, subsidies for climate-friendly energy sources, or an emissions trading system (see Chapter 19)

leave greater freedom of choice to the regulated agents. Even less inva-
sive measures are public *information and motivation campaigns*. Therefore the strong contrast between state coercion and voluntary personal
initiative is exaggerated.

The duty to mitigate climate change should thus be implemented primarily at the political, rather than the individual, level. However, this
does not mean that personal initiative is completely relieved of responsibility. Individual efforts to mitigate climate change are still called for in
three areas. First, laws can provide only rough guidelines for regulating
the complexities of real-life behavior. The state can hardly force us to
switch off unnecessary lights in the office or compel a solar energy
researcher to make optimal use of his or her research funds. What slips
through the net of the law falls back into the area of responsibility of
personal initiative.

Second, the state often fails to perform its task. Climate policy has
failed at both the national and the international level. When political
action fails, individual action must step into the breach as a stopgap
measure. The situation is analogous to the pond example in Chapter 17,
in which one agent's failure to save a drowning child means that another
agent has a duty to step into the breach. The only difference here is that
we are talking about agents at different levels: If the state, as the agent
at the political level, does not perform its tasks, then agents at the individual level must assume responsibility for them.

Third, no political action against climate change will be undertaken
unless the state is empowered to do so by individuals. In a democracy,
by far the most important individual actions on behalf of the climate
consist, on the one hand, in declaring one's support for official climate
mitigation measures by voting for the relevant political candidates and,
on the other, in engaging in political activism to motivate as many of
one's fellow citizens as possible to do likewise.

A detailed assessment of political and personal climate mitigation
depends, of course, on the concrete measures under consideration. We
will now address this topic by examining three strategies—namely, the
population, technology, and affluence strategies.

First strategy: population

Global CO_2 emissions from fossil energy rose by 108 percent between
1970 and 2010. Surprisingly, this occurred even though the emission
intensity—that is, the emissions per unit of GDP—underwent a significant
decrease over the same period. Thus even though production processes
have become cleaner, we are nevertheless generating more emissions.
There is a simple explanation for this: The global population increased by

87 percent during this period, with per capita GDP (adjusted for purchasing power parity) even increasing by 103 percent (Blanco et al. 2014: 365). Population and economic growth therefore seem to be the main culprits, while there has even been a decrease in emission intensity.

Admittedly, the population growth figures are somewhat misleading as regards their climate relevance. This is because the population growth is occurring mainly in those global regions that currently still have low per capita emissions. When an American woman gives birth, this can give rise to well over 100 times as many emissions in the long run—descendants included—as when a Bangladeshi woman has a child (Murtaugh and Schlax 2009). Nevertheless, we should not downplay the issue of population growth. It is estimated that the population of the world will increase by around 50 percent between 2000 and 2050 (United Nations 2009). Moreover, the public discussion tends to sweep this topic under the carpet. It is, of course, understandable to a certain extent that controlling population growth is a taboo subject. In 1968, the UN Conference on Human Rights proclaimed the right of all parents to freely and responsibly choose how many children they have. Therefore policies such as compulsory sterilization programs, or China's one child policy, are infringements of important freedoms. Some religions are opposed to family planning through condoms, the pill, or abortions, and for many people a large family is part of their conception of a fulfilled life. When critics of population policies stress these points, they are not casting doubt on the claim that slowing down population growth would contribute to climate mitigation; instead, they doubt whether it is possible to regulate the size of the population in ethically unproblematic ways. For critics of population policies, it is not the goals of the policies that are problematic, but the means that they employ.

But this criticism rests on a shaky foundation. Just as there are clearly unacceptable methods for regulating the size of the population, there are also clearly acceptable methods. For example, poverty alleviation measures, and measures to promote gender equality and women's education, slow down population growth (UNFPA 2011; Cafaro 2012). In contrast to some ways of employing the technology strategy to achieve climate mitigation, these measures do not have negative, but rather positive, side effects. Except in the eyes of certain conservative critics, promoting family planning through access to birth control also has a twofold benefit: It not only promotes the autonomy of women, especially in developing countries, but it could also be an especially cheap method for reducing emissions (see Wire 2009: table 5.0.1). Given these ethically unproblematic methods of slowing down population growth, there is hardly any need to seriously entertain coercive measures.

But even if we leave coercive measures out of account, difficult issues remain open for discussion. Thus one might wonder whether financial incentives to have fewer children already amounts to an unacceptable interference in personal freedom of choice. When parents hold a newborn in their arms, they have not only given someone the gift of life, provided everyone around them with grounds for celebration, and brought a new creative being into the world who may one day have ingenious ideas for solving social problems; they have also incurred costs for society and for themselves. A child needs food and education, it needs space, and it is a burden on the climate. Should society compensate the parents for the costs that they have incurred? Or should the parents, on the contrary, compensate society for the costs that it incurs as a result of the child? How can the burdens be shared fairly between the parents and society? Subsidies and taxes influence how these costs are distributed—often in hidden ways—and create incentives to have more or fewer children. This question arises not only between parents and society, but also in an analogous way between individual states and the global community. A country that permits, or even promotes, a high level of population growth thereby claims a larger share of natural resources. Should this country compensate the other countries for this or should they, on the contrary, show solidarity by contributing to meeting the environmental costs of this decision? In climate policy, this question can be made more specific by asking whether a country's emission rights should be increased in proportion to its population growth. And should countries be allowed to count measures to reduce population growth as climate mitigation measures?

One objection against reducing population growth comes from a completely different direction (and is independent of whether we adopt coercive population planning measures or whether the costs of population growth are distributed fairly). Let us imagine that, some 50 years ago, humanity had set itself the goal of radically reducing the size of the population: Half of the people alive today would never have seen the light of day. Would something of value have been lost as a result? It is true that forgoing the birth of many human beings would have reduced the pressure on the climate. But it is equally true that something wonderful would have been lost as a result—namely, human life, with all of its moments of happiness, its relationships, and its ambitions, would never have existed. Those who believe that the birth of a human being brings something of value into the world, who conclude from this that the birth of *more* human beings brings *more* value into the world, and who combine this with the claim that it is our task to create value wherever possible cannot avoid playing off two aspects of population policy against each other: On the one hand, population growth means a greater number of people, which is something positive; on the other hand, it also means increased pressure on the climate, which is something negative, because the average well-being of this greater number of people is reduced. When population growth is discussed in the context of climate change, attention is often paid only to the second aspect (more people are bad for the climate), while the first aspect (more people represent something inherently valuable) is ignored. Admittedly, it is also far from easy to take the first aspect into account. Hardly anything opens the door to confusing philosophical paradoxes as much as this topic (see Parfit 1984: pt. IV; Broome 2012: ch. 10).

The bottom line is that population policy can make a certain contribution to climate mitigation. And we should take advantage of this—as long as we adopt acceptable measures to influence population size.

Second strategy: technology

The second climate mitigation strategy we would like to discuss is technological progress. Its goal is to reduce emission intensity and thereby allow affluence to increase in spite of falling emissions, or at least to prevent it from decreasing. While the population and affluence strategies are often taboo subjects, the technology strategy cannot complain that it receives too little attention. Politicians from across the political spectrum extol a greening of the economy as the least painful and only realistic way in which to mitigate climate change.

Which clean technologies are currently up for debate? Most of the measures aim to generate either the same economic output with less energy (energy efficiency) or equal amounts of energy with fewer emissions. Some examples are: replacing fossil energy sources with nuclear, wind, and solar power; reducing the fuel consumption of automobiles; using hydrogen and bioethanol as fuels; increasing the efficiency of coal-fired power plants and replacing them with gas-fired power plants; constructing buildings that are more climate-friendly; and cultivating arable land in ways that conserve the soil. A somewhat different example is carbon capture and storage (CCS), which is closely related to climate engineering (see Chapter 4). Instead of reducing emissions, the idea of CCS is to capture them directly at source and store them in underground repositories. In view of the enormous range of possible forms of technological progress—from small, tested, and successful improvements in everyday life that not only protect the climate, but also save money, to large-scale projects that are utopian and risky—it would be absurd to try to force them all into a single ethical mold. While it is beyond doubt that certain aspects of technological progress must be part of any future climate mitigation strategy, in the remainder of this section we want to ask how we should evaluate large-scale promotion of technological progress as the main pillar of climate mitigation.

The technology strategy stands in stark contrast to the motto "Back to nature." According to its critics, it tries to solve the problem of climate change by means of the same way of thinking that gave rise to it in the first place. Sometimes, this criticism reflects a nonanthropocentric worldview. The claim is that faith in progress expresses an arrogant belief in technological domination of the world that lacks respect for natural processes. It exploits the environment in a calculated way and neglects, not least, the repercussions for the animal world. Instead of nurturing fundamental distrust of the attitude that informs the technology strategy, one can also—somewhat less radically—simply be skeptical about the prospects of technological progress in fact delivering the results for which we hope.

Is this skepticism justified? Is it really true that a way of thinking that has given rise to a problem cannot contribute to solving it? In fact, there are good reasons to be skeptical about the effectiveness of technological progress as an instrument for solving the problem of climate change—reasons that go beyond a general distrust of progress. For example, there is the problem of the rebound effect: Using energy more efficiently does not necessarily mean that we end up using less energy. If automobiles consume less fuel, then driving becomes cheaper, and this has the effect that people drive more. Thus improvements in energy efficiency do not fully translate into emission reductions, but may also result in increases of affluence. Another problem is that, although many forms of "clean" energy reduce emissions, they also have side effects: Wind turbines sometimes disturb the natural landscape, while biofuels involve even graver dangers, the cultivation of crops for biofuels competing with the cultivation of food crops. The associated increases in the price of foodstuffs constitute an existential threat for people living in poverty. The dangers of nuclear power are also prominent: reactor accidents, health and environmental damage in uranium mining, the need to store radioactive waste for thousands of years, and the risk of civilian nuclear energy programs being used for military purposes. CCS also entails risks that are difficult to assess: For example, there is no reliable guarantee that there will not be uncontrolled leaks of the CO_2 stored underground.

In addition, making long-term forecasts of technological progress is often like gazing into a crystal ball. Estimates of the potential of clean technologies are often based on intuition and, as a result, are exposed to distorting influences. On the one hand, skepticism about progress may be rooted in a fearful attitude toward the future, lack of imagination, or resistance to anything that is new; on the other hand, it is tempting to exaggerate the potential of new technologies in political debates, because the technology strategy seems to be particularly comfortable when compared to the alternatives. The climate mitigation effects of the population and affluence strategies are easier to estimate. The technology strategy, by contrast, is tantamount to making a bet that we could win or lose. On the one hand, there *might* be a technological breakthrough just around the corner that will solve the climate problem cheaply and painlessly. On the other hand, the development of clean technologies and their wide-scale implementation may equally be a long time coming and have serious side effects. However, the fact that optimistic and pessimistic forecasts are possible does not mean that they balance each other out from an ethical point of view. In Part II, we concluded that climate mitigation is a matter of avoiding excessive risks for future generations. Given this goal, a "strategy" that, first, only *partially avoids* climate-related risks ("the residual risk of ineffectiveness") because of the uncertainty surrounding its effectiveness and, second, *replaces* climate-related risks *in part with new risks* ("the risk of new dangers") because of its side effects cannot even count as a real strategy in the full sense of the term; rather, it is tantamount to an experiment. In the final analysis, it is immaterial for future generations who have to live with the consequences, whether a threat to their human rights can be traced back to climate-related risks, to radioactive waste, or to an increase in food prices.

It could be objected that the impacts of climate-related risks would be more global and that their worst-case scenarios would be worse by comparison with the side effects of the new technologies. Above all, one might object that ultimately everything is a question of money: If we were willing to spend more on developing new, and on implementing the existing, clean technologies, then the risks of the technology strategy could probably be reduced to a tolerable level. Solar energy, for example, involves hardly any risks, but at present it is not the cheapest option. If we were willing to pay this price, then the technological transformation would not simply replace the risks of climate change, but would instead actually reduce them. But then the strategy would also be more expensive than it appears at first sight. The same objection cropped up in Chapter 4 when we compared climate mitigation, adaptation, and climate engineering: If adaptation and climate engineering were implemented in such a way that they ultimately reduced the risks as much as climate mitigation, then they would no longer seem so cheap.

This insight sheds new light on the technology strategy. If the strategy is expensive, then it is ultimately equivalent to forgoing affluence. For example, if we spend money on developing and implementing solar energy, then we cannot spend this money on other goods for consumption. Thus technological progress seems to be a version of the affluence strategy rather than an alternative to it. And whether it is the most attractive version has not been conclusively clarified: For example, it could very well be more attractive simply to heat less rather than to spend a lot of money on developing and implementing clean heating technologies.

Third strategy: affluence

Whereas the aim of the first strategy is to ensure that fewer people are born and that of the second strategy is to generate the affluence of these people with less emissions, the aim of the third strategy is to limit their affluence. Examples of the affluence strategy include making do with limited living space, traveling moderately, extending the useful life of objects, switching to a plant-based diet, and the like. Indirectly, the affluence strategy manifests itself in lower, or possibly even negative, economic growth as a result of regulating greenhouse gas emissions.

Is forgoing economic growth a sensible strategy for mitigating climate change? That depends on a number of factors: on whether the strategy is applied by the poor or the rich, and on how it is implemented. If the richest billion people in the world were to volunteer to adopt a more modest lifestyle, this would be one of the least problematic and most reliable strategies for mitigating climate change. In contrast to the technology strategy, it has no dangerous side effects, and in contrast to the population strategy, there are no further sensitive ethical considerations at stake. In addition, it is quite possible that a lower level of affluence would entail hardly any sacrifice in terms of quality of life. While some questions about the link between wealth and satisfaction with one's life still remain open in happiness research, there are some indications that, beyond a certain level, additional increases in prosperity give rise to little additional life satisfaction; on the contrary, the connection between certain immaterial and hence low-emission factors—such as stable relationships, democracy, and sleep—and a happy life is well documented. It is even the case that a focus on material values can be detrimental to a sense of well-being (on which, see Diener and Seligman 2004; Stoll et al. 2012).

However, the affluence strategy encounters an objection even in rich countries: A state that decrees a simpler lifestyle from the top down restricts freedom and must count as illiberal. However, this objection does not fully hit the mark. A policy that is hostile to growth does indeed favor certain lifestyles while impeding others. If a country advocates less economic growth, this influences, for example, the design of its public infrastructure, its attractiveness as a location for doing business, and its priorities for public school curricula. Moreover, these aspects influence in turn the opportunities of individual citizens to choose freely between a more and a less prosperous lifestyle. But the tables can be turned, since the same criticism also applies in many respects to a growth-friendly policy: By aggressively promoting economic progress, and hence materialistic values, a country makes it difficult for citizens with other goals to pursue their conception of the "good life." Even a "drop-out," for example, cannot escape aircraft noise or a price level geared to high earners. By opting for more or less growth, politics cannot avoid doing right by some and not by others.

The state can, however, uphold respect for individual freedom by not imposing *specific* simpler lifestyles. In a liberal state, it should be a matter of personal decision which aspects of prosperity one does without and for what reasons. Some people will accept the limits on levels of affluence only resentfully, as a necessary evil; others will attach a positive value to them. They will appreciate a simpler lifestyle as an ideal supplement to values such as a sense of community, love of nature, or spirituality. But a modest lifestyle need not have such connotations. Such a lifestyle can also assume quite different forms. Spending the day playing computer games in a small urban apartment, and feeding oneself on pasta and cheap cola, is presumably less resource-intensive than living on a large farm, eating organic meat, and traveling to the meditation center on weekends. In a liberal state, the law should prescribe certain limits on levels of afflu-ence only as necessary to protect the climate, but not the choice of one or another path to achieving these limits nor the corresponding change in mentality.

At this point, one could object that this restriction—that the state should prescribe only the destination, but not the route—attaches too much weight to liberal respect for the value of freedom. Is it really wrong to imbue children in public schools with a nature-loving attitude, for exam-ple, or to ban Formula One racing? We do not develop our values, norms, and habits in isolation, but always acquire them as part of a community. In particular, if certain fundamental values were not widely shared, the viability of the liberal state itself would be placed in question. If the cli-mate crisis now calls for a "green transformation" of our values, it could be criticized as too individualistic if everyone were to make this change in mentality in accordance with their personal preferences. Making the change in our values, norms, and habits as independently as possible from the impetus provided by a collective and politically shaped rethinking process would not only be artificial, but also excessively burdensome (or, if you will, inefficient). Therefore whether we regard legal regulations—not to mention informal social pressure—to adopt specific aspects of a simpler lifestyle as an unacceptable interference in our personal affairs depends on our understanding of liberalism.

The bottom line, however, is that limiting affluence as a strategy for mitigating climate change is especially unproblematic from an ethical perspective—at any rate, if it is confined to the circle of wealthy people.

For people living in poverty, the evaluation of the affluence strategy must be precisely the opposite. In the case of poor people, it is hardly controversial that material values such as more goods, more energy, and more mobility are conducive to quality of life; at a more fundamental level, they are even a precondition for fulfilling these people's human rights in the first place. While forgoing economic growth means reducing luxury emissions for the wealthy, it denies people living in poverty subsistence emissions (see Shue 1993). For people in poverty, therefore, the main options are the population and technology strategies—insofar as they have any duties to mitigate climate change at all (see Part III). This insight leads to a further conclusion: Given that people living in poverty account for such a large portion of humanity and given that the contribution of the population strategy to climate mitigation cannot be increased indefinitely (see O'Neill et al. 2010), it follows that the technology strategy is unavoidable for people living in poverty. Therefore an especially convincing way for rich people from industrialized countries to limit their affluence is to finance the research, development, and diffusion of clean technologies in developing countries (see Chapter 16). In the next chapter, we will discuss a policy instrument—namely, emissions trading—that could promote precisely this objective.

Arguments box 15: emission reduction: three strategies

This chapter has not discussed *how much* we should reduce emissions, but rather *what means* we should employ. Global emissions can be calculated by multiplying the number of people by the level of affluence per person and the emissions required to produce one unit of affluence. Accordingly, a climate mitigation strategy can address either the size of the population, the emission intensity, or the level of affluence.

(1) *The population strategy*: Population policy can make a genuine contribution to climate mitigation. There is a sound objection to population policy if ethically sensitive coercive measures are used to reach its goals. However, political decision-makers do not have to resort to such measures and can instead make use of instruments such as poverty reduction that are valuable in themselves. One crucial consideration is difficult to assess from an ethical point of view: the fact that reducing population growth inevitably means that fewer people receive the gift of life.

(2) *The technology strategy*: The main objection to the technology strategy consists in doubts about whether it will achieve the ultimate aim of climate mitigation—namely, reducing the risks for future generations. This is so for two reasons: because it is hard to predict how successful low-emission technologies will be, and because they often give rise to new risks as side effects. If the technology strategy were actually to achieve the objective, this would entail substantial costs, which calls its status as the politically least painful option in question.

(3) *The affluence strategy*: The affluence strategy is not an option for people living in poverty; for wealthy people, by contrast, it is the least problematic climate mitigation strategy. This means that the technology strategy is unavoidable for developing countries and part of the affluence that richer countries forgo should be used to finance the relevant measures. The objection that political limits on economic growth conflict with respect for liberal values is weaker the less specific the changes in lifestyle that are prescribed.

One can ask, regarding all strategies, whether the main emphasis should be on *implementation by the state* or on *personal initiative*. Implementing climate mitigation through political programs is *less burdensome* than leaving it up to individual action. Because greenhouse gas emissions violate rights, state restrictions on individual freedom are also *justified*. Striking a balance between legal coercion and voluntary initiative allows for many gradations in order to minimize the loss of freedom. However, voluntary initiative is indispensable if the state is unable or unwilling to act. Finally, voluntary initiative—through voting and activism—is also necessary to empower the state to become active in the field of climate policy in the first place.

References

Blanco, G., Gerlagh, R., Suh, S., Barrett, J., de Coninck, H. C., Diaz Morejon, C. F., Mathur, R., Nakicenovic, N., Ahenkorah, A. O., Pan, J., Pathak, H., Rice, J., Richels, R., Smith, S. J., Stern, D. I., Toth, F. L., and Zhou, P. (2014) "Drivers, trends and mitigation," in O. Edenhofer et al. (eds.) *Climate Change 2014: Mitigation of Climate Change—Contribution of Working Group III to the Fifth Assessment Report of the Intergovernmental Panel on Climate Change*, Cambridge: Cambridge University Press, 351–411.

Broome, J. (2012) *Climate Matters*, New York: W. W. Norton & Co.

Cafaro, P. (2012) "Climate ethics and population policy," *Wiley Interdisciplinary Reviews: Climate Change*, 3(1): 45–61.

Diener, E., and Seligman, M. E. P. (2004) "Beyond money: toward an economy of well-being," *Psychological Science in the Public Interest*, 5(1): 1–31.

Murtaugh, P. A., and Schlax, M. G. (2009) "Reproduction and the carbon legacies of individuals," *Global Environmental Change*, 19(1): 14–20.

O'Neill, B. C., Dalton, M., Fuchs, R., Jiang, L., Pachauri, S., and Zigova, K. (2010) "Global demographic trends and future carbon emissions," *Proceedings of the National Academy of Sciences*, 107(41): 17521–6.

Parfit, D. (1984) *Reasons and Persons*, Oxford: Clarendon Press.

Shue, H. (1993) "Subsistence emissions and luxury emissions," *Law & Policy*, 15(1): 39–59.

Stoll, L., Michaelson, J., and Seaford, C. (2012) *Wellbeing Evidence for Policy: A Review*, London: New Economics Foundation.

United Nations (2009) *World Population Prospects: The 2008 Revision*, New York: Population Division of the Department of Economic and Social Affairs of the United Nations Secretariat.

United Nations Population Fund (UNFPA) (2011) *The State of World Population 2011*, available online at http://foweb.unfpa.org/SWP2011/reports/EN-SWOP2011-FINAL.pdf [accessed April 29, 2016].

Wire, T. (2009) *Fewer Emitters, Lower Emissions, Less Cost*, London: London School of Economics.

19 The market for emissions

A modern sale of indulgences?

Climate policy can have recourse to a variety of instruments in order to implement its strategies. One particularly prominent—but also a particularly controversial—strategy is emissions trading.

The basic idea of a market for emissions can be illustrated using the example from Chapter 15.

> A town with a population of 200 is situated on a lake that is very well suited for bathing—but the use of the lake has to be restricted to 2,000 bathing sessions per summer. The town community decides to issue a ten-session swimming permit to each of the town's residents. Soon, the children of the town start to buy permits from each other. The water lovers are happy that they can use the lake more than ten times, whereas the homebodies are happy to be able to cash in on their permits.

If the trade of permits becomes commonplace, then we may even see the emergence of a price that one must expect to pay for a permit. There are three core elements in this example: a total budget of swimming permits, the distribution of the budget among the individual residents of the town, and the trade with the permits. Analogous elements can be found in emissions trading, only here what is involved is the atmosphere, rather than a lake, and emission permits, rather than swimming permits. In the classical case of emissions trading, the political authorities first stipulate a total budget of emission rights (the size of the "CO_2 cake"—a so-called *cap*); second, this budget of emission rights is divided up into a budget for each individual agent (the "pieces of the cake"); third, the agents—countries, companies, or individuals—can trade their emission rights. Those agents who can easily reduce their emissions, and hence have a preference for income over emission permits, sell their permits. The agents who need the emission permits, and hence are willing to pay for them, purchase additional emission permits. The emission permits acquire a market price depending on supply and demand.

The basic idea of a market for emission permits—or for reduction obligations—also has different manifestations from the classical case of emissions trading. The Clean Development Mechanism (CDM) of the

Kyoto Protocol, for example, differs from emissions trading in the narrower sense in that there is no cap on the emissions budget for all of the agents involved, but only for the industrialized countries. The latter can buy emission reductions in developing countries, provided that they can demonstrate that the reduction in emissions has, in fact, been achieved *because of* the measure financed by an industrialized country and would not have been achieved in any case. Another manifestation of a market for emissions is voluntary offsetting. In this case, individuals or firms offset their emissions for air travel, consumer goods, events, and so on, and thereby achieve "climate neutrality." This form deviates from emissions trading in the classical sense, because the buyers pay voluntarily for the emission reductions without their emissions budget having been restricted by the political authorities through a cap. However, this voluntary market accounts for only a fraction of the total emissions market (on which and on the following statements, see Kossoy and Guigon 2012). By the end of 2011, the voluntary market comprised trade in around 10 billion tons of CO_2-equivalent (on this unit of measure, see the Glossary) valued at around US\$176 billion. The lion's share of this trade occurs in the European Union, because it has established the first major cross-border greenhouse gas trading system for companies.

The question to be answered in this chapter is whether a market for emissions should be supported or rejected, from a moral point of view. In the case of classical emissions trading, ethical questions arise regarding all three elements, although the first two elements raise the weightiest questions: Is the total "CO_2 cake" (the cap) as small as it should be, given our duties toward future generations? And are the "pieces of the cake" distributed fairly? Because we have already discussed these two questions in the parts on intergenerational and global justice, we will exclude them for the most part in this chapter and will return to them only briefly at the end. Here, we will concentrate instead on the third aspect of emissions trading: the *tradability* of the "pieces of the cake." This is the core idea of a market for emissions in all of its manifestations. The tradability of emissions means that we do not necessarily "first have to clean up our own backyard" when fulfilling our duties to reduce emissions, but can instead pay others to reduce emissions in our place. Emission rights become a tradable good, like apples or shares. When we address the question in this chapter of whether it makes a morally relevant difference if we reduce emissions ourselves or pay others to do so, we are relying in many places on the arguments of Caney and Hepburn (2011).

What speaks in favor of a market for emissions?

Emissions trading has two major advantages by comparison with other instruments: First, it makes climate mitigation cheaper; and second, it grants the agents more freedom over how they implement climate mitigation. In contrast to the arguments *against* a market for emissions, these two points are not particularly subtle, but they are by no means unimportant for that reason.

Let us consider the first advantage. An emissions market enables us to reduce emissions wherever this is cheapest. If a Canadian company can achieve a massive reduction in emissions through a small tweak, while an American company can achieve the same objective only through costly measures, it would seem to make sense that the American company should reduce its emissions less and the Canadian company more than it would otherwise have to, and that the Canadian company should be compensated for this by the American company. This is a win–win situation. If we were to require each company to "first clean up its own backyard," then the same amount of climate mitigation would cost more. Conversely, we can say that, thanks to the emissions market, more climate mitigation can be accomplished at a given cost, which is especially advantageous when the political will to promote climate mitigation is very weak. In that case, it is important to stretch the limited financial resources as far as possible in terms of emission reductions.

But a market for emissions not only reduces the costs of climate mitigation; it also places fewer restrictions on the freedom of those who must protect the climate. The agents are not tied down to a specific *kind* of climate-friendly action (for example doing without automobiles that do not fulfill certain efficiency standards); instead, they "merely" have to ensure *that* emissions are reduced. *How* exactly the emissions are reduced is left up to each individual agent and *who* exactly carries out the reductions is a function of cost advantages—namely, those for whom it is cheapest. By contrast, direct regulation in the form of requirements and prohibitions lay down detailed guidelines in specific economic domains and areas of life; an instrument such as emissions trading leaves virtually every other decision—except whether or not to attain the objective—up to the individual agents and subject to coordination by the market mechanism.

What speaks against a market for emissions?

The trade in emissions is, however, often met with skepticism in spite of its advantages as regards costs and freedom. The unease is palpable in the Kyoto Protocol when, immediately after affirming emissions trading, it emphasizes that this is allowed at most as a supplemental measure to domestic mitigation efforts. So what are the ethical arguments against a market for emissions?

The objections against buying and selling emissions build on the widespread view that not everything that *can* be traded on markets *ought to* be traded on markets. This is a familiar view in many areas of life. We intuitively agree that, although organ donations are a good thing, the trade in human organs is problematic; that a labor market makes sense, but that the slave trade is bad; that a millionaire may buy many privileges, but not the service of a poor person to serve a prison sentence in his or her place.

Even if a market transaction is voluntary and advantageous for both buyer and seller, it is not for this reason necessarily morally unobjectionable; on the contrary, an exchange may be morally problematic for at least three reasons. First, it should not be possible to have ownership—or at least to have private ownership—of certain goods (a *property-related criticism*). And if property in a good is questionable, then so too is the trade in that good. The example of slavery can be understood in this sense: No one should claim ownership of other human beings, let alone buy and sell other human beings on markets.

Second, there are goods that are such that claiming ownership of them does not present any problems, but which nevertheless should not be traded on markets and certainly not for money (a *goods-related criticism*). This is because the trade would convey an inappropriate attitude toward this good or give rise to such an inappropriate attitude. The example of organs can be understood in this sense: Selling our bodily organs for money on markets would devalue the special and intimate relationship that we have with them as parts of our body.

Third, there are duties that one should perform oneself instead of paying others to fulfill them (a *duty-related criticism*). The prison example can be understood in this sense: The wealthy criminal has a personal duty to serve his or her punishment. One should no more be allowed to transfer it to others for money than one should sell certain other goods.

Do these three forms of criticism of certain market transactions also apply to the specific case of the market in emissions? The property-related form of criticism could appeal to the fact that we should not regard the atmosphere as human property. In a somewhat weaker form, one could criticize not ownership of the atmosphere as such, but only private ownership. This weaker form of the criticism concedes that the atmosphere is the collective property of all human beings, but denies exclusive—and hence tradable—rights to parts of the atmosphere. However, neither the stronger nor the weaker form of the criticism provides a conclusive argument against emissions trading. First, it is not obvious that we should not have ownership of the atmosphere—after all, we do not object to the idea of ownership of many other aspects of nature (such as land or plants).

Second, and more important, it is far from clear that emissions trading really depends on the idea of ownership of the atmosphere—for what is bought and sold in emissions trading is not a *property right*, but instead a *right of use* in the atmosphere. An emissions permit is not an entitlement to do whatever one likes with a certain cubic meter of the atmosphere; instead, it confers a right to utilize the capacity of the atmosphere to absorb CO_2 for a certain time. In the American emissions trade in sulfur dioxide, it was even explicitly laid down that it was a matter of a limited authorization to emit and that the permits do not constitute property rights (Tietenberg 2006: 193). But hardly anyone will object to a *right to use* the atmosphere. How would we even survive without using the atmosphere? Emissions trading merely restricts this right and makes it tradable.

Third, the market for emissions—at least in some cases—can also be interpreted as a market for emission reductions rather than as a market for emission rights. If this interpretation is correct, then the property-related criticism is even less persuasive.

Those who are skeptical about the trade in emissions could also base their argument on the goods-related criticism and claim that, regardless of whether the trade in emissions is a matter of property rights, rights of use, or emission reductions, it in any case involves the *purchase* of these goods. A market for emissions, it could be argued, "commodifies" the atmosphere by hanging a price tag on it. Taken literally, this criticism is not easy to uphold. When we charge admission for a piano concert, we are neither expressing the value of the music performed in monetary terms nor are we "commodifying" the beauty of the music; the price of admission is merely a way of preventing a rush on the concert, of being able to pay the pianist, or of ensuring that those who attend the concert are predominantly people who appreciate music more than others. Something similar holds in the case of emissions trading: The trade in emission rights need not symbolize that we regard nature merely as an object of use and trade. In principle, the price paid for emission permits could even express respect for nature, because it testifies to the fact that we have voluntarily made emission permits into a scarce (and tradable) resource, or that we want to achieve the most extensive emission reductions possible at a given cost. In particular, no one forces us to make the extent of our appreciation for nature in any way dependent on the price of emission permits.

The critic of emissions trading could now acknowledge that, in some cases, it would certainly be appropriate to pay for producing emissions; it is just that the payment must be understood *as a fine rather than a fee*. An example can illustrate the difference between a fine and a fee. Imagine a concert promoter who puts up posters and must pay a fee of $100 per poster for the use of public walls. If he also had to pay a fine of $100 for illegal billposting, these two cases would nevertheless have to be *interpreted* differently: The payment for the legal posters is a *fee*; the payment for the illegal posters a *fine*. Similarly, the critic of emissions trading could claim that if someone emits CO_2 and buys an emission permit for this purpose, then he or she should not understand this payment as the price for a right to emit, but instead as a penalty for wrongdoing (namely, the wrong of having emitted too much). The claim is that the person is not in the clear with the purchase of the emission permit, because his or her duty was to reduce the emissions *him or herself* and not merely to ensure, by means of a payment, that emissions were reduced elsewhere. The purchaser has committed an "environmental sin," so to speak, and the payment is not an "indulgence" for this.

This brings us to the duty-based criticism of emissions trading. How should we evaluate this criticism? First of all, we must ask whether there is an argument for regarding reducing emissions in particular as a duty that must be fulfilled in person. After all, in everyday life, we allow many of our duties be performed by strangers: Our duty to care for our children, for example, is often performed by a babysitter. That climate mitigation, of all things, should be regarded as a personal duty is questionable, because the point of emission reductions is their *effect*. The atmosphere does not care *who* reduces emissions. Why, then, should it be the case that we must *personally* comply with our duty to reduce emissions?

A potential argument for this could appeal to the example of ration cards, through which all citizens may be obligated to limit their consumption of certain foods to a specific amount per month in times of war. Many find it morally problematic when, at such times, rich citizens are able to buy up the ration coupons of their destitute fellow citizens; rather, it should be an expression of a cooperative ethos when even the rich have to confine themselves to one egg per month. A ban or prohibition on trading with ration coupons symbolizes that all are pulling together in hard times. Similarly, in the case of climate mitigation, one could also require that the rich may not buy themselves out of the necessary change in lifestyles by paying the poor to reduce emissions; instead, all should follow the same path toward a less emissions-intensive lifestyle together. This criticism is sometimes presented in an excessively crude form, as though the wealthy purchasers of emission permits would not bear any burden at all, but instead shift it entirely onto the sellers. Of course, this is not the case: The rich *pay* the poor for their efforts. Although this is not the same as forgoing emissions, it does involve forgoing wealth. And this does, in fact, mean sacrificing something. In emissions trading, therefore, burdens are borne by both the rich and the poor, and it is not readily apparent why both parties should have to bear the burdens in the form of emission reductions. A personal duty to *reduce emissions* instead of *paying for emission reductions* makes little sense in particular when it comes to emissions trading between companies. Companies are not persons, after all, and hence the idea of a cooperative ethos between companies also makes less sense. But even when it comes to trading between nations and between individuals, it is questionable whether the plausibility of a prohibition on trading in the case of ration coupons does not rather constitute an exception. On the one hand, it might not represent any great sacrifice for the agents involved to do without this trade in ration coupons; on the other hand, doing without emissions trading might well amount to a major sacrifice, especially for the poor who were not allowed to convert surplus emission permits into money.

Although the three versions of the market criticism do indeed have a certain persuasive power at first sight, on closer inspection they hardly apply to the market for emissions. It is surprisingly difficult to identify *fundamental* ethical problems with the trade in emissions. This is not to deny that buying and selling emissions could represent a small part of a larger and problematic trend—namely, the trend to extend the market mechanism to more and more areas of life. The "economic colonization" of many separate areas of life taken together could be problematic, even if each individual example viewed in isolation could be unproblematic. If all aspects of human interactions are understood exclusively as an exchange of services, then clearly something important in our lives does get lost. However, in that case, it would not be obvious why the market for emissions in particular would have to be abandoned instead of, for example, the extension of the market logic to education and health care.

Thus, by itself, the theoretical idea at the core of emissions trading—including its market-oriented character—provides little reason for ethical criticism. The problems with emissions trading must be sought instead in its *practical* implementation.

Does the market for emissions work?

Emissions trading is based on the idea that it makes no difference whether we reduce emissions ourselves or pay someone else to reduce them—and yet it *does* make a difference. In practice, the tradability of emission permits influences the extent to which total emissions ultimately decrease and how the related costs are distributed. That may come as a surprise, because by comparison with other policy instruments—such as taxes or technical standards—emissions trading allows more direct control of the reduction target and the burden-sharing scheme.

The reasons for the practical problems are diverse. Emission reductions are difficult to observe, quantify, and monitor, especially in countries with weak and corrupt governance structures. For emissions trading to work, a regulatory framework relating to the cap, the allocation of emissions, and measurement and monitoring needs to be negotiated. In this respect, reliance on the cooperation of companies is unavoidable and they tend to influence such frameworks in their own interest. For example, the companies in the emissions trading system of the European Union were able to ensure that the emission permits were originally issued free of cost. But because the introduction of emissions trading meant that CO_2 simultaneously acquired a price, the companies were then able to sell their emissions-intensive goods at a higher price. At the end of the day, this had the undesirable effect that emissions did not become more expensive for the companies, but at the same time companies could sell their emissions-intensive products more expensively—and they pocketed the difference as profit (so-called *windfall profits*). But even if companies refrain for the most part from influencing the regulatory framework in their own interests, a single weak link in the chain is enough to allow for emission reductions being paid for that ultimately do not amount to any reduction at all. For example, if a company in Switzerland pays to conserve an area of forest in Brazil, then this benefits the atmosphere only if the forest is not cut down five years later anyway. And even if the forest is conserved in the long term, it is open to question whether it is in fact conserved *because of* the payment by the Swiss company. Otherwise, of course, forgoing defor-estation does not make up for any emissions in Switzerland. In the spe-cialist jargon, this is known as the so-called *additionality problem*, which can arise in the context of the CDM and of voluntary offsetting. If agents who do not face an upper limit on their emissions sell a reduction in emis-sions, then this should not be a reduction that would have been under-taken *in any case*. Of course, there is a lot of latitude in estimating which reductions would have been made anyway—that is, even without the opportunity to cash them out on the emissions market. Especially prob-lematic is the incentive to intentionally build climate-damaging facilities in order to make money later through the reduction of the greenhouse gases produced by these same facilities.

In addition, the market for emissions could lead to *motivation crowd-ing* (for a critical overview, see Page 2011). Many people protect the climate to a certain degree even without financial incentives, but simply out of personal conviction. Studies have shown that financial incentives do not always *supplement* this intrinsic motivation, but can also *replace and eradicate* it. By rewarding climate-friendly behavior financially, emissions trading sends a signal to society that such intrinsic motivation is not even necessary. As a result, we wean ourselves off our conscien-tiousness and reduce emissions only in exchange for remuneration. Through this motivation crowding, the market for emissions can delay,

or even prevent, the change in mentality toward regarding climate mitigation as the normal and voluntary thing to do. Emissions trading
removes the stigma from the emission of greenhouse gases by placing
the focus on the *right* to pollute. At the very least, it can be accused of
diverting attention: It invests climate mitigation with the connotation of
growth opportunities and shifts the focus from the central aim of actually reducing emissions sufficiently toward ensuring that this aim can be
achieved at the least cost.

These examples of some of the practical problems inspire doubt as to
whether the core idea of a market for emissions really works in practice.
If we emit 1 ton of CO_2 above our cap and pay someone to emit 1 ton
under his or her cap, then it remains uncertain whether this is really a
zero-sum game in practice—or whether, in the end, even more emissions find their way into the atmosphere than if both parties had reduced
their emissions to the level of their respective caps. In addition, there is
the problem that, in emissions trading, opportunities are missed to
reduce emissions by *more* than is required, so that they fall below the
level of the cap. Thus the countries of the former Soviet Union were
issued more emission permits in the Kyoto Protocol than they even
needed. Without emissions trading, these permits would simply have
expired—that is, the emissions would have sunk below the targeted
level—but, thanks to emissions trading, they were able to sell these permits and thereby facilitate other emissions (known as the so-called *hot
air problem*). The missed opportunity for additional reductions is also
illustrated by the fact that Western countries would have been compelled
to make much more extensive innovations if they had had to fulfill their
reduction obligations at home instead of being able to offset their emissions in other countries. These innovations in technology and lifestyle
would have had multiplier effects, and would have lent an additional
impulse to the transition to a low-carbon economy. Emissions trading is
also called into question if one assumes that we will have to leave the
fossil fuel era behind us completely, in the medium term at any rate, and
that the earlier this happens, the better (not least in our own self-interest).
If the cap does not take into account the long-term benefits of making
this transition quickly, then the wealthy can continue to produce emissions blithely in the short term only to have to make even more painful
adjustments later.

In the real world, therefore, emissions trading may well come into
conflict with the goal of reducing emissions. And not only the size of
the CO_2 "cake," but also the burden-sharing sought by means of the
distribution of the "pieces of the cake" can ultimately turn out to be less
fair than intended for a variety of reasons. Thus emissions trading does
not typically take place between individuals, but between states or

companies. Even if the emission permits were divided up fairly among the different *states*, this would not necessarily mean that there would ultimately be a fair distribution of the costs of climate mitigation among *individuals*. Corrupt elites can exploit the emission permits—which can be turned into cash, after all—for their own benefit instead of granting the population a fair share in them. And, as already mentioned, companies that are better informed about their own emissions and possibilities for reducing them than any political regulatory authority can try to shape and exploit the system in their own favor. In addition, there are concerns that emissions trading has regressive effects—that is, that, relatively speaking, the poor are burdened more than the rich (Shammin and Bullard 2009). Through emissions trading, CO_2 emissions acquire a price; because the poor are less able to pay this price, and in addition use a larger share of their total expenditures for energy, they can be affected disproportionately by emissions trading. However, these negative effects can also be avoided, for example, through accompanying redistribution measures (such as social transfers to cover basic energy needs) or by excluding the emissions that serve to cover basic needs completely from trading. In addition, a market for emissions might well also have positive effects for people living in poverty. If the West makes the innovations in clean technologies in developing countries rather than at home, this should be welcomed from the perspective of justice. Whatever the outcome of the interplay between these various effects at the end of the day, the complications illustrate that the distributive effect of emissions trading is less easily and directly controllable than it may appear at first sight. Emissions trading needs to be carefully implemented in order to avoid the risk of new injustices.

What does all of this mean in the larger picture? In theory, pursuing climate mitigation with the help of a market for emissions has advantages in terms of costs and freedom. In practice, however, it is beset by a range of problems: Neither the intended level of climate mitigation nor the desired pattern of distribution of costs can be achieved as easily as it seems. One of two conclusions can be drawn from this: that we must either abandon or improve the emissions market. If one thinks that the problems of practical implementation cannot be solved, then the first conclusion is preferable. In that case, other policy instruments must be entertained: CO_2 taxes, subsidies for climate-friendly technologies and their transfer to developing countries, prohibitions, standards, a research push in the field of renewable energy, motivation and information campaigns, and so on. If one believes, by contrast, that the practical problems of the emissions market can be overcome, then the task would be to develop a better version. Thus the final word has not yet been heard on this topic.

Arguments box 16: the market for emissions: a modern sale of indulgences?

In addition to the two central questions of how many emission permits should be issued in total and how they should be distributed, emissions trading raises the ethical question of whether it is justifiable to trade emission rights—in other words, whether we may pay others to reduce emissions instead of reducing them ourselves.

The ethical argument in favor of a market for emissions is that this makes climate mitigation cheaper and provides greater freedom in the choice of the means of reducing emissions.

Three objections can, however, be put forward against the trade in emissions from a market-skeptical perspective.

(1) *Objection*: "It is wrong to have (private) property in the atmosphere."
Reply: Emissions trading does not presuppose property rights in the atmosphere.

(2) *Objection*: "The atmosphere, as part of nature, is a resource that should not be bought and sold for money."
Reply: As the example of the admission price for a concert showed, using the market mechanism does not imply anything about how we value the atmosphere as part of nature.

(3) *Objection*: "Reducing emissions is a personal duty."
Reply: What ultimately matters about emission reduction measures is their effect. Thus, in the absence of a compelling argument to the contrary, paying for a reduction in emissions must also count as fulfilling one's duty. Basing a counterargument on the analogy to special cases, such as the prohibition of the trade with ration coupons, would fail to appreciate that doing without an emissions market could represent a significant sacrifice and that the talk of personal duties is in any case unconvincing in the case of trade between companies.

Therefore these principled ethical objections against a market for emissions are not convincing.

In practice, however, emissions trading is fraught with a variety of problems, in particular as regards its effectiveness for climate mitigation and its unintended effects on the distribution of burdens. This can either serve as motivation to improve the market for emissions or justify using alternative policy instruments.

References

Caney, S., and Hepburn, C. (2011) "Carbon trading: unethical, unjust and ineffective?" *Royal Institute of Philosophy Supplements*, 69: 201–34.

Kossoy, A., and Guigon, P. (2012) *State and Trends of the Carbon Market 2012*, Washington, DC: World Bank.

Page, E. (2011) "Cosmopolitanism, climate change, and greenhouse emissions trading," *International Theory*, 3(1): 37–69.

Shammin, M. R., and Bullard, C. W. (2009) "Impact of cap and trade policies for reducing greenhouse gas emissions on US households," *Ecological Economics*, 68(8–9): 2432–8.

Tietenberg, T. H. (2006) *Emissions Trading: Principles and Practice*, Washington, DC: RFF Press.

20 Procedural justice

Democracy in times of climate change

Up to now, we have focused on the following question: What is a just climate policy? In doing so, the focus was on just *outcomes*. However, we must also pay attention to the ethical character of the *procedures* that give rise to these outcomes. We can illustrate this by returning once again to the example of the lake and bathing rights: *One* question (the question of justice regarding outcomes) is which distribution of the limited bathing rights is just; a *different* question (the question of justice regarding procedures) is through which procedures agreement is supposed to be reached among the townspeople on one of the possible distributions. Should the town hold a referendum on the distribution of the bathing rights? Should the mayor be allowed to decide on his or her own? Should the town administration decide on the basis of principles laid down in national law? Or should they draw lots to decide between the different possible distributions? Which procedure would be morally justified?

The procedure by which international climate policy decisions are currently reached is a complex negotiation process based on the UNFCCC. Such negotiation processes can also be judged from the perspective of justice. Thus a number of countries have rejected the result of the 2009 Copenhagen Climate Conference precisely on these grounds. From their perspective, the outcome of the Copenhagen Conference was problematic for the simple reason that it was the result of an unfair negotiation process (Eckersley 2012: 34). Is this view justified? And if so, how should the negotiation processes be reformed? In short, what would a fair decision-making procedure in climate policy look like? This is the topic of the present chapter.

In Chapter 18, we already excluded one specific procedure as a possible answer to this question—namely, the "anarchist" idea that the outcome should be determined solely by the unregulated interplay of voluntary contributions by individuals. However, excluding anarchy is not enough; we also need to know how an alternative procedure should be designed. An appealing alternative for many is democracy—and more of it than we currently have. According to some critics, political processes at the international level exhibit significant democratic deficits (Bäckstrand 2011: 670). Thus, time and again, we hear calls to make climate policy more democratic. But is democracy a suitable procedure for decision-making in climate policy? The mills of democracy grind slowly, after all, whereas the problem of preventing climate change must be addressed as quickly as possible. Moreover, in a democracy, everyone has a vote—even the foot draggers, the obfuscators, and the enemies of justice. It is therefore not surprising that, to date, democratic states have not managed to prevent climate change or even to bear their fair share of the costs. Would it therefore not be more appropriate to take power away from the parliaments and hand over all decision-making authority to green expert councils, or even to an eco-dictator? Is democracy perhaps a luxury decision-making procedure that we can ill afford in view of the impending climate catastrophe? It seems worthwhile to examine the relationship between democracy and climate justice more closely.

Two criteria of procedural justice

In the eyes of skeptics about democracy, political decision-making procedures can be compared to a defective machine. If a machine produces defective goods, it must be replaced by a different model; similarly, if a decision-making procedure gives rise to injustice, it must be replaced by a different procedure. Insofar as democracy gives rise to intergenerational and global injustice in climate policy (or at least does not prevent it), therefore, we should replace it as we would a defective machine.

However, this inference is too quick. A first problem is that the poor track record of democratic states in terms of climate justice is, of course, not yet evidence that the track record of undemocratic states is any better. We simply do not have any experience with states that have rejected democracy specifically for reasons of environmental protection. We do have experience, however, with undemocratic regimes in general and their track record looks pretty bleak. Undemocratic regimes do not achieve better results in environmental policy than democracies (Burnell 2012: 823*ff*), but they often produce very unjust results in other policy areas. Even if it seems that democracies hardly bring about justice in the field of climate policy, it is questionable in the extreme whether an undemocratic green regime would give rise to more justice, all things considered.

A second problem with the skeptic's unease about democracy is more fundamental in nature: Should decision-making procedures such as democracy really be measured only by their fruits? Unlike the case of the machine in which only the quality of the output counts, we do believe that democracy is something good *in and of itself*. For example, someone who champions the expansion of opportunities for democratic participation (for instance through the right to vote) will hardly want to grant a vote only to those whose voting behavior also leads to better results. Similarly, one might believe that, in the field of climate policy too, democratic participation by all is required even if it does not serve the cause of climate justice. However, the objection of the skeptics concerning democracy is based on precisely the opposite view.

Thus skepticism about the suitability of democracy faces at least two problems that rest on two different standards for assessing a political decision-making procedure from the perspective of justice. The first standard judges a procedure by whether it is an efficient and reliable instrument for producing just results—that is, it is an *instrumental* criterion of procedural justice. The second standard, by contrast, judges a political procedure by whether it is just in and of itself—regardless of the probability of its leading to just results—and this is an *intrinsic* criterion of procedural justice.

The intrinsic criterion consists, strictly speaking, in a whole cluster of criteria. A central criterion, for example, is that all those who must adhere to a political decision should have a say about its introduction. As citizens, it is important to us not only that the climate policy process results in an outcome that grants us a fair share of emission rights as "recipients", but also that we can shape this process and that, in doing so, our views have equal weight to the views of others.

A second criterion of intrinsic procedural justice includes not only those who must adhere to a political decision in the decision-making process, but also all those who are *affected* by it. If, for example, a country prescribes that fossil fuels should be replaced by biofuels, then this not only has repercussions for drivers of automobiles in the country in question; it also affects the workers in oil refineries in Saudi Arabia or poor people around the globe (because increased demand for biofuels can lead to an increase in food prices). Although a just procedure need not necessarily grant all those affected a *vote*, it should at least *give them a voice* in the process leading up to a decision. These two criteria of intrinsic procedural justice—vote and voice—can be fulfilled only if certain preconditions are met: If citizens and those affected are to be able to form an opinion about the impacts of different climate policy proposals, political procedures must be transparent, information must be widely available, and an open discourse must take place that is not distorted by financially powerful lobbies.

A third criterion, finally, is respect for the legitimate scope of application of political procedures. Not every matter should be regulated by a collective decision; every agent is entitled to certain domains in which to make his or her own decisions, and procedures for arriving at collective decisions should be applied only where political regulation is justified. For example, every citizen should be able to decide freely *how* he or she reduces emissions; a political process should prescribe only *that* he or she should do so. Similarly, the world community should regulate collectively only that every state should reduce emissions, but not what policy instruments a state uses to achieve this goal.

One could continue this list of criteria for intrinsic procedural justice. By now, it should be clear that these criteria obviously speak for, and not against, democratic procedures. This applies in particular to the first two criteria. In contrast to an undemocratic, green regime, they include those affected extensively in the formation of opinions and decision-making. Of course, one could respond that an undemocratic regime, by contrast, fares better with regard to the instrumental criterion, which counterbalances the deficiencies in intrinsic procedural justice. However, this rests on unfounded hopes: To repeat, there is simply no evidence that undemocratic countries take more reliable care of the environment and hence perform better with respect to the instrumental criterion. In light of both criteria, therefore, there is scarcely any reason for serious or fundamental skepticism about democracy on grounds of climate mitigation.

On the contrary, if we want to better promote climate justice, it may even turn out to be a matter of strengthening, rather than weakening, democracy. Strengthening democracy, in particular, would mean adapting democratic institutions to the global and intergenerational challenges posed by climate change. Our current political procedures are located at the national level and geared in the short term to the next election. Thus their focus is much too narrow in both spatial and temporal terms to cope successfully with climate change. It may therefore be that the decision-making procedure we need is a more global and a more intergenerational democracy. In what follows, we want to examine whether this proposal can withstand scrutiny in terms of the two criteria of procedural justice.

A more global democracy

Let us briefly review a previous argument. In Chapter 18, we argued for a political (over an "anarchist," individual) solution on the basis of two points: First, it is easier to solve the problem with common rules; and second, implementing these rules is justified in order to prevent rights violations. These arguments by no means apply only to interaction between individuals *within* a state, but also to the interaction between states at the global level. However, whereas within states there are often long-standing and efficient legislative processes, at the global level there is a lack of political procedures that can effectively and fairly coordinate joint action against climate change. Although there are elaborate climate negotiations, these function according to the consensus principle: Each state is free to reject any proposal. And if such different states as Iran, France, and China must reach agreement, it is hardly surprising that only modest steps emerge as a lowest common denominator. Therefore the consensus principle fares poorly from the perspective of instrumental procedural justice. Are there better alternatives? Let us consider two: a "coalition of heavyweights," and the majority principle.

The first alternative is based on the insight that the ten countries with the largest greenhouse gas emissions alone are responsible for around 60 percent of global emissions (see WRI 2014). Such a critical mass of the most important countries could simply decide on the next steps among themselves, rather than engaging in a consultation process with the rest of the world. That would represent a shortcut compared with the arduous consensual process involving almost 200 countries within the framework of the UNFCCC. The hope would be that the remaining countries would use the measures of such a "coalition of heavyweights" as a point of orientation and voluntarily follow suit. Of course, this model already reflects reality to a certain extent. Thus, for example, the final document of the Copenhagen Climate Conference was ultimately penned by India, China, Brazil, South Africa, and the United States (Eckersley 2012: 34). However, relying on the initiative of such a coalition of heavyweights is problematic from the perspective of procedural justice. Even though it may be admirable if the largest countries take measures to combat climate change without the certainty that others will follow, we should not forget that these countries are thereby ultimately deciding global climate policy on their own. Even if these are steps in the right direction, the "lightweights" are nevertheless entitled to be asked about their views and to have a say. It would be especially problematic if the action of the large countries were to diminish the importance of the UNFCCC process, for the UNFCCC guarantees certain participation rights to all—in particular, the most vulnerable and poorest countries.

This lack of participation is a problem from the perspective of intrinsic procedural justice. Even from the instrumental perspective, the "coalition of heavyweights" is more questionable than it may seem at first sight. If such a coalition does not cover the vast majority of global emissions, then the emissions could simply move to the countries outside the coalition (*carbon leakage*—see Chapter 17). In addition, it would be naive to think that all that counts for an effective climate policy is that agreements should be reached and not whether the countries actually abide by the agreements. Without incentives, monitoring, or even sanctions, many solemn pledges will never become a concrete reality. But if a voluntary coalition reaches legally nonbinding agreements outside of the UNFCCC and the excluded countries in addition perceive this process as unfair, then this might well lead to a particularly large gap between intention and implementation. From the perspective of justice, a coalition of heavyweights is thus a dubious alternative to the consensus principle.

A second alternative is the majority principle. The consensus principle requires unanimity in order to adopt a proposal. This gives the supporters of the status quo an advantage over the supporters of change: Progress is possible only if no single country objects. By contrast, if votes in the climate negotiations (as originally planned, but in the final analysis never introduced) require only a two-thirds majority, urgently needed decisions can be taken more easily. From the instrumental perspective, therefore, the majority principle fares better than the consensus principle. But the majority principle is also to be welcomed from the perspective of intrinsic procedural justice. It stands for the idea of equal participation rights for all—or, at least, it realizes this idea *better* than some alternatives. In practice, much depends on how the majority principle is elaborated in concrete terms. A crucial point, in particular, is how well it realizes the principle "one person, one vote" and not only the principle "one state, one vote." These two principles differ, for example, when all states have equal votes: If India and Luxembourg have equal weight when it comes to votes, then the views of an Indian person have much less weight than the views of a person from Luxembourg. The two principles also differ when the delegates of a state do not represent the views of its own people. When an authoritarian regime such as Saudi Arabia votes at the climate conference, then Saudi citizens do not necessarily have a vote as a result. And even in the case of democratic states "one state, one vote" does not necessarily mean "one person, one vote." In democratic states, there are sections of the population who are continually in the minority and whose views therefore are not represented by the majority. It is questionable, for example, whether the Canadian or Australian governments adequately represent the concerns of their indigenous peoples at the climate negotiations. How well the majority principle implements the idea of equal participation rights for all therefore depends heavily on the specific details.

One might also try to formulate a fundamental criticism of the majority principle even if its practical design implemented the idea of equal participation rights of all people perfectly. A critic could prefer the consensus principle because the majority principle places restrictions on national self-determination. If a state is in the minority on a vote, then it has to submit to the will of the majority of the world community. However, this criticism rests on a shaky foundation, because it presupposes an excessively strong right of self-determination of states. Should we really regard emissions—which cause cross-border damage, after all—as an internal affair of each state that it may regulate without involving others? Rather than indicating a problem of the majority principle, the critic's unease about the loss of sovereignty may instead indicate that our historically developed conceptions of the importance of independent nation states must be regarded as excessive in an interdependent world such as ours. These conceptions still stand firm, however: The direction of travel of international climate policy over the last two decades has even been to become more, rather than less, accommodating toward national self-determination. This can be seen in the increasing emphasis on bottom-up processes and the decreasing emphasis on achieving legally binding outcomes.

Thus we can state that the majority principle—in contrast to a "coalition of heavyweights"—would represent progress over the consensus principle. However, when it comes to extending democracy at the global level, the consensus principle and its possible alternatives represent only one side of the coin: They concern the *formal* elaboration of global decision-making procedures. But the less formal aspects of global climate policy are equally important. For example, strengthening civil society is also relevant from the perspective of procedural justice. Civil society consists of associations, initiatives, trade unions, religious groups, and so forth. Given their diversity and their commitment, they ensure greater attention for the voices of those who are usually underrepresented in formal procedures, such as indigenous peoples, women, and nonhuman nature. Civil society contributes to ensuring that the perspectives of all those affected are heard. This enhances intrinsic procedural justice by bringing a wider range of viewpoints into the procedure. But it should also be advocated from the instrumental perspective: A process that incorporates more ideas, expertise, and perspectives will tend to be more successful in bringing about a just solution. For example, women are underrepresented in climate negotiations (at the annual climate conference in 2014, almost three-quarters of the heads of delegations were male—UNFCCC 2015: 9), although they often have a different perspective and are often more conscious of the environment than men (Gifford and Nilsson 2014). In addition, the more the political result is shaped by views "from below," the more support the implementation will meet with in daily life. There are, however, also grounds for reservations about the strengthening of civil society based on the two criteria of procedural justice. Greater openness to more voices can also act as a brake—and this is a significant disadvantage from an instrumental perspective, if one considers that the climate negotiations are already cumbersome. The Copenhagen Conference, for example, numbered more than 30,000 registered participants (Fisher 2010: 12). From an intrinsic perspective, the lack of democratic legitimacy is also problematic. Civil society is neither representative of, nor accountable to, the population. Just as in formal procedures, the privi-leged can also exercise greater influence in the informal forums of civil society. Therefore strengthening civil society must be undertaken with caution.

A second informal, but relevant, feature of decision-making procedures is the resources that states have at their disposal to feed their views effec-tively into the existing decision-making procedures. What is involved here are such concrete aspects as the size of the negotiating delegations, mastery of English as the language of negotiation, and advice from scien-tific support staff, and so on, but also access to informal discussions behind closed doors. Investing in the capabilities of countries with low levels of influence to introduce their interests and positions effectively into the negotiations is one of the least controversial ways in which to strengthen procedural justice.

The global climate policy processes are complex. Accordingly, it is difficult to make a straightforward ethical recommendation on the appropriate design of these processes (for a more detailed discussion of which, see Tomlinson 2015). The upshot is that global procedures must be reformed in such a way that they are more effective at achieving ambitious results and that they do so without compromising intrinsic procedural justice. As regards the formal aspects, therefore, we should put our weight behind the introduction of the majority principle rather than placing our hopes in a "coalition of heavyweights." When it comes to the informal aspects, it is particularly important to boost the voice of the insufficiently represented parties. This means, for example, more space for civil society and more resources for strengthening the negoti-ating power of poor countries.

A more intergenerational democracy

Adapting democracy to the global character of climate change already represents a major challenge. Adapting democracy to the intergenera-tional character of climate change is an even more difficult task. In order to allow the people of the 22nd century to participate in present-day votes, we would have to overcome the laws of physics. As a result, the Brundtland Report on Sustainable Development considers that it is not surprising that future generations receive short shrift: "We act as we do because we can get away with it: future generations do not vote; they have no political or financial power; they cannot challenge our decisions" (Brundtland Commission 1987: 8). Does this mean that a central require-ment of procedural justice—involving all those affected by a decision in the decision-making process—must remain unfulfilled across genera-tional boundaries? Not necessarily. For example, we could strengthen the political power of young people, or we could even include unborn generations, by reserving some seats in parliament for members who are tasked with defending their interests. Unfortunately, neither proposal is as promising as it appears at first sight.

Regarding the first proposal, the political power of the young could be strengthened by implementing dedicated measures to promote young voters, candidates, and Members of Parliament. One could also reduce the voting age or give parents additional voting rights to exercise on behalf of their children. Because the young are particularly seriously affected by present-day decisions, but are at the same time underrepresented in the decision-making processes, that would constitute progress from the perspective of intrinsic procedural justice. However, it must be conceded that the underrepresentation of the young is less serious than the political underrepresentation of other social minorities: In contrast to gender or skin color, age is a feature that changes for all of us over the course of our lives; thus the underrepresentation has a foreseeable end. But the call for more influence for the young can also be justified in instrumental terms. The argument is that because the young are more seriously affected by climate change than the old, they are also more committed to climate mitigation. However, this consideration is not well supported empirically: The young do not necessarily take better care of the future simply because they are more seriously affected (Karnein and Roser 2015). And even if they did, this would be only a modest advance when it comes to the representation of people in the distant future. A young voter will be affected by climate change for only around three decades longer than the average voter. As a result, the self-interest of the young does in fact provide a somewhat stronger reason for climate mitigation than the self-interest of the old, but the difference is not great. When it comes to climate damage in the *distant* future, then, the young are affected just as much as the old— namely, not at all. The bottom line is that, although strengthening the voice of the young should indeed be evaluated positively, this would not solve the fundamental problem of adequately representing people in the distant future.

The second proposal—to include representatives of future generations in parliament—takes this problem as its starting point. The crux, of course, is who elects these representatives and the answer is inevitably: "The present generation." Thus future generations do not enjoy any *real* participation as a result. If we describe democracy in terms of the famous dictum "government of the people, by the people, and for the people," then it becomes clear that parliamentary representation for future generations does not give rise to intergenerational democracy in the sense of a government *by* the (future) people, but at most in the sense of government *for* the (future) people. In other words, representatives for future generations may promote instrumental procedural justice, but not intrinsic procedural justice. They may be an instrument for ensuring that future interests are better heeded in the present-day political processes, but they do not give future generations real voice in decisions. Such representatives even imply a step backwards in terms of intrinsic procedural justice. The reason is that political power is shifted to representatives who cannot be held accountable by the people they represent; moreover, these representatives do not have any firsthand knowledge of the views of those they represent.

But if such representatives can serve at best as a means to an end, then we can broaden our view to include additional institutional reform proposals that do not claim to be anything more than instruments for strengthening the orientation of our political procedures to the future. There is no shortage of examples. If an ombudsman for future generations (as in Hungary) can examine complaints about violations of the law, or if the constitution (as in Japan) enshrines future-oriented rights, then in this way a political community *binds itself* to its good intentions and voluntarily restricts its scope for action. Other reforms are aimed at *creating good intentions* in the first place. This can be accomplished by improving the availability of relevant information through binding future impact assessments for important political decisions; or by having a future committee (as in Finland) or a future or sustainability commissioner (as in Wales or as discussed in the United Nations) initiate and provide supportive advice for legislative processes and discuss them with the population; or by using mechanisms, such as national vision days or binding consultations with children's or youth councils, to support us in acquiring a more vivid grasp of the long term.

Such institutional innovations are, for the most part, positive. Granted, there is little evidence for their effectiveness, in particular when it comes to taking the distant future into account. But because they also entail few risks, even the chance of a positive effect already counts. If some of these reform proposals have any disadvantage at all, then it is that they shift some political power from parliaments into the hands of agents with weaker democratic legitimacy. However, a parliament can, of course, abolish or weaken a future commission or an ombudsman at any time (as happened in Israel and Hungary). Many of these mechanisms can also be seen as strengthening democracy: If they improve the availability of relevant information or make the future less abstract, then they support present-day decision-makers in forming autonomous opinions. This must be regarded as a plus from the perspective of procedural justice.

In summary, aiming to include the future reveals the limits of intrinsic procedural justice. People in the distant future who are affected by present-day climate policy cannot enjoy real participation in the present; hence

present-day decision-makers have no option other than to take responsibility for future generations on their own initiative. There is a range of
institutional reforms that can support them in this regard. Most of these
reforms involve low risks, but there is also little evidence of their use-
fulness.

Arguments box 17: democracy in times of climate change

Not only the outcomes of climate policy, but also the procedures that
lead to these outcomes, must be assessed from the perspective of
justice. Instrumental and intrinsic criteria are relevant for this assessment. The decisive question from an instrumental perspective is to
what extent a political procedure produces just results. From the
intrinsic perspective, the decisive issue is to what extent a political
procedure is inherently just: For example, how much participation in
the decisions does it allow those who must adhere to the decisions,
and how much voice does it give to all who are affected by them?

In this chapter, we have examined whether we should challenge
democracy with regard to these criteria, or whether we should
instead strengthen it by orienting it better toward the global and
intergenerational character of the climate change challenge.

(1) *Less democracy*: Fundamental criticism of democracy is not
    justified. First, there is no evidence—from an instrumental
    perspective—that undemocratic regimes would realize more
    (climate) justice; and second, democracy clearly performs bet-
    ter when assessed by the intrinsic criteria of procedural justice.
(2) *More democracy—globally*: The cumbersome global negotia-
    tions based on the consensus principle are unsatisfactory. Prom-
    ising steps forward from the instrumental and/or the intrinsic
    perspective include the majority principle, and a better hearing
    for underrepresented voices by strengthening civil society and
    the negotiating power of resource-poor countries. By contrast,
    it would be less just if a "coalition of heavyweights" were to set
    the course for climate policy without the participation of others.
(3) *More democracy—intergenerationally*: A genuine strengthen-
    ing of intrinsic procedural justice across generations is
    scarcely possible. However, a series of reform proposals that
    support present-day decision-makers in according better con-
    sideration to the future are worthy of consideration.

The dissatisfaction with the unjust results of current climate policy is one of the primary motivations for placing the spotlight on the political procedures that lead to these results. However, we should not forget that even the best procedures cannot achieve justice unless the population feeds the necessary inputs into the political process.

References

Bäckstrand, K. (2011) "The democratic legitimacy of global governance after Copenhagen," in J. S. Dryzek et al. (eds.) *The Oxford Handbook of Climate Change and Society*, Oxford: Oxford University Press, 669–84.

Burnell, P. (2012) "Democracy, democratization and climate change: complex relationships," *Democratization*, 19(5): 813–42.

Eckersley, R. (2012) "Moving forward in the climate negotiations: multilateralism or minilateralism?" *Global Environmental Politics*, 12(2): 24–42.

Fisher, D. R. (2010) "COP-15 in Copenhagen: how the merging of movements left civil society out in the cold," *Global Environmental Politics*, 10(2): 11–17.

Gifford, R., and Nilsson, A. (2014) "Personal and social factors that influence pro-environmental concern and behaviour: a review," *International Journal of Psychology*, 49(3): 141–57.

Karnein, A., and Roser, A. (2015) "Saving the planet by empowering the young?" in J. Tremmel et al. (eds.) *Youth Quotas and Other Efficient Forms of Youth Participation in Ageing Societies*, Berlin: Springer, 77–92.

Tomlinson, L. (2015) *Procedural Justice in the United Nations Framework Convention on Climate Change: Negotiating Fairness*, Berlin: Springer.

United Nations Framework Convention on Climate Change (UNFCCC) (2015) *Report on Gender Composition*, available online at http://unfccc.int/resource/docs/2015/cop21/eng/06.pdf [accessed April 29, 2016].

World Commission on Environment and Development (WCED/Brundtland Commission) (1987) *Our Common Future: Report of the World Commission on Environment and Development*, Oxford: Oxford University Press.

World Resources Institute (WRI) (2014) "Climate analysis indicators tool: WRI's climate data explorer (CAIT 2.0)," available online at http://cait2.wri.org [accessed April 29, 2016].

21 Looking back and checking up with reality

In this book, we have offered resources for assessing climate policy from an ethical perspective. In particular, we provided arguments that help to answer the three key questions of climate ethics.

(1) Do we have a duty to do anything at all in the face of climate change?
(2) Assuming that we must do something: How much must we do?
(3) And how ought these duties to be distributed?

Answering these questions is anything but straightforward. Traditional ethics has not equipped us well for dealing with a challenge like climate change—a challenge that combines features such as global inequalities, major uncertainties, fragmented causes, and effects across generations.

The response to the first key question—whether we have a duty to mitigate climate change at all—allowed for clearer answers than the other parts of the book. In Part I, we dismissed objections to the effect that there is no man-made, bad, and avoidable climate change, or that there are no duties toward future generations, or that, if there are, our duties consist only in pursuing adaptation and climate engineering rather than mitigation. Thus the duty to mitigate climate change was strongly affirmed and the objections refuted.

However, this affirmation of the duty to mitigate climate change does not in itself tell us how much we must do—the second key question of climate ethics. An answer to this question needs to be based on theories of intergenerational justice. In Part II, we criticized arguments for a duty to bequeath a better world to our descendants. We suggested that rather there is a duty to bequeath enough to our descendants—for example enough for human rights to be fulfilled—and that there might well also be a duty to ensure that they are not worse off than we are. How much effort is needed on our part if we are to leave enough or equally much for our descendants depends crucially on two further factors: uncertainty about the future, and inequality in the future. Taking these two factors into account points toward a strong duty to protect the climate.

This led to the third key question of climate ethics: If there is this strong duty to protect the climate, how should we distribute the corresponding responsibilities? An answer to this question needs to be based on theories of intragenerational distributive justice. In Part III, we analyzed several principles for distributing mitigation, adaptation, and compensation costs. Three of them—grandfathering, the beneficiary pays principle, and emissions egalitarianism—proved not to be well-founded despite their initial plausibility. In contrast, the ability-to-pay principle and a restricted polluter pays principle proved to be more convincing. We sketched how these principles can be combined if climate policy is regarded as but one piece in the larger puzzle of fairly distributing global prosperity and "clean development." When combined in this way, the two principles ascribe more extensive responsibilities to people in developed countries than in developing countries.

Not everyone will live up to their responsibilities, however. In the last part of the book, we suggested that if some do not pull their weight, others have a duty to step into the breach. We also looked at the pros and cons of various means of implementing these duties in practice: voluntary action versus political action, limiting economic growth and population growth, pushing technological progress, and market mechanisms. The very last chapter of the book then highlighted that it matters not only whether the outcome is just, but also how the decision on an outcome is reached. Achieving democratic decision-making procedures in the climate context is particularly challenging given its global and intergenerational scope.

Admittedly, the ideals discussed in this book are fairly visionary. Both individual and political action have fallen massively short of what even minimalist answers to the key questions of climate ethics would prescribe. Given the unique combination of challenges that climate change poses, this is perhaps not too surprising. At the same time, there has been progress in recent years—in particular, at the Paris Conference in late 2015—and it is instructive to look at the political developments in the light of the considerations put forth in this book.

A first point to note is that the moral dimension of climate change is increasingly acknowledged. Whereas, in 2007, the lead US negotiator proclaimed that "if equity's in, we're out" (US Department of State 2011), in Paris even the final decisions had a reference to "climate justice," which many perceive to be an even stronger expression than "equity" (UNFCCC 2015). This was the first appearance of the expression "climate justice" in the outcomes of climate negotiations under the UNFCCC. Also, a diversity of factors served to increasingly frame climate change as a moral issue in the public mind. Some examples of such factors are the divestment movement, which had the effect of stigmatizing fossil fuels, a heightened focus on liability for loss and damage resulting from climate change, increased action in the judicial sphere, or the Pope strongly weighing in on the issue.

Second, even though the skepticism about the basics of climate science has not subsided (Boussalis and Coan 2016), recent years have witnessed a more widely shared agreement that there is a straightforward answer to the question whether we must take action at all: "Yes, we must." There is, however, less univocal agreement on what exactly our duty consists in: Given the slow progress on mitigation in recent years (IPCC 2014: 5), the question of adaptation and climate engineering as complements, or even alternatives, to mitigation have become more relevant. This is not to say that there have been no hopeful signals at all in the area of mitigation: The Paris Agreement of 2015, for example, settled on the goal of keeping warming well below 2°C and even on pursuing efforts to limit it to 1.5°C. But we have to remember that we ultimately have to spell out what needs to be done in terms of specific emission paths, for example a 50 percent reduction of global greenhouse gas emissions until 2030. And the relationship between these paths and reaching the goal of keeping global warming below 2°C is probabilistic: Some paths are more likely to overshoot the goal; others are less likely to do so. Both in our ethical assessment and in the sphere of political negotiations, we therefore still have to settle the question of which probability of reaching the Paris goal (and which risk of not reaching it) is acceptable—and as the chapter on uncertainty has shown, this is a crucial, but difficult, question. Also, as the conclusion to Part II has indicated, these official goals are clearly aspirational when taking into account the effort that countries are actually willing to make.

The conclusions that we reached are visionary not only when it comes to intergenerational justice, but also when it comes to the global distribution of responsibilities. An element of the morally least plausible principle—grandfathering—is clearly discernible in political reality. And of the two morally plausible principles, one is highly controversial in the arena of real-world politics: the polluter pays principle, understood as a principle for making present people pay for past emissions. It is particularly sensitive, or even taboo, to expressly speak of compensation for past wrongs—a topic that has come up in the context of the emerging discussions about responding to loss and damage resulting from climate change. In contrast, differentiating responsibilities among countries according to the ability-to-pay principle has proven to garner broader political acceptance. While developed countries undoubtedly have taken the lead in the climate action effort—not least by committing to mobilizing US$100 billion annually by 2020 to support developing countries—their shortfall from the benchmark of a fair share is arguably still much larger than the shortfall of developing countries (see, for example, Civil Society Review 2015). The issue of interpreting the notion of "common but differentiated responsibilities and respective capabilities" remains deeply divisive, and many countries even resist precisely what we tried to achieve in Part III of this book: to be more explicit about different distributive principles. Some countries prefer to remain vague on these matters rather than to receive clear benchmarks against which to measure their efforts.

What can be said about the various means of achieving climate justice that we discussed in Part IV? Given how political will limits the extent to which the population and the affluence strategies allow for significant emission reductions, the focus lies strongly on the technology strategy. While there are some genuinely hopeful signs in this respect—such as the costs of solar power dropping dramatically—political discourse also provides plenty of examples of calculated optimism regarding technologies that seem indispensable for reaching the mitigation targets, but which are not proven to actually work safely and at scale, such as various negative emission technologies. When we turn to market mechanisms—such as emissions trading—we can observe that they have not come to dominate the field as strongly as economists might have wished them to. Still, part of our analysis in Chapter 19 also applies to the more general concept of one agent reducing emissions, but being paid for doing so by another agent. This more general concept is certainly at the heart of any future climate solution, and it manifests itself not only in emissions trading and offsetting, but also in broader ways, for example in developing countries pledging to undertake emission reductions conditional on climate finance provided by developed countries.

Finally, how has procedural justice fared in recent years? Finding effective ways of global decision-making in climate policy remains a big stumbling block. In the lead-up to the 2015 conference in Paris, countries even backtracked by shifting the focus to nationally determined contributions. This shift was based on past experience—particularly the 2009 climate conference in Copenhagen, which indicated that countries are resisting submission to jointly taken "top-down" climate decisions. They are willing to make efforts only if they can do so in a voluntary, "bottom-up," way. From a procedural perspective, there was also a positive aspect in the Paris Agreement: Countries bound their future decision-makers to regularly assess their contributions in global stocktakes, and to update and enhance their effort in that light. Such mechanisms can be instrumental in enhancing intergenerational justice. This does nothing, however, to diffuse the more general point made in the last section of Chapter 20: Genuine intergenerational democracy was, is, and will be out of reach. The discussion of the limits of intergenerational democracy can also serve to raise awareness of a more general truth: Ultimately, democracy can process only the political will that voters feed into the political process in the first place; even the best procedure cannot conjure a just output out of an unjust input. Therefore the responsibility for just outcomes can be delegated only to a limited extent to those who design political procedures. The fundamental decision between self-interest in the here and now and justice across space and time therefore ultimately remains in the hands of the voters—that is, in our hands and in your hands.

References

Boussalis, C., and Coan, T. G. (2016) "Text-mining the signals of climate change doubt," *Global Environmental Change*, 36: 89–100.

Civil Society Review (2015) *Fair Shares: A Civil Society Equity Review of INDCs*, available online at http://civilsocietyreview.org/wp-content/uploads/2015/11/CSO_FullReport.pdf [accessed April 29, 2016].

Intergovernmental Panel on Climate Change (IPCC) (2014) "Summary for policymakers," in *Climate Change 2014: Synthesis Report—Contribution of Working Groups I, II and III to the Fifth Assessment Report of the Intergovernmental Panel on Climate Change*, available online at http://www.ipcc.ch/pdf/assessment-report/ar5/syr/AR5_SYR_FINAL_SPM.pdf [accessed April 29, 2016].

United Nations Framework Convention on Climate Change (UNFCCC) (2015) *Adoption of the Paris Agreement*, available online at http://unfccc.int/resource/docs/2015/cop21/eng/l09r01.pdf [accessed April 29, 2016].

US Department of State (2011) "United Nations Climate Change Conference in Durban, South Africa: Special Briefing—Todd Stern, Special Envoy for Climate Change," December 13, available online at http://www.state.gov/r/pa/prs/ps/2011/12/178699.htm [accessed April 29, 2016].

Suggested further reading for Part IV

Cafaro, P. (2011) "Beyond business as usual: alternative wedges to avoid catastrophic climate change and create sustainable societies," in D. G. Arnold (ed.) *The Ethics of Global Climate Change*, Cambridge: Cambridge University Press, 192–215.

This chapter proposes tackling economic growth and population growth as solutions to climate change rather than focusing exclusively on technological solutions.

Caney, S., and Hepburn, C. (2011) "Carbon trading: unethical, unjust and ineffective?" *Royal Institute of Philosophy Supplements*, 69: 201–34.

This paper provides a rich examination of carbon trading from an ethical and an economic perspective.

Cripps, E. (2013) *Climate Change and the Moral Agent: Individual Duties in an Interdependent World*, Oxford: Oxford University Press.

This book provides an in-depth discussion of individual and collective climate action, including a treatment of duties in response to the failure of others to act according to their duties.

Mulgan, T. (2011) *Ethics for a Broken World*, Durham: Acumen.

Part IV presents arguments on democracy in the context of current environmental challenges.

Tomlinson, L. (2015) *Procedural Justice in the United Nations Framework Convention on Climate Change: Negotiating Fairness*, Berlin: Springer.

This book offers a thorough examination of decision-making procedures in international climate policy from the perspective of justice.

A more comprehensive list of further readings for this part is available at http://climate-justice-references.christianseidel.eu

Glossary

"Ability-to-pay" principle A distributive principle according to which the costs associated with addressing a problem should be distributed (among all agents living above the sufficiency threshold) in proportion to each agent's ability to pay.

Adaptation Refers to human or natural adjustments to actual or expected changes in the climate.

Anthropocentrism An ethical position according to which only humans matter fundamentally; other sentient beings, organisms, or ecosystems matter only insofar as they affect human concerns.

Atmospheric concentration The number of molecules of a **greenhouse gas** per million molecules in the atmosphere. It is measured in parts per million (ppm).

"Beneficiary pays" principle A distributive principle according to which the costs for coping with a problem (such as climate change) should be divided up in proportion to the benefits derived from the causes of this problem (such as past emissions).

Carbon dioxide (CO_2) The **greenhouse gas** that is most responsible for anthropogenic climate change. The atmospheric concentration of this naturally occurring gas has risen strongly in recent times mainly owing to the creation of a fossil-fuel-based economy and land-use changes.

Carbon dioxide equivalent (CO_2eq) **Greenhouse gases** differ in their global warming effect. To allow comparability, a certain amount of one greenhouse gas (such as 1 ton of methane) can also be expressed in terms of the amount of **carbon dioxide (CO_2)** which would have an equivalent global warming effect (over a certain period of time), for example 1 ton of methane corresponds to 21 tons of CO_2eq.

Climate engineering (or geoengineering) Refers to intentional, large-scale interventions in the climate system.

Discounting   Consists in giving less weight to future values than to present values. The so-called *discount rate* expresses how much less weight is given to a value that accrues in a year when compared to the same value accruing today, for example a discount rate of 5 percent means that US$100 in a year counts as the equivalent to $95 today.

Emissions egalitarianism   A distributive principle that allocates equal per capita shares of the remaining emissions budget to all people.

Emissions market   Allows the purchase of emission rights and the sale of emission reductions. Emissions trading, more specifically, is a climate policy instrument that sets a cap on emissions and distributes the emissions allowed under the cap to various agents (countries, companies, individuals), who can subsequently trade in them.

Expected value   Whenever a variable can take different values with different probabilities, the expected value of the (random) variable is the probability weighted average of all possible values. Imagine that you toss a fair coin and you will receive $2 if it lands as heads (and receive nothing otherwise); the expected value of this lottery is $1—that is, (50% × $2) + (50% × $0).

Grandfathering   A distributive principle according to which all agents must reduce their emissions by the same percentage.

Greenhouse gases (GHGs)   Components of the atmosphere that absorb and reflect part of the radiation that is reflected by the earth. The most important (and naturally occurring) GHGs are water vapor, **carbon dioxide (CO_2)**, nitrous oxide, methane, and ozone. Many human activities add GHGs to the atmosphere and thus change the climate.

Gross domestic product (GDP)   A measure of a nation's economic activity. It represents the value of goods and services produced within a country's (or, in the case of global GDP, all countries') territory over a certain time period.

Intergovernmental Panel on Climate Change (IPCC)   A scientific body under the auspices of the United Nations. It reviews and assesses the most recent scientific, technical, and socioeconomic information produced worldwide relevant to the understanding of climate change. It is particularly known for the five major assessment reports that have been published since 1990.

Justice, global   Refers to justice between people across all geographical, political, and cultural borders.

Justice, intergenerational   Refers to justice between people of different generations.

Justice, procedural   Refers to justice regarding decision-making processes.

Kyoto Protocol   A supplement to the **United Nations Framework Convention on Climate Change (UNFCCC)**; adopted in 1997 and entered into force in 2005. With this binding agreement, virtually all industrial countries (with the notable exception of the United States) committed themselves to reduce their **greenhouse gas** emissions (although Canada withdrew from the Protocol in 2012).

Mitigation   Refers to actions that reduce **greenhouse gas** emissions or increase the capacity of natural carbon sinks (such as forests) to absorb greenhouse gases.

Paris Agreement   The most important agreement in international climate policy since the **Kyoto Protocol**. Adopted in 2015, it aims (among other things) at a temperature increase well below 2°C and it hopes to achieve this goal on the basis of a bottom-up process of nationally determined contributions.

"Polluter pays" principle   A distributive principle according to which agents should bear the burdens of addressing a problem in proportion to their contribution to causing the problem.

Sufficiency requirement   Refers to the duty to make sure that others have at least enough (where the notion of "having enough" can be spelled out in various ways).

Two-degree (2°C) target   Refers to the intention to limit the global mean temperature rise to a maximum of 2°C above preindustrial levels. In order to derive policy implications from this, one must specify the probability with which the target must be met.

United Nations Framework Convention on Climate Change (UNFCCC)   Adopted in 1992 and entered into force in 1994, the UNFCCC establishes the foundational principles of international climate policy and forms the basis for subsequent agreements such as the **Kyoto Protocol**.

Universal Declaration of Human Rights (UDHR)   Adopted by the United Nations General Assembly in 1948, the UDHR is one of the most important human rights documents. It consists of thirty Articles on the civil, political, socioeconomic, and cultural rights to which all humans are entitled.

Utilitarianism   A moral theory that claims that an action or policy is morally right if—and only if—it maximizes utility.

Index